Knots

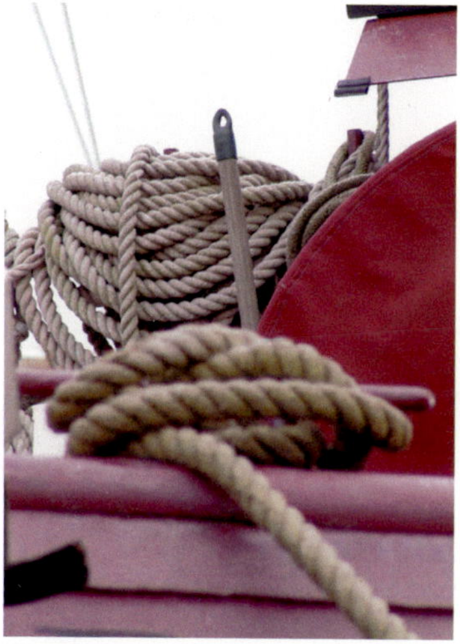

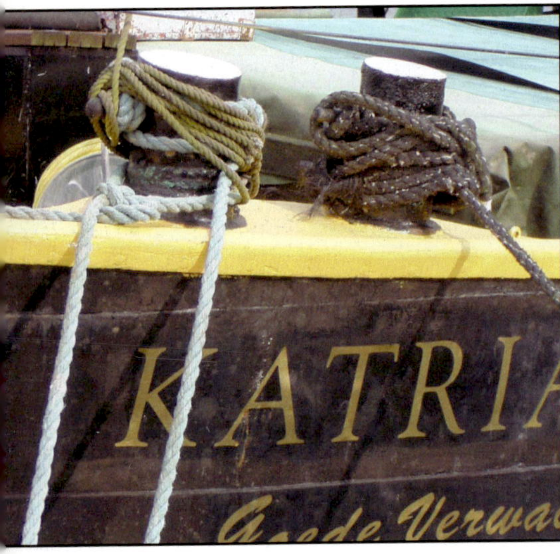
KATRIA

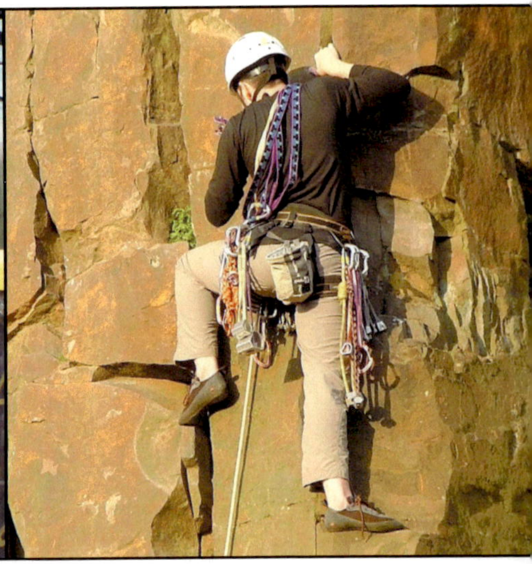

Collins need to know?

Knots

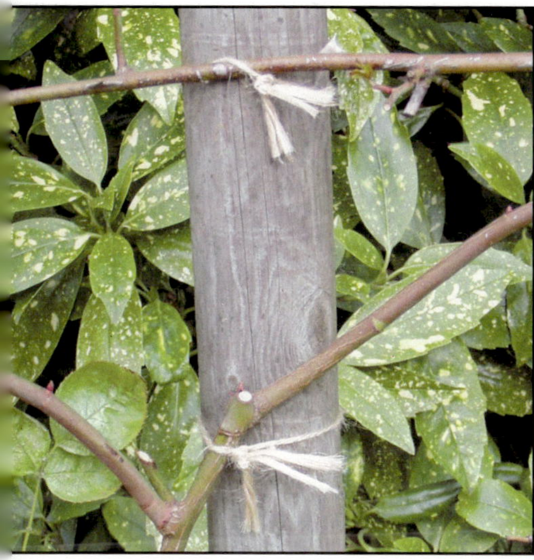

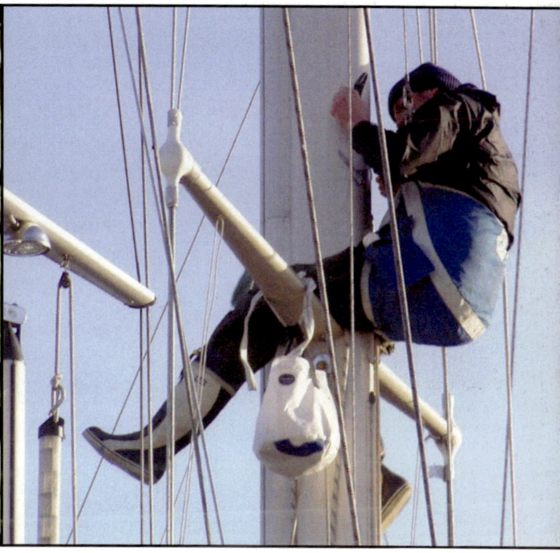

All the kit, techniques and tips you need to get you started

Geoffrey Budworth

First published in 2005 by
Collins, an imprint of
HarperCollins*Publishers*
77–85 Fulham Palace Road
Hammersmith, London W6 8JB

The Collins website address is:
www.collins.co.uk

Collins is a registered trademark of HarperCollins Publishers Limited.

09 08 07
6 5 4 3 2 1

A catalogue record for this book is available from the British Library

Created by: m&n publishing
Editor: Nina Sharman
Designer: Martin Hendry
Photographer: Colin Sherwin
Cover design: Cook Design
Back cover photographs: Colin Sherwin

ISBN-13 978 0 00 779350 1

Colour reproduction by Colourscan, Singapore
Printed and bound by Printing Express Ltd, Hong Kong

This book is intended to be a safe and simple introduction to knot tying. Do not use any of the knots, bends or hitches that appear in this book for activities which involve foreseeable risk of loss, damage or injury without first seeking the advice and guidance of a qualified practitioner and obtaining the proper training and equipment.

contents

Introduction

Remember that it is no use waiting until you need a knot before learning to tie it.

Richard Hopkins IGKT

Learn to tie at least one knot from this book, use it often, and it will more than repay the cost. Learn several and your life will be transformed. For knot tyers are self-reliant individuals who, given a length of string, cord or rope, are never at a loss when it comes to assembling a gift-wrapped parcel or contriving a first-aid tourniquet; safely crossing a swollen river; replacing the broken string on a musical instrument; or training to be a tree surgeon. Knotting can also be an absorbing handicraft.

It is a science too, about which we may know less than half of all there is to be discovered. In 1990, Professor Vaughan Jones of New Zealand was awarded a Fields Medal (the mathematician's equivalent of a Nobel

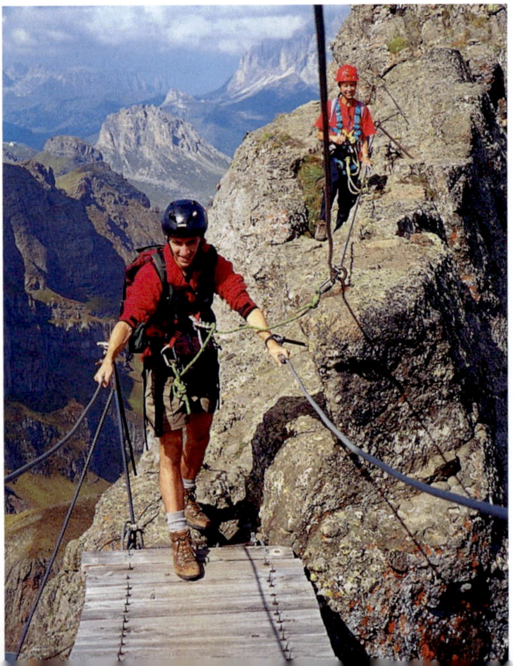

◀ **Suspension bridges (made from fibre or wire cordage) make useful shortcuts in many wild and rugged terrains throughout the world.**

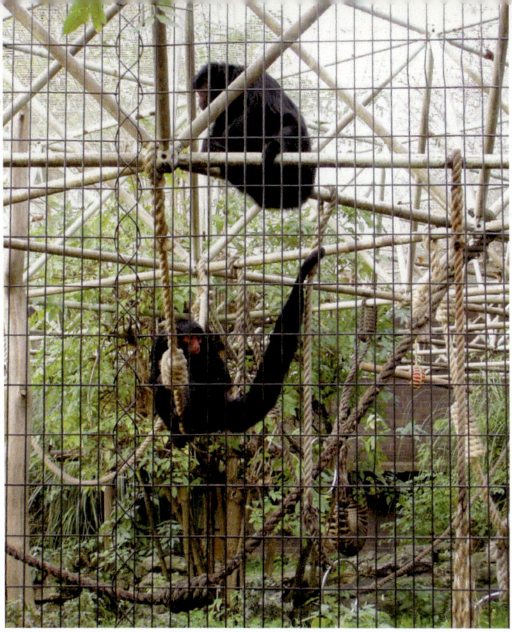

◀ The eye-spliced ropes here add interest to the artificial habitat of these zoo-based primates.

Prize) for his original contributions to the study of knot theory.

If you cannot tie knots, it is only because you have not discovered how to do so. No special aptitude is necessary. You do not even have to want to climb mountains, enjoy messing about in boats, or have been a girl guide or boy scout

▼ You cannot simply park a boat and walk away from it. Even a dinghy, like this one, with fenders in place, must be tied up to the jetty or quayside by means of bow and stern lines.

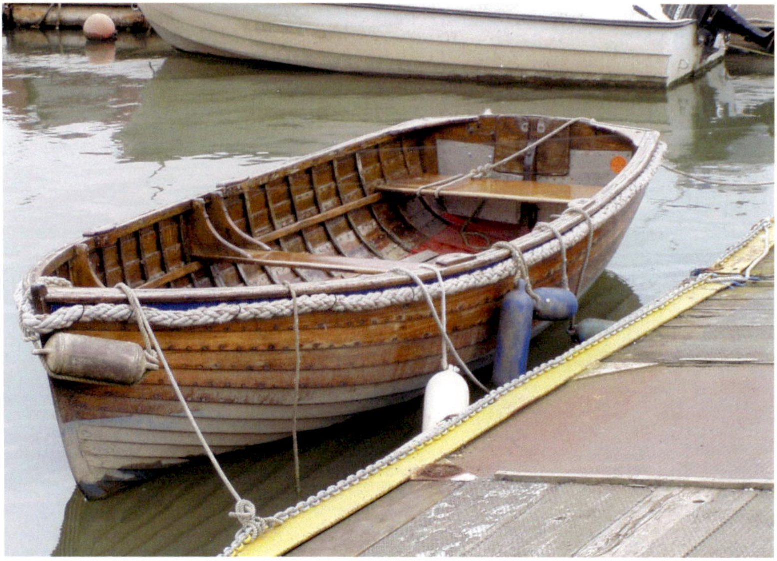

(pursuits often assumed, wrongly, to foster knotting know-how).

Knotting can be a pleasing pastime, a creative handicraft, a practical tool and, at its most esoteric, a rigorously demanding field of theoretical and experimental study. Some 'knottologists' even appear as expert witnesses to give evidence in court about knotted clues found at scenes of crime.

All of the knots contained in this book are innocent enough and may be enjoyed alone, or collectively through membership of the International Guild of Knot Tyers.

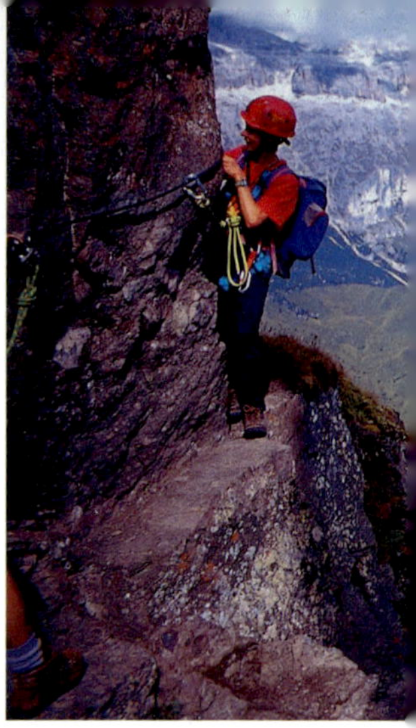

INVENTORY OF KNOTS

How to use this table

As well as putting the knots in this book to the tasks described in each chapter, many knots are versatile and can easily be adapted for other activities. This chart gives an indication of the other categories from the book that the knots can also be used for.

B = Boating and maritime usage
F = Fishing purposes
H = Home and hobby applications
L = Life support situations
W = Webbing and tape usage

Getting started

Reef knot B H
Overhand knot B H W
Noose B H
Double overhand knot B H L
Triple overhand knot B H L
Multiple overhand knot B H
Two half-hitches B H
Two reversed half-hitches B H
Half hitching B H
Marline hitching B H
Common whipping B H

Boating knots

Figure eight stopper knot H L
Ashley's stopper knot H L
Back splice (with Crown knot) H
Sheet bend H
Zeppelin bend H L
Clove hitch H W
Rolling hitch H W
Anchor bend H L W
Bowline/Water bowline H L
Eye splice H
Scaffold knot H
Midshipman's hitch H L

Fishing knots

Albright knot
Clinch knot
Blood knot
Blood knot loop
Blood loop dropper knot
Perfection loop B H L
Tube knot
Offshore swivel knot B H
Palomar knot
Berkley braid knot
Snelling
Lock knot

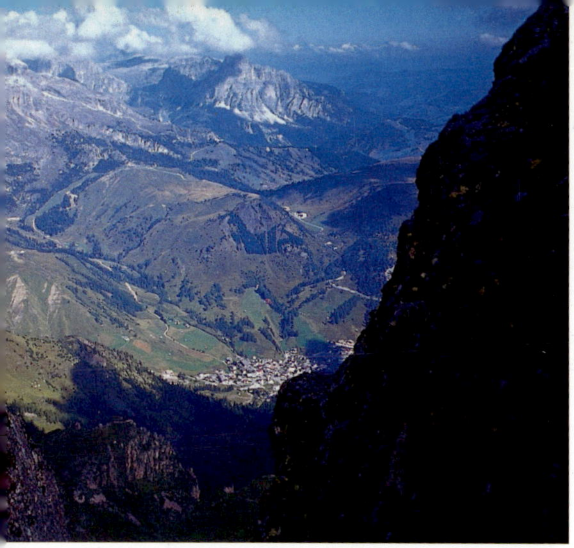

◀ Climbing not only requires specialist tools but also an understanding and knowledge of a wide variety of knots.

Home and hobbies

Strangle knot (B)(L)
Constrictor knot (B)(L)
Boa knot
Short splice (B)
Asher's bottle sling (B)
Tarbuck knot (B)(L)
Sheepshank (B)
Braid knot (B)
Lapp knot (B)
Harness bend (B)(L)(W)
Fisherman's knot (B)(L)
Knute hitch (B)
Pedigree cow hitch (B)(W)
Ring hitch (B)(W)
Round turn and two half-hitches (B)(L)
Highwayman's hitch (B)
Killick hitch (B)

Life support knots

Reinforced reef knot (B)(H)
Reever bend (B)(F)(H)(W)
Double fisherman's knot (B)(F)(H)
Triple fisherman's knot (B)(F)(H)
Alpine butterfly loop (B)(F)(H)
Prusik knot (H)
Figure eight loop (B)(F)(H)(W)
Double figure eight loop (B)(H)
Bowline on a coil (B)
Round turn bowline (B)(H)
Bowline in the bight (B)(H)
Triple bowline (B)(H)

Webbing knots

Ring or water knot (B)(F)(H)(L)
Overhand shortening (B)(H)(L)
Frost knot (L)
Overhand loop (B)(H)(L)
Sling hitch (B)(H)(L)
Reinforced ring hitch (B)(H)(L)
Reinforced cow hitch (B)(H)(L)
Pile hitch (B)(H)
Ground line hitch (B)(H)
Buntline hitch (B)(H)
Ossel hitch (B)(H)
Collared hitch (B)(H)(L)
Boom hitch (B)(H)(L)
Slide-and-grip hitch (end-loaded, one-way) (B)(H)(L)
Slide-and-grip hitch (centre-loaded, two-way) (B)(H)(L)

Cordage facts

Basic coil tie (B)(H)(L)

getting

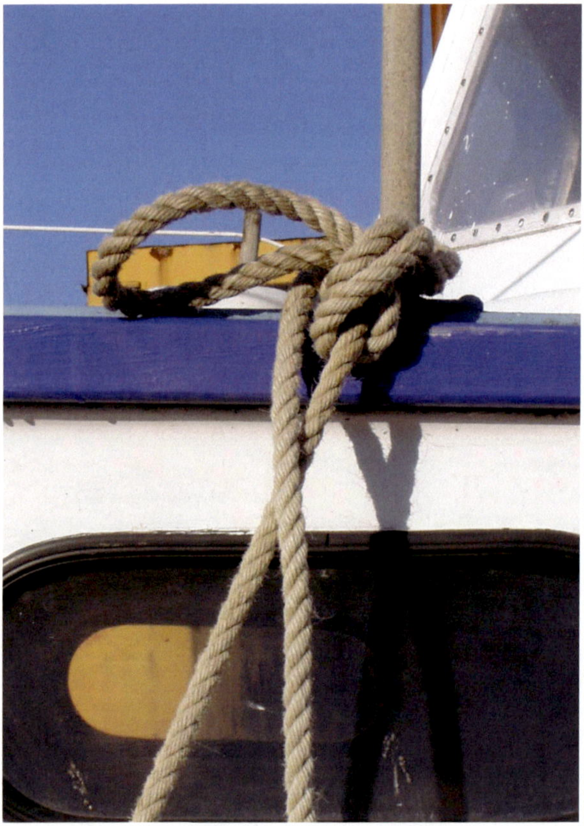

started

Learning to tie knots is a fundamental but fascinating art, craft and science. Knots pre-date written history; some are rediscovered and new knots are always being invented. This section shows how to tie some basic knots, illustrates the different types of knots, explains the terms and techniques used, and provides information on tools and accessories.

Knotting history

Knots predate mankind's ability to start a fire and maybe even to talk intelligibly. Ancient cave dwellers were probably knot tyers.

Primitive cultures used knots to snare and net food, to make clothing and shelters, to drag loads, to bind enemies, and to strangle human sacrifices. Some knots altered the course of history; the arrow that killed King Harold at the Battle of Hastings in October 1066 was propelled by a knotted Norman bowstring.

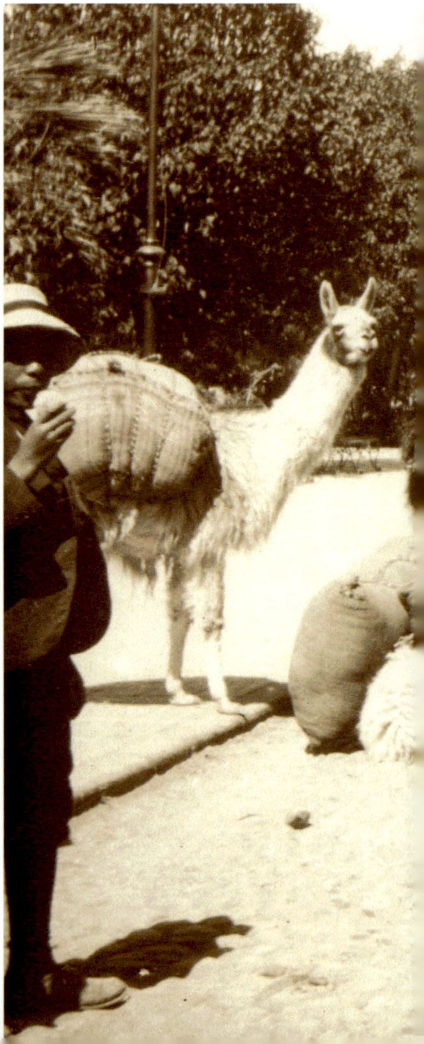

Early uses

The construction of the legendary Tower of Babel and the Colossus of Rhodes, as well as medieval castles and cathedrals, all required knotted ropes; so, too, did early ascents of the earth's high places (seeking birds' eggs) and descents into the depths (after valuable mineral ores). Bookbinders, cobblers and conjurors, hangmen and lynch mobs, all relied upon a knot or two, as did (and still do) bell-ringers, escapologists, kite fliers, poachers, surgeons, trapeze artists and the water carrier at the well.

Sailors and dockyard riggers devised increasingly complicated knots to manoeuvre wooden ships with canvas sails and cordage, while Spanish vacqueros and American cowboys tied more complex rawhide and leather ones in their horse harnesses, lariats and whips.

Knotting books

The first printed knot books were the formal seamanship manuals of the late 1700s and early 1800s. Popular knot publications are a 20th-century development (one internet bookseller's website claims there are 500 books about knots available) and it is certainly a fact that, in the past 20 years or so, more than 100 fresh and original ones have been written and published. Knotting – its lure and lore – is now a hot topic, keenly pursued on land as well as water, by both sexes and all ages.

▼ Pack animals, such as these llamas in early 20th century South America, can still be seen with loads lashed onto them in many regions of the world.

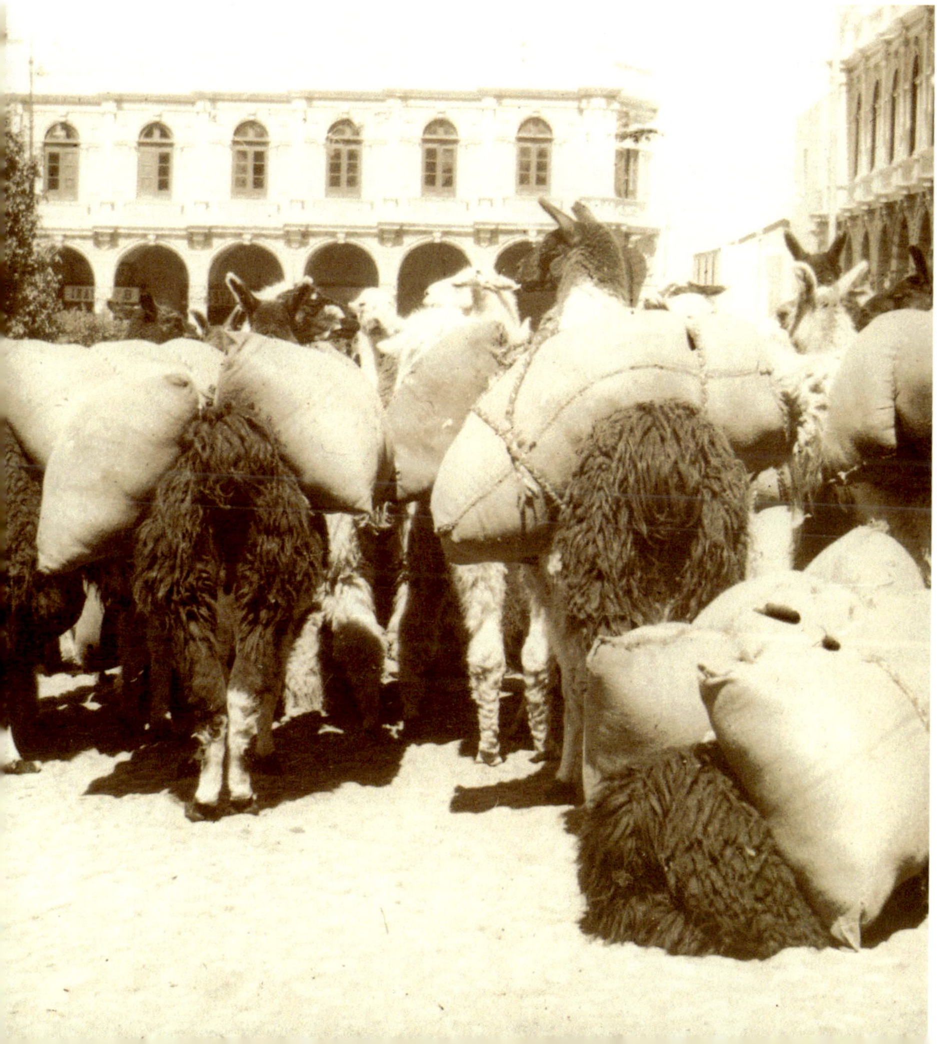

Knotting terms

Knotting is 'nodology' (Latin) or 'kompology' (Greek). However, no knot tyer would be caught using either of these pretentious words, although some quite like 'knottology' and call themselves 'knottologists'.

Parts of a rope

The active end of a line used to tie knots is the **working end**, and the other end is the **standing end**, between which two extremities lies the **standing part** of the line. However, anglers refer to the working end of a fishing line as the **tag end**, whether it is active in the tying process or merely protruding (trimmed) from the completed knot.

A U-shaped section is a **bight**, and a bight twisted to create a single **crossing point** becomes a **loop**. If you are forming a loop in the end of a line, it is an **overhand loop** when the working end lands on top of the standing part, and an **underhand loop** if the working end lies beneath the standing part.

A twist with two crossing points forms **interlocking elbows**.

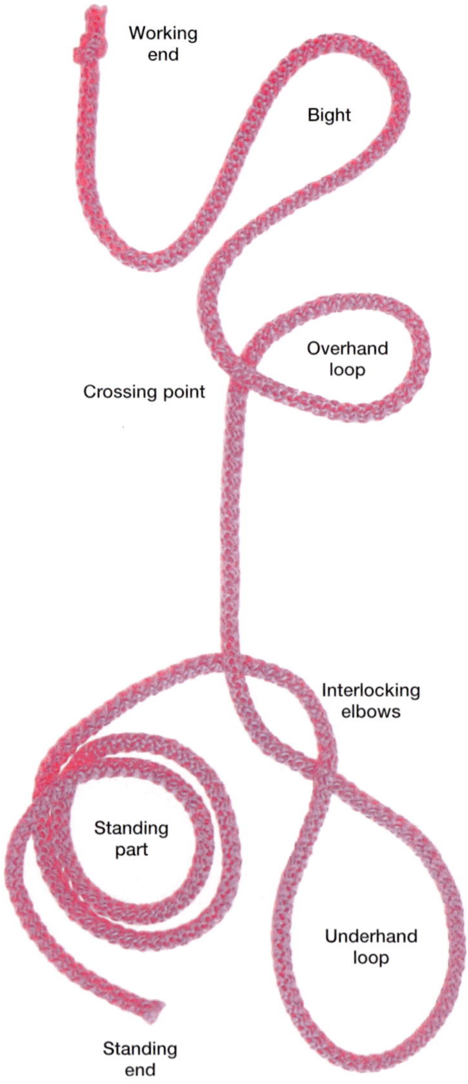

S-laid and Z-laid knots

When two working ends are twisted together with three crossing points, the result is a **half-knot** which will be either **S-laid** or **Z-laid** depending upon whether it spirals left-handed (counter-clockwise) or right-handed (clockwise). The terms S-laid and Z-laid are lifted from rope-making where three-strand hawsers are laid up either left- or right-handed.

▼ The two vertical ropes (left) show how the S and Z lay form of ropes is also applied to the spiralling parts of half-knots.

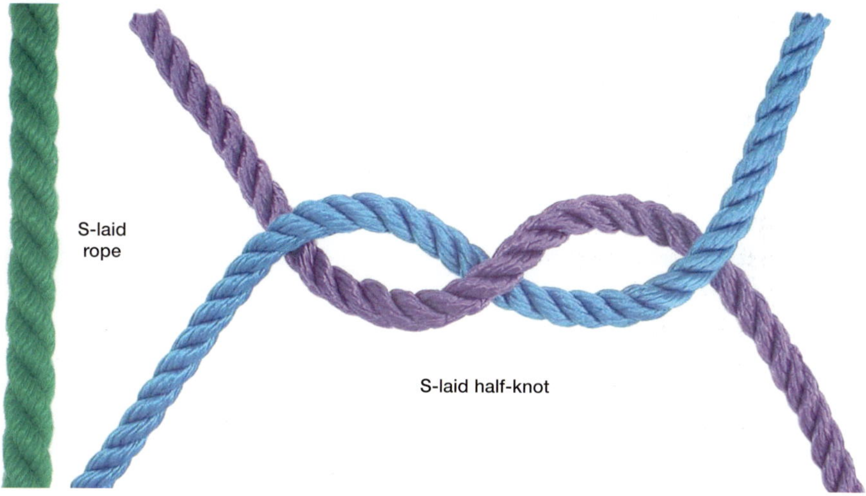

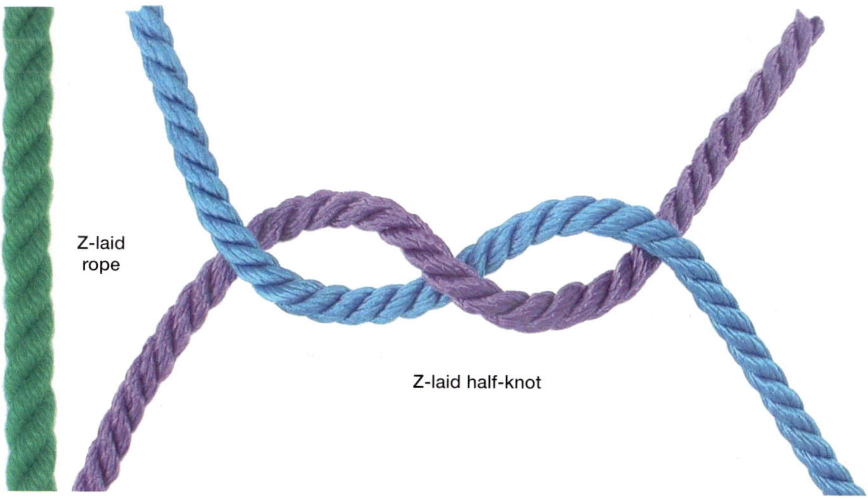

Knot uses and their names

Knots are divided by function into three main groups - bends, hitches and knots.

Knots joining two ropes together are called **bends**, while any knot that attaches a rope or line to a post, rail or other anchorage point is referred to as a **hitch**. The catch-all term for those that are not bends or hitches is **knots,** and this group is sub-divided into stopper knots, bindings, shortenings, loops and nooses.

Anything tied in thin braid, twine, thread or fishing line is referred to as a 'knot' (even when it is used as a bend or hitch).

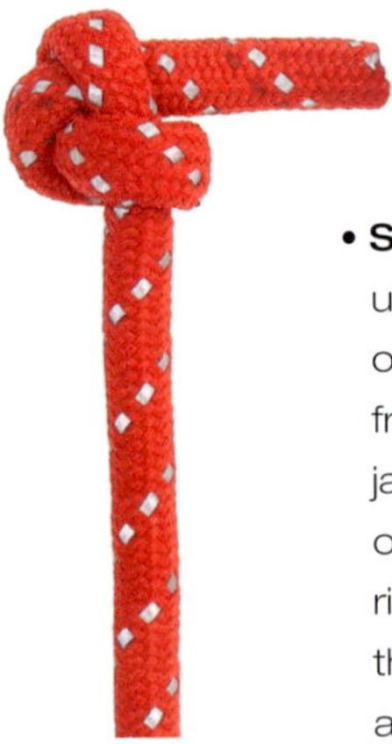

- **Stopper knots** are used to prevent a rope or cord pulling free from a pulley sheave, jam cleat, fairlead or other item of rope and rigging hardware but they also stop twine and thread fraying.

- **Bindings** typically use both ends of the same lace or lashing to wrap and tightly seize ropes' ends and the necks of bags or sacks, but they can also be applied to bandages and parcels of all kinds.

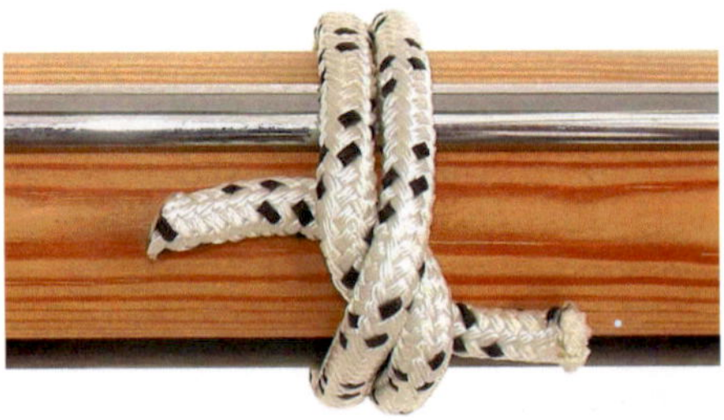

- **Shortenings** remove the need to cut over-long rope or other cordage, preserving it intact for use another time.

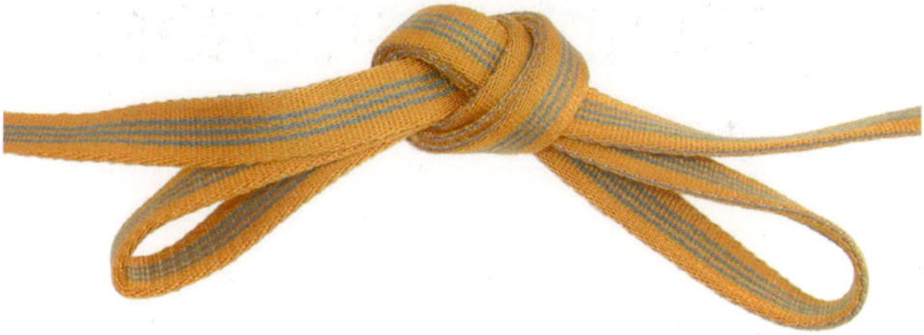

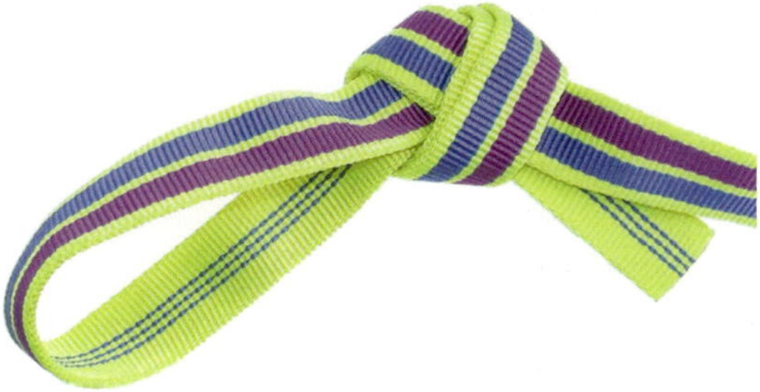

- **Loops** act as hitches, or start lashings.

- **Nooses** are loops that either tighten themselves under load or can be adjusted to size by hand.

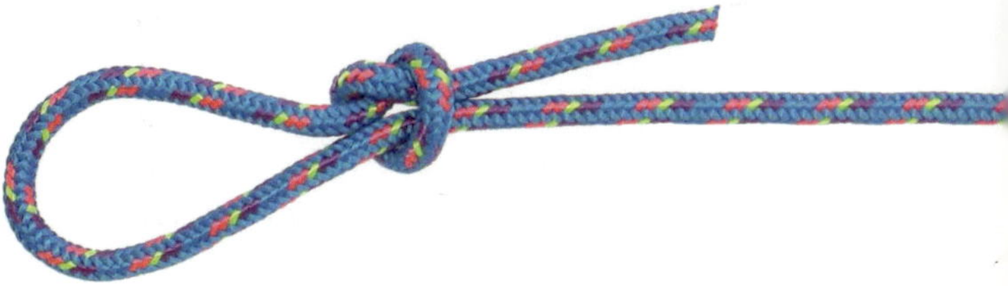

Knot names

While many knots do not have names, over time some have acquired more than one. For example, the figure eight knot is also known as the Flemish knot, and the double fisherman's knot is called a grapevine knot by climbers and a grinner knot by anglers.

A knot's name may suggest its appearance (round turn and two half-hitches), its use (bottle sling) or the person who might use it (highwayman's knot). Some, such as the Alpine butterfly loop, imply a region of origin, others are named after a person, for instance, the Tarbuck knot, and a few are whimsical, such as the knute hitch.

Starting to tie knots

Knotting is a practical skill that can be acquired only by active involvement in tying knots.

To learn any one, or all, of the knots described and illustrated in this book, equip yourself with a couple of 2 metre (6 ft) lengths of soft braided cord, about 5 or 6 mm (¼ in) in diameter, but two long thick laces from a pair of walking boots will do just as well. It can help if they are different colours. Learning the three splices takes no more than 2 metres (6 ft) of three-strand rope between 10 mm (⅜ in) and 15 mm (½ in) diameter.

Converting knots on the page into knots with real cord becomes easier with practice.

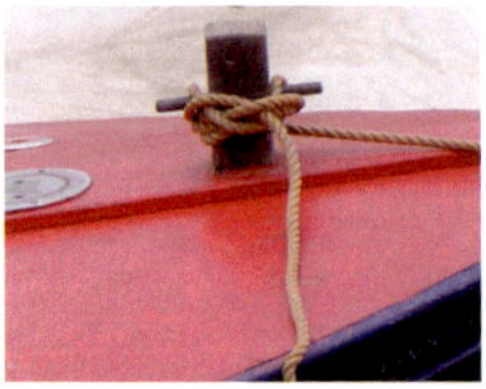

▲ An anchor warp or other mooring line is belayed (made fast) to a small boat's single bitt or wooden post by its 'bitter end' (hence the expression).

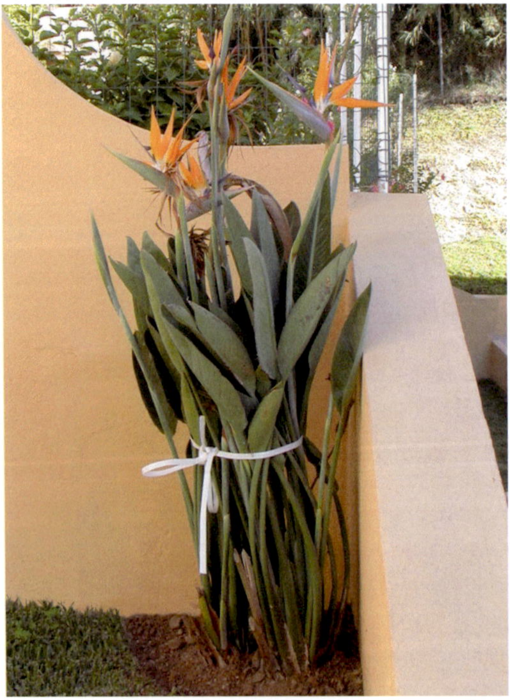

◀ When it comes to tying things down, or tying them up, a knot will do the trick, as is shown here with these bird of paradise flowers.

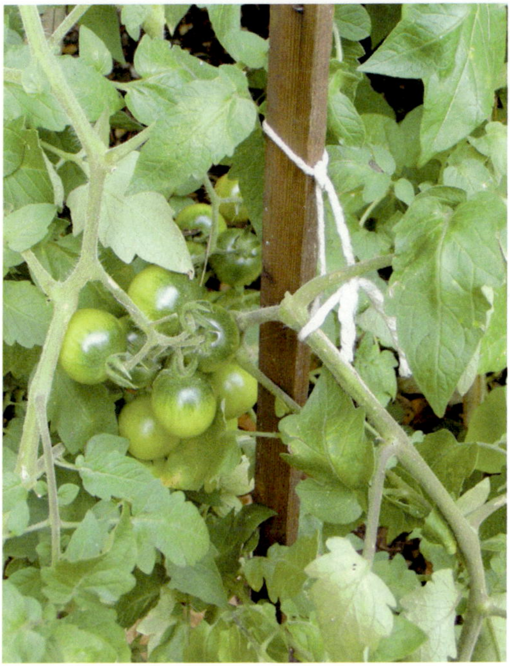

◀ Gardeners need to know how to tie simple knots in order to support plants when necessary. A versatile piece of string should always be at hand.

Through this, you will acquire eye-to-hand coordination and your knot tying will improve.

The method of tying each knot described in this book was chosen because it is straightforward to learn and easily depicted on the page. When it is particularly useful, a second tying method is shown, for example, tying the constrictor knot both with an end and in the bight (see pages 88–9). There are various ways to tie many knots – such as the alpine butterfly loop (see pages 122–3) – you should experiment to discover if there is one that suits you better. Try undoing the knot, step-by-step, and sometimes a shortcut will occur to you that results in more fluent re-tying. Adopt it, for practice does not make perfect, practice makes permanent. Whether clever or clumsy, if you repeat an action often enough, it becomes habitual. Strive to make a habit of doing your dextrous best.

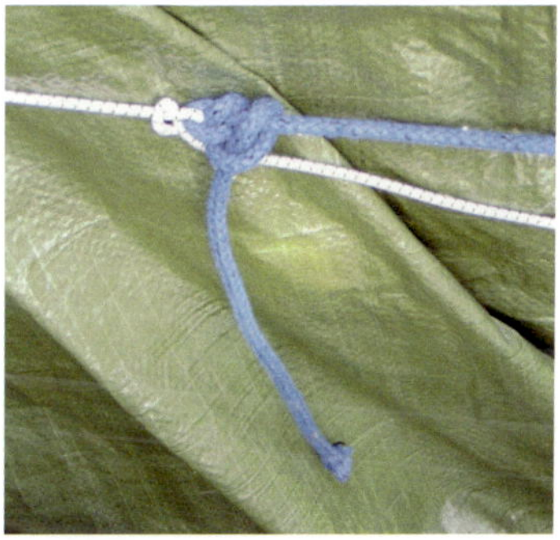

▲ An overhand knot plus a couple of half-hitches are equal to just about anything. However, they serve a purpose in holding a tarpaulin in place.

Need to know basic knots

It is important to know how to tie basic knots because they form the foundation of more complicated ones.

A handful of very simple knots (including half-knots, half-hitches and overhand knots) are all interrelated. They are also, curiously, knots that many of us 'just know', probably because we learnt them when very young.

They are included here as they are essential components of some other more elaborate knots featured in later sections.

Reef knot

In prehistoric times knotting must have been clumsy and haphazard, made up each time a need arose. Later, after some primitive genius discovered 'left-over-right, then right-over-left' (or vice versa), a reef knot would always be a reef knot. It was one of the world's early inventions.

However, the reef knot is merely a binding knot tied in both ends of the same lace, lanyard or lashing and works best when pressed against something – a parcel, a foot in a shoe or a bandaged body part. Do not use it as a bend to join separate ropes, except with certain safeguards while climbing (see Life-Support Knots).

MUST KNOW

SZ and ZS

An SZ reef knot is one where the S-laid half-knot is tied first, then a Z-laid one added to complete the knot (see Step 3). A ZS knot has its two half-knots tied in the reverse order.

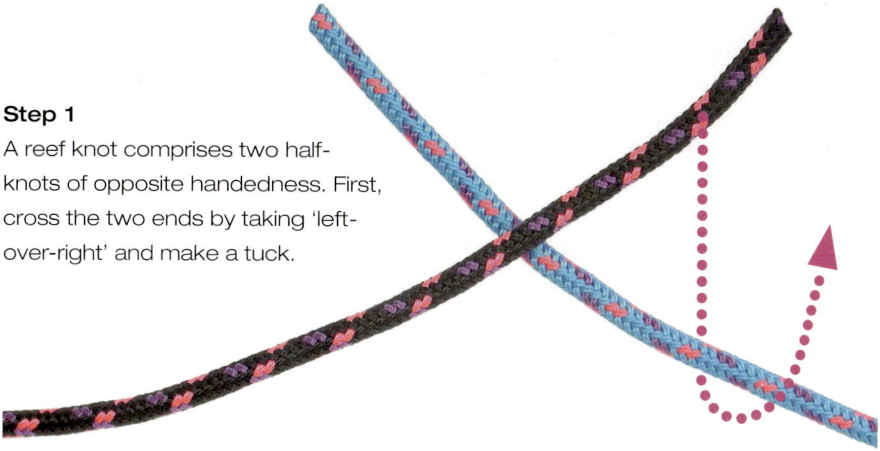

Step 1

A reef knot comprises two half-knots of opposite handedness. First, cross the two ends by taking 'left-over-right' and make a tuck.

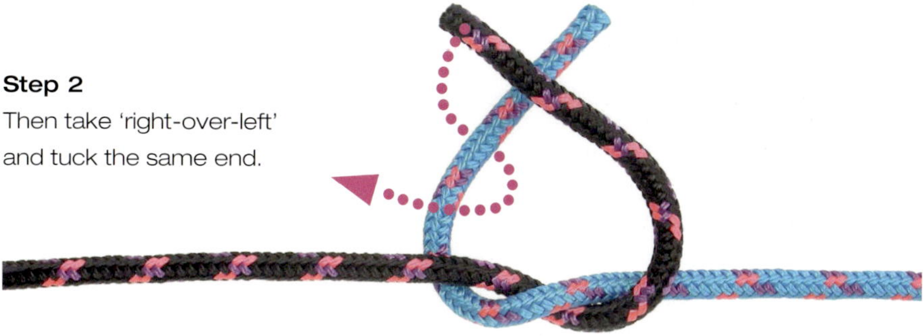

Step 2

Then take 'right-over-left' and tuck the same end.

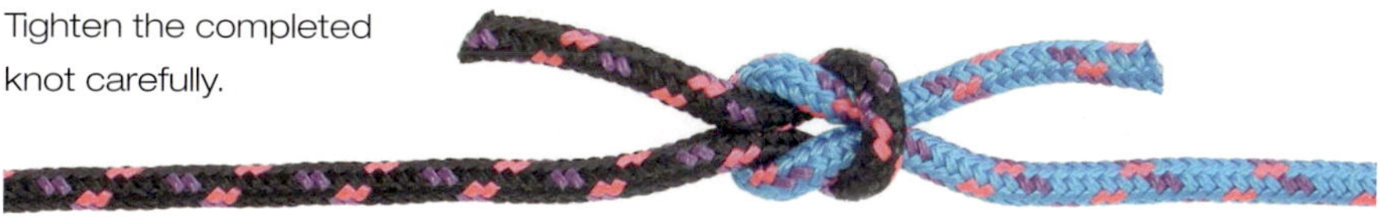

Step 3

Tighten the completed knot carefully.

This is the SZ version of the knot. If it does not come easily to you, try going 'right-over-left', then 'left-over-right', to produce the ZS version.

Most knots come in two mirror-images and, as a general rule, you will prefer one to the other and have to think hard in order to tie the one that does not come easily.

Overhand knot

This is an elementary knot but is the basis of many more complex knots. A simple overhand or thumb knot makes a stopper knot and can be tied in the end of rope, cord or twine as an easy alternative to a whipping (see page 32), or to stop it pulling free from an anchorage point. This knot, too, may be S-laid or Z-laid.

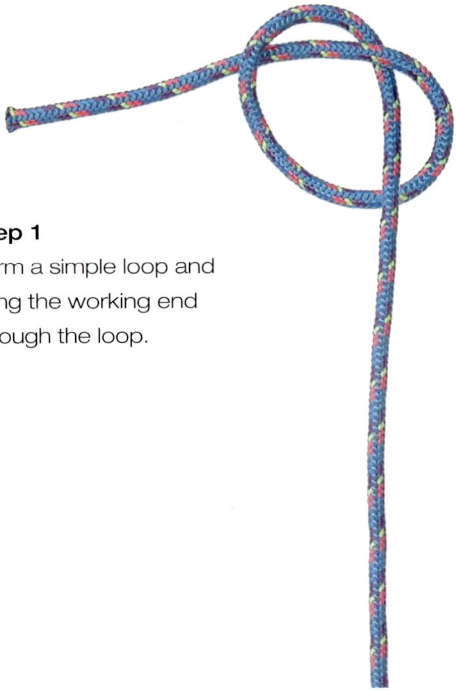

Step 1

Form a simple loop and bring the working end through the loop.

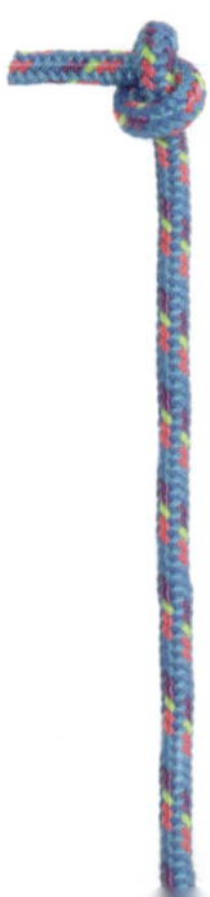

Step 2

Work the knot tight and notice how, when tightened, the working end tilts over almost at a right-angle to the standing part. Let it happen. Always heed what a knot wants to do.

MUST KNOW

Thumb knot

The other name for an overhand knot is a thumb knot, because (in twine) some people tie it around their thumbs.

Draw loop

To form a draw-loop, when you are in the final stage of tying an overhand knot (or other knots), do not pull the working end fully through the knot before tightening.

Draw loops should be used more often than they are. They add bulk to a knot, which can strengthen it, and make it easier to untie.

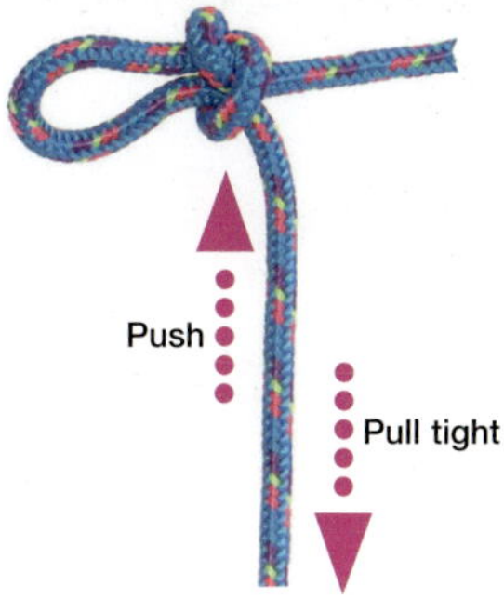

Noose

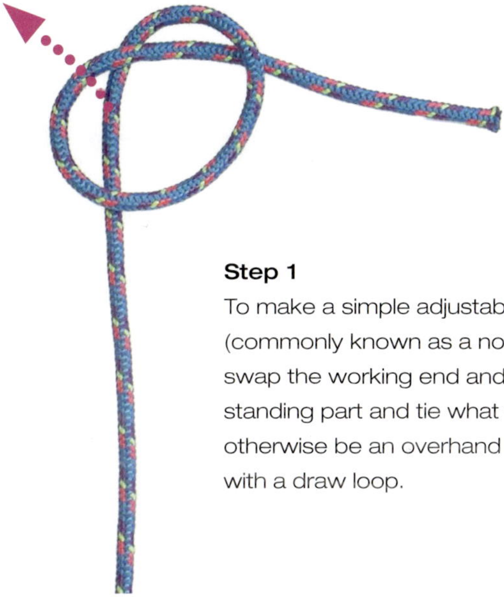

Step 1

To make a simple adjustable loop (commonly known as a noose), swap the working end and standing part and tie what would otherwise be an overhand knot with a draw loop.

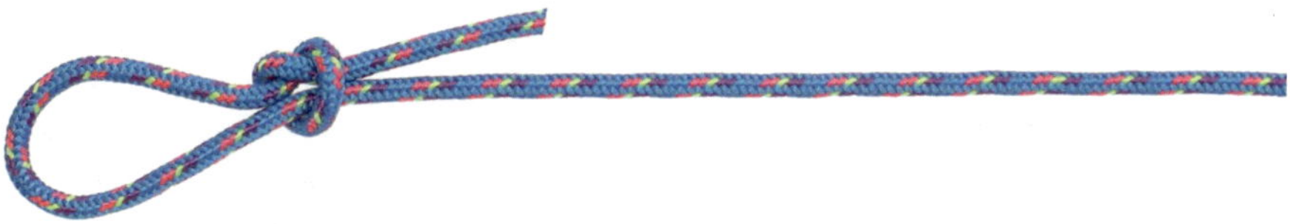

Step 2

First tighten the knot, then adjust the noose to the required size.

Double overhand knot

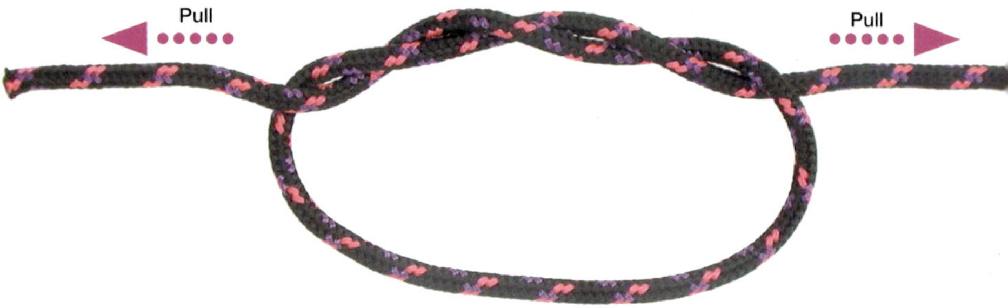

Step 1

Tie an overhand knot and tuck the working end a second time before pulling the working end and standing part gently in opposite directions.

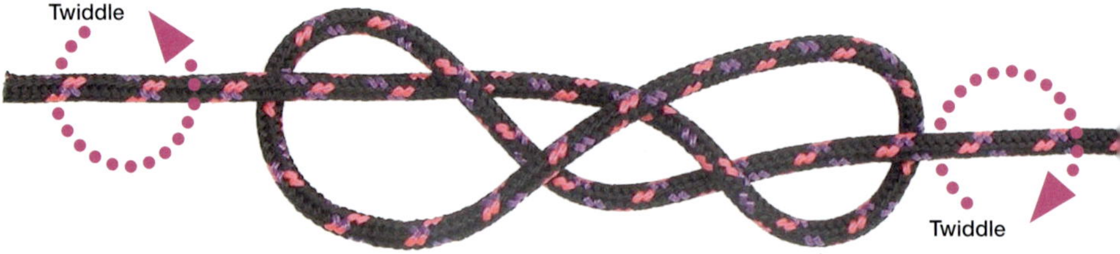

Step 2

Counter-twiddle the ends around (as shown) to generate a chunkier stopper knot.

Step 3

The tightened knot is ideal when you want the working end in line with the standing part rather than projecting sideways.

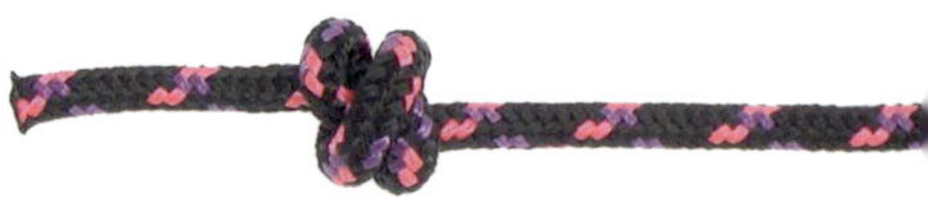

MUST KNOW

Flyping (sounds like typing)

The process of wrap and trap, turning double and triple overhand knots inside-out, akin to peeling off a sock or glove, is known as flyping. Flyping was first used as a knotting term in the late-19th century by the Scottish physicist Peter Guthrie Tait. It was resurrected in the mid-1980s as a succinct term for a knot tying technique that otherwise needs a great deal of explaining.

Triple overhand knot

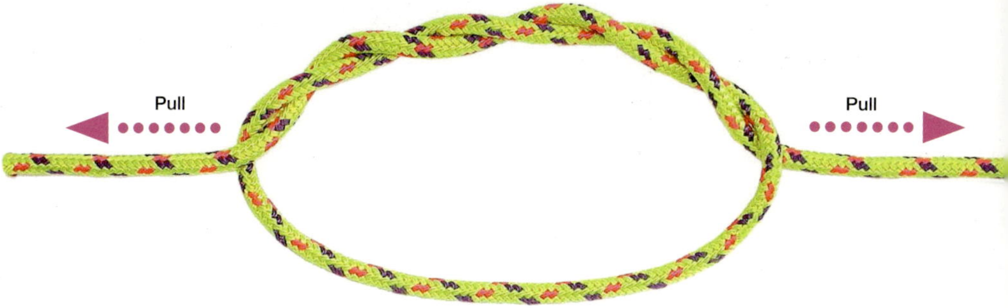

Step 1
Tie a double overhand knot and tuck the working end a third time before pulling the ends gently.

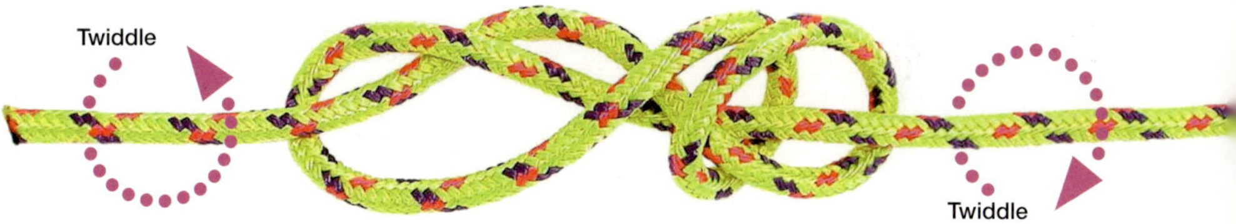

Step 2
Repeat the second stage of the double overhand knot.

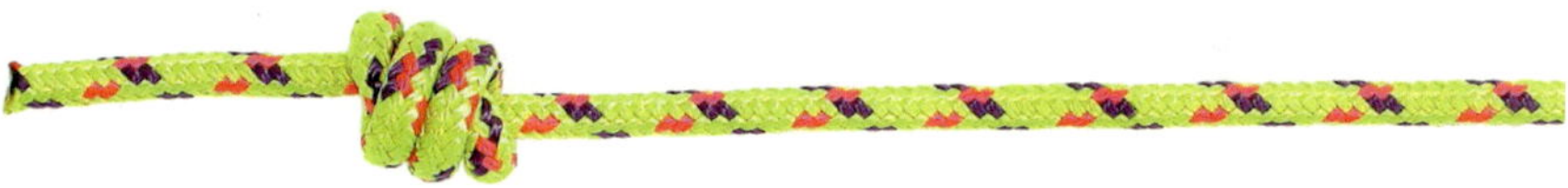

Step 3
Tighten to create a triple overhand knot. Learn this trio of core-and-wrap knots now, because they are essential elements of even more ambitious knots later.

Multiple overhand knot

In thick cordage this is better tied directly in the hand, rather than by flyping (see page 24). Use a finger or other object to hold the preformed turns in place until the working end can be tucked to complete the knot. In fine fishing lines, however, flyping is often the preferred technique.

Step 1

With the standing end in a diagonal position, wrap the working end around the foundation (or finger), say, five times. Tuck the working end back through the turns and beneath the standing part to complete the knot.

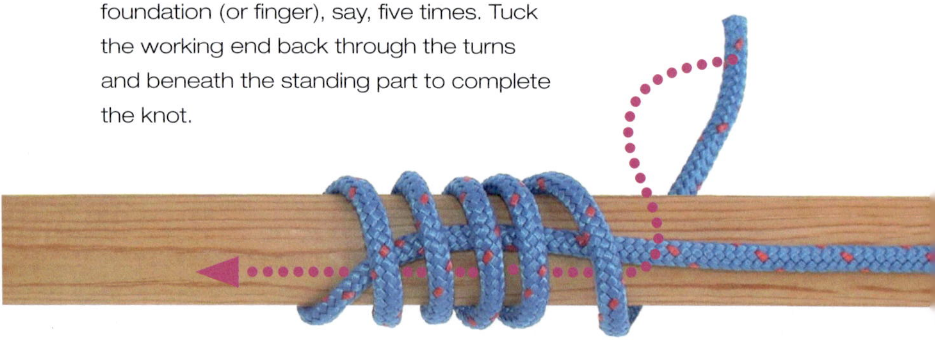

Step 2

Withdraw the retaining foundation (or finger) and work the knot so that the turns lie neatly next to one another and then tighten the knot.

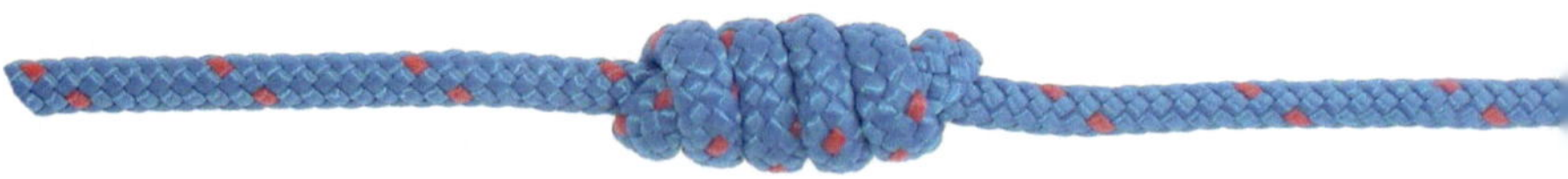

MUST KNOW

Bloody history

Overhand knots, when tied in the lashes of a cat-o'-nine-tails, were called 'blood knots' because they lacerated the victim's skin.

Anglers, who like the strength and streamlining that this knot gives them, still refer to them as blood knots.

They also harmlessly embellish the ropes tied by monks and nuns around their waist to signify that they are bound by vows of poverty, celibacy (or chastity) and obedience.

Two half-hitches

Step 1

Tie an overhand knot around a rail, ring or post (or another rope), bring the working end down alongside the standing part, and a half-hitch results.

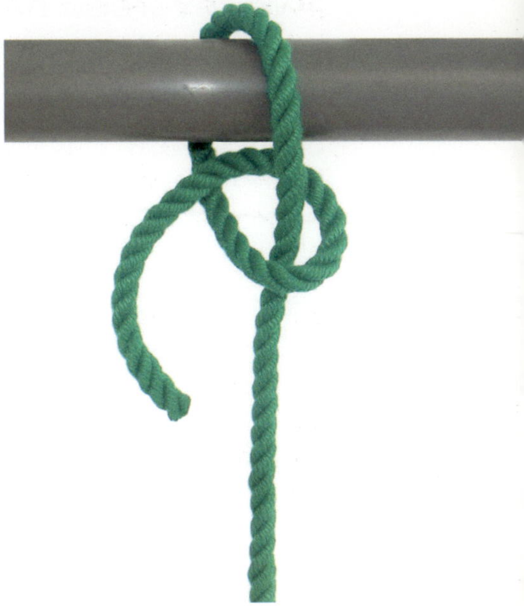

MUST KNOW

Elementary knots

Two half-hitches are also used for both the round turn and two half-hitches (see page 110) and the anchor (or fisherman's) bend (see page 53).

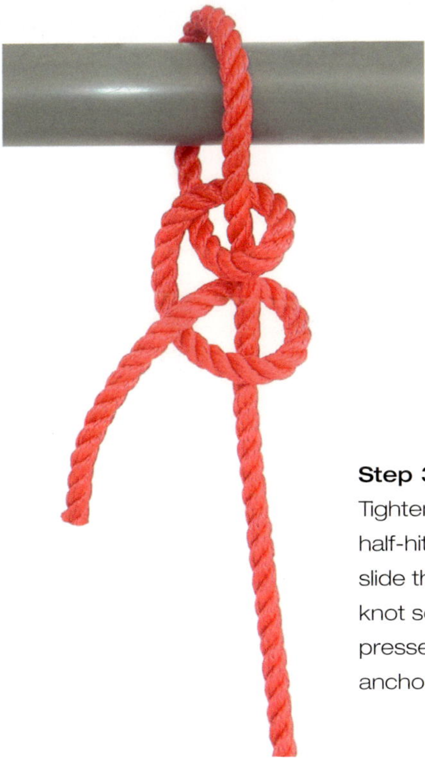

Step 2

Add a second identical half-hitch for a fairly secure holdfast.

Step 3

Tighten both half-hitches and slide the resulting knot so that it presses against its anchorage point.

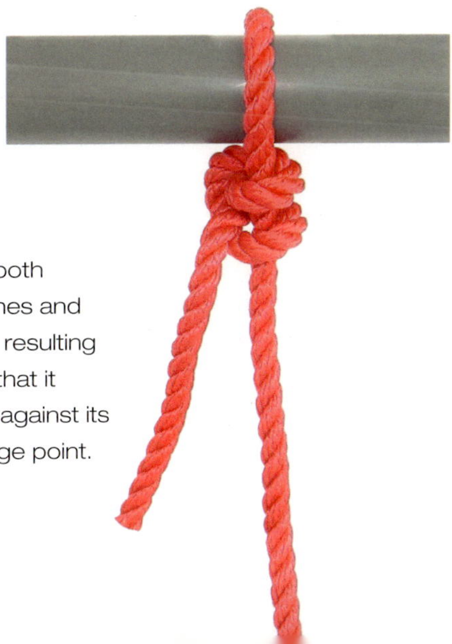

Two reversed half-hitches

Two reversed half-hitches are just as effective but they tend to be viewed with disfavour and suspicion, in part because sailors see them as lubberly, but also because they may be a sign that the tyer cannot be depended upon to tie two orthodox half-hitches correctly.

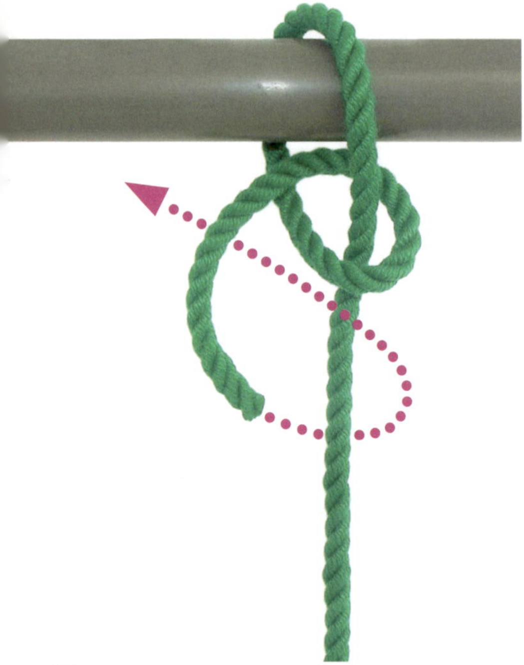

Step 1
Repeat step 1 as for two half-hitches (see page 27).

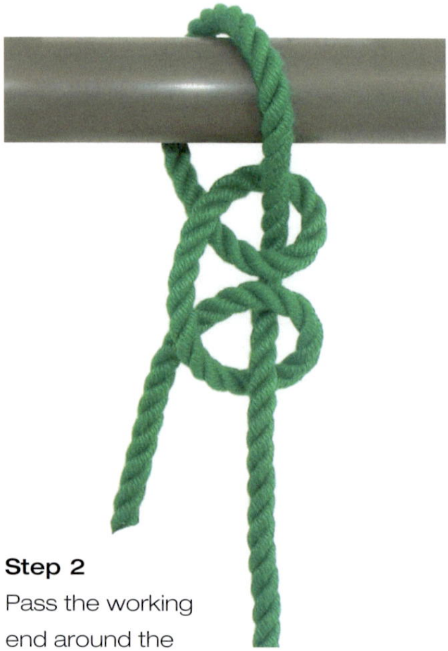

Step 2
Pass the working end around the standing part, but this time counter-clockwise (instead of clockwise) to tie the second half-hitch.

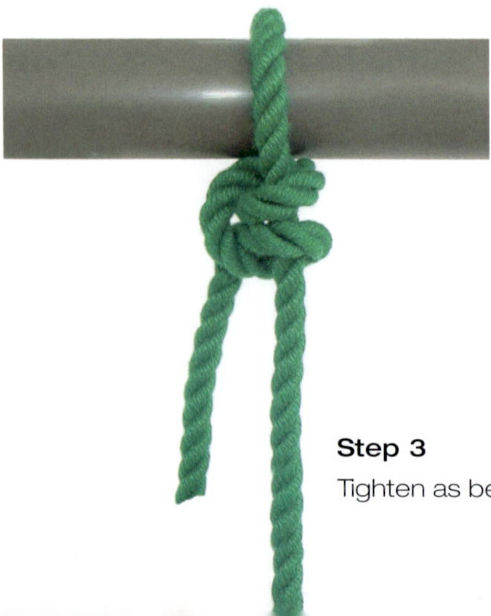

Step 3
Tighten as before.

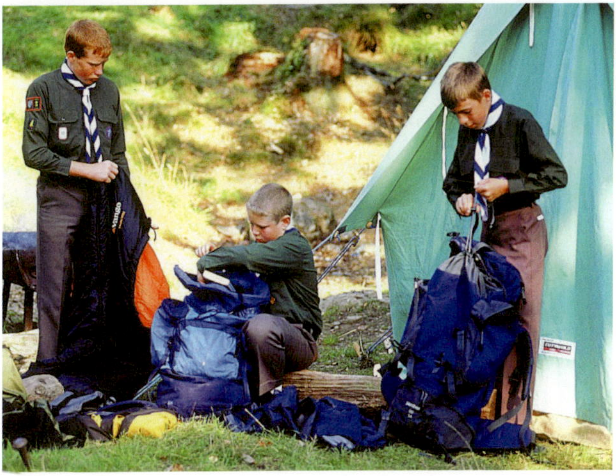

◀ Camping, with its opportunities for allied outdoor pursuits, always involves the chance to practice tying a few knots.

The parsimony principle

There is an economical, miserly or parsimonious streak to knotting, with tying techniques limited to the same few manoeuvres and manipulations, while the knots themselves are usually combinations of recurring components – bights, loops, elbows, twists, turns and tucks, half-hitches and overhand knots. This is the parsimony principle. The bowline and the sheet bend (see Boating knots), for instance, share a common layout. Two half-hitches and a clove hitch (see Boating knots again) are similar. Whipping (see page 32), a nail knot and snelling (see Fishing knots) are all just different applications of the same basic binding. In each case, learn one and get one free.

The law of loop, hitch and bight

The law of loop, hitch and bight is a knot-tying litmus test, letting us know when to look for a way of tying in the bight and when not to bother. For example, the constrictor knot (see pages 88–9) can be tied in the bight, but the strangle knot (see pages 86–7) cannot. Removed from its foundation, it is a double overhand knot. Where possible, tie knots in the bight. Sometimes it is easier to learn a knot by tying with an end but, when possible, you should graduate to tying it in the bight.

Half-hitching

A series of linked half-hitches (see page 27) is a handy way to parcel up a roll of worn-out linoleum to take it to the local refuse and recycling depot or, alternatively, to take an antique Persian carpet to an auction house. Then again, for boating purposes, it will temporarily furl a sail while you go ashore.

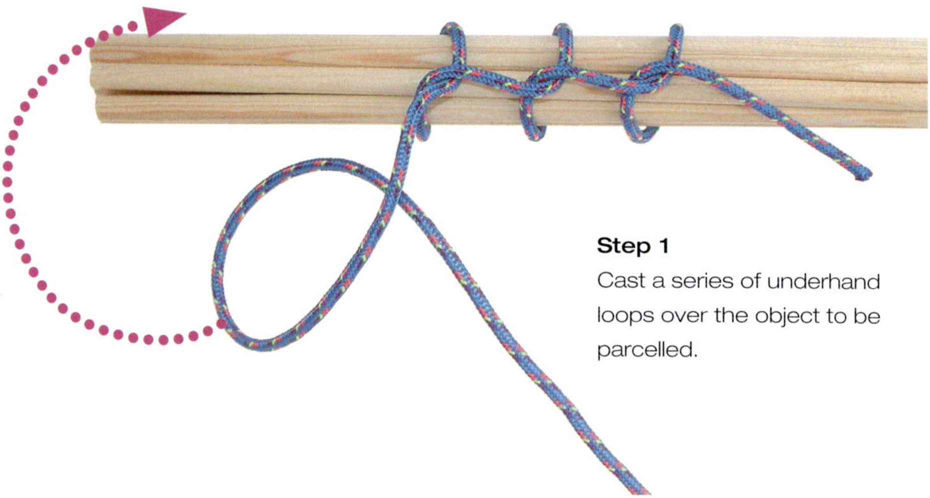

Step 1

Cast a series of underhand loops over the object to be parcelled.

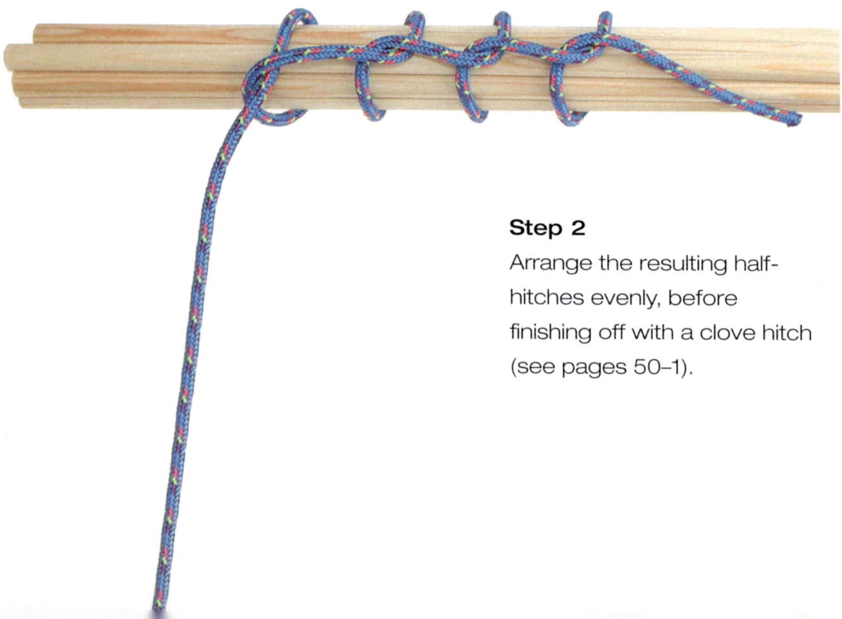

Step 2

Arrange the resulting half-hitches evenly, before finishing off with a clove hitch (see pages 50–1).

Marline hitching

Marline hitching is superior to half-hitching: although at first glance the two appear identical, it is subtly different. Slide half-hitching off its foundation and it falls apart leaving only a memory. Do the same with marline hitching and you are left with a row of overhand knots. It is for this reason that marline hitching grips and holds better than half-hitching. The disadvantage is that it must be tied with an end, while half-hitching can be assembled in the bight (that is, without using an end).

This is a demonstration of the law of loop, hitch and bight. All hitches that collapse to nothing when deprived of their foundations (in other words, 'untie themselves in the bight'), such as half-hitching and the clove hitch, can be tied in the bight. Loop knots, for instance, the perfection loop (see pages 72–3), that fall apart if a bight is withdrawn, can also be tied in the bight.

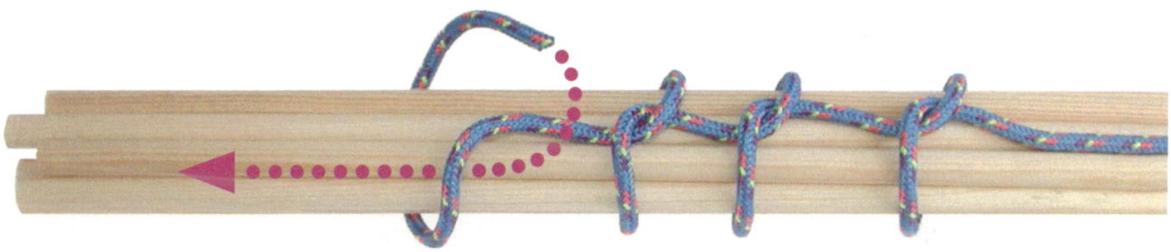

Step 1

Tie a series of half-knots around the object to be parcelled.

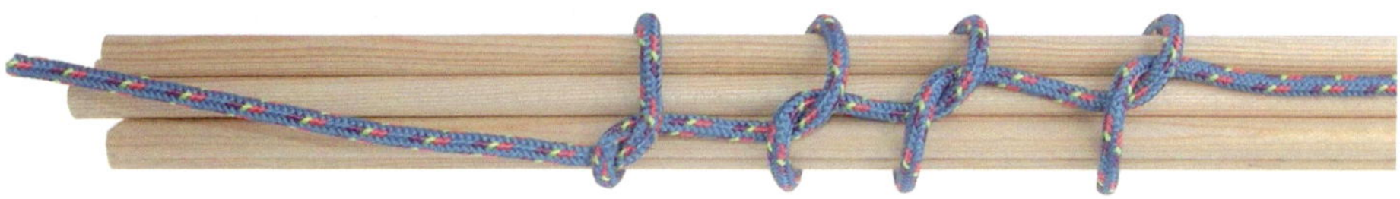

Step 2

Arrange the knots evenly, before finishing off with a clove hitch (see pages 50–1).

Protecting rope ends

Failing to guard against unravelling is a careless waste of costly rope as you can never reassemble the ruined section.

A rope or cord unravels when cut. Synthetics are worse than natural fibre in this respect because their filaments, yarns and strands may be very hard-laid and cling less firmly to each other. Therefore, before you take a knife to any cordage, seize it temporarily with a strangle knot (see pages 86–7) or a constrictor knot (see pages 88–9), either side of where you are going to cut it, or bind it with adhesive tape. Synthetic cordage can always be heat-sealed (see Alternative Treatments opposite).

Common whipping

A neater treatment, especially for natural fibre rope, is to whip it. Purists still regard a whipping as the only proper remedy for rope ends. Use natural fibre whipping twine on natural fibre cordage, and synthetic on synthetics.

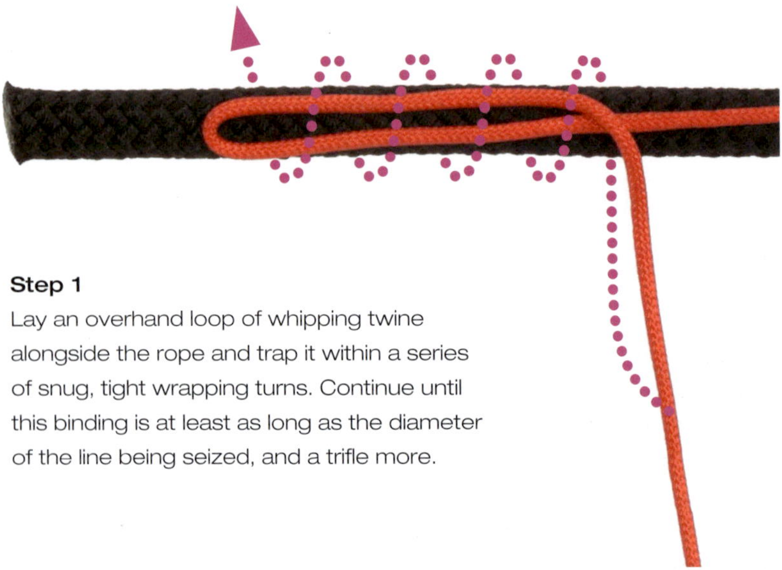

Step 1

Lay an overhand loop of whipping twine alongside the rope and trap it within a series of snug, tight wrapping turns. Continue until this binding is at least as long as the diameter of the line being seized, and a trifle more.

Step 2
Then tuck the working end through what remains of the original bight. (So as to make the next step easy, keep the last wrapping turn slacker than those preceding it.)

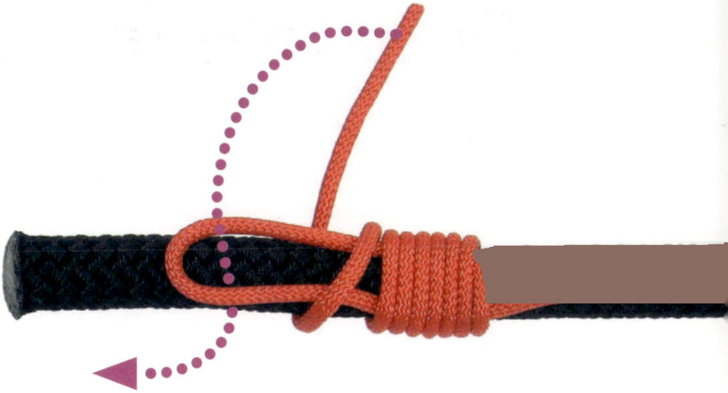

Step 3
Now pull the unused end of the twine so that it drags the working end beneath the whipping.

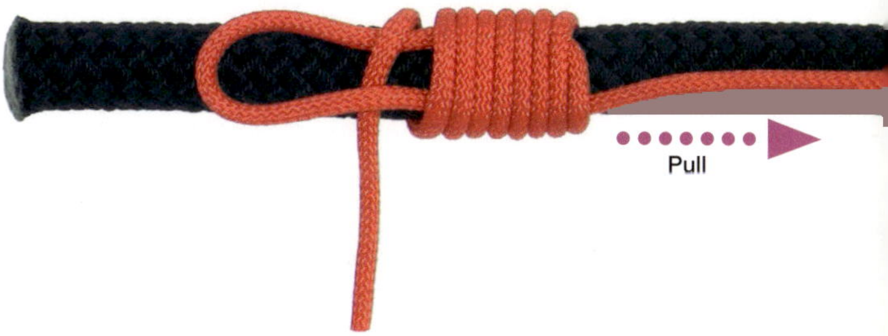

Step 4
Stop pulling when the interlocked end parts are located at the centre of the whipping.

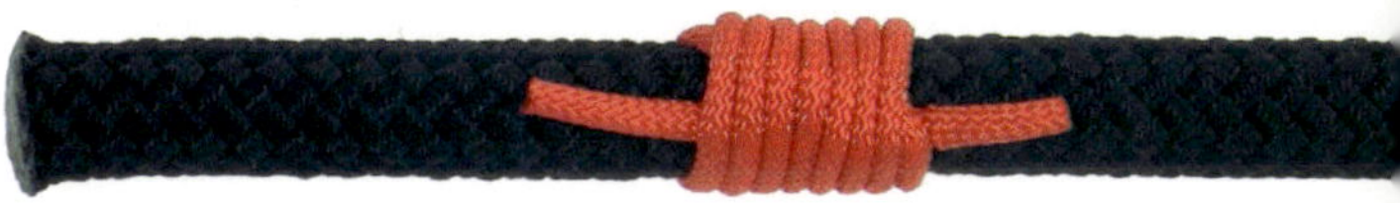

Alternative treatments

Another type of whipping is snelling (see page 81) and this, too, can be used on a rope's end.

Synthetic cords can be melted, heat-sealing both ends in the process, with a lighted match or the flame from a cigarette lighter, but make sure to do this in a well ventilated room and take care to protect your hands. Rope stockists achieve a neater cut using a proprietary brand of electric rope guillotine with a heated blade, either bench-mounted or hand-held, which the amateur can also purchase; but any old knife blade, heated cherry-red in a flame, will also achieve the same result.

WATCH OUT!

Melting synthetic cordage gives off acrid fumes and is both hot and sticky. Work in a ventilated area and take care not to burn yourself. Let the ends cool and harden for just a minute or so before handling them.

Knot strength and security

All knots weaken cordage, however, some retain a higher breaking strength and others maintain greater security.

The simple overhand and reef (or square) knots halve the unknotted breaking strength of rope. A bowline (the so-called 'King of knots') retains only 60 per cent and a figure eight loop around 70 per cent. It is how sharply the line curves where it first enters the body of the knot that determines its strength or weakness.

Bulky core-and-wrap knots, such as the double and triple fisherman's knots and the so-called blood knots, are stronger, preserving as much as 90 per cent or more of a rope's breaking strength, because the first curve of the most heavily loaded segment is well inside those knots.

Hitches, too, are strong because the friction of their initial wrapping turns absorbs the stress and strain, before any tucks or half-hitches are applied to secure them. As strong knots often take longer – and may be trickier – to tie and can be harder to untie, choosing which knot to use is always a compromise between strength, weakness and effectiveness.

Secure knots

Knot security is a measure of how well a knot, bend or hitch can withstand intermittent jerking and shaking without slipping, capsizing and spilling. It is a distinct and disparate consideration from knot strength.

Some knots, such as climbing and fishing knots, have to be strong and secure. Indeed, climbers habitually back-up or lock-off the

MUST KNOW

Security risk
When you wish to assess if a knot is secure enough for what it has to do, try tying it in shock elastic (bungee cord). It can be a revelation. A bowline (see page 54) falls apart, but the perfection loop (see pages 72–3) holds firm. A sheet bend (see pages 46–7) fails, but the zeppelin bend (see pages 48–9) does not.

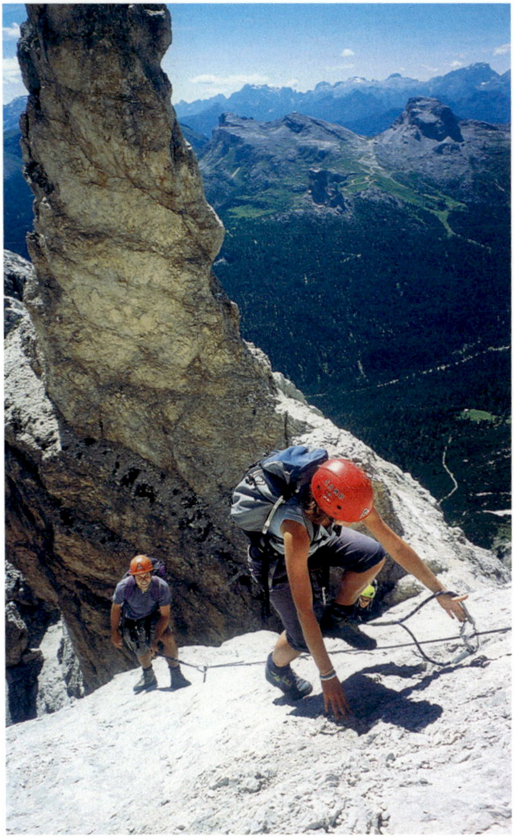

◀ To scale and descend from heights, choosing the best knots for the purpose is a crucial consideration.

▼ The combined strength and security of any tether or harness arrangement is only as good as the weakest knot used.

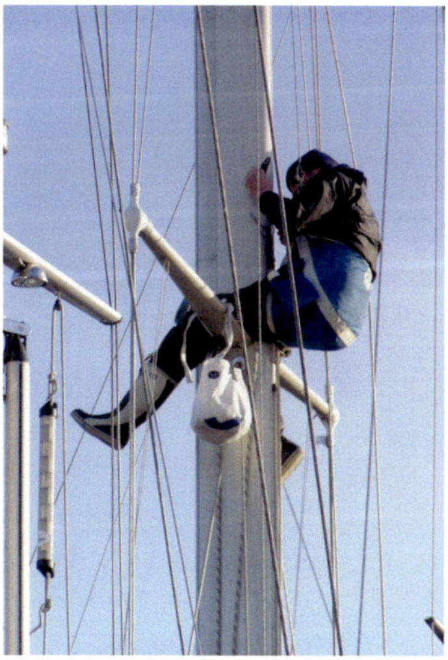

working ends of their knots (see Life-Support Knots) with a double overhand knot, or tape them to the standing part of the line, for reassuring extra security. In contrast, boating knots must be easy to cast loose in a life-saving second, which is why the common sheet bend (see pages 46–7) and the bowline (see page 54) remain popular, despite poor test data. The sheepshank (see page 98) is a very insecure shortening, unless the end bights are somehow tied or toggled. Then there are knots such as the Lapp knot (see pages 100–1) and the highwayman's hitch (see page 111) that are secure enough but which melt away at the tug of a draw-loop.

Tools and accessories

It is advisable to acquire a range of tools that can be used on more ambitious knots later.

All of the knots and splices in this book can be tied with the fingers unaided by any tools. Sometimes, however, tightening knots is best done with pliers (or the deft application of thumb and spike) and knots often have to be poked and prised loose to untie them. Cordage has to be cut with a knife and the severed ends whipped, taped or heat-sealed.

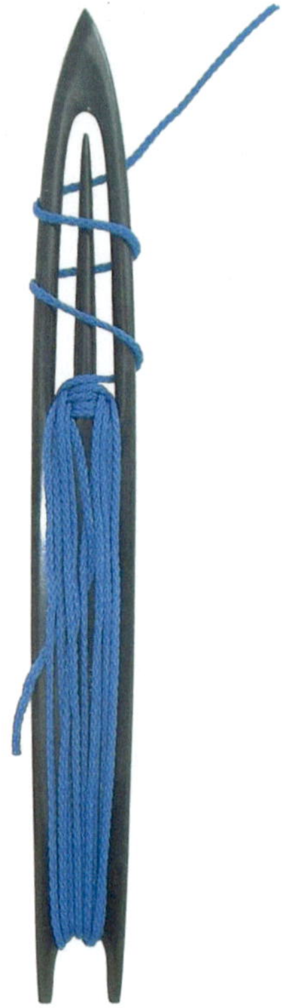

Netting needle

Useful tools

- **Craft knife (with replaceable blade)** trims the ends of completed knot work.
- **Fids (wooden)** force open hawser-laid ropes to tuck each working end or strand when knotting or splicing.
- **Fids (steel, hollow, nesting)** are essential for some splices and handy for tying knots too.
- **Gripfids (small, large)** overcome the disadvantage of solid wooden fids, which must be removed before a working end can be tucked (when the hard-won gap may close up again), because the gripfid not only creates a space but then traps and pulls the working end through as the tool is withdrawn.
- **Marlinespike** is a metal fid for heavier splicing work, also hauls tight spliced strands and marline hitching or half-hitching.
- **Netting needles (small, medium, large)** are excellent for storing tangle-free lengths of cords and twine (even if you never use them to make a knotted net).
- **Pliers (round-billed, small, medium)** are invaluable for tightening, and later untying, knots.

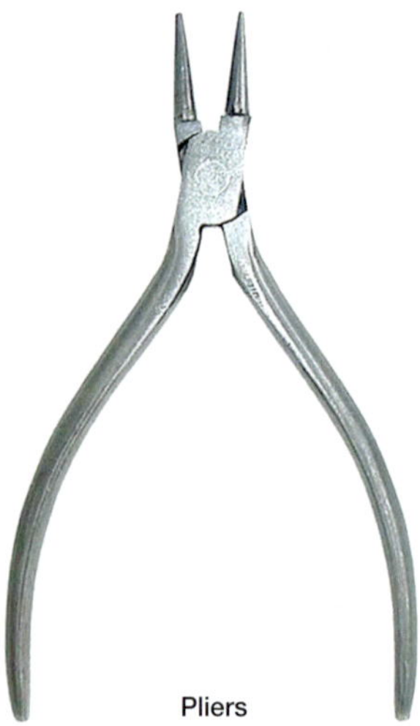

Pliers

- **Pocket knife** any folding knife is handy, but one with a sharp blade and a spike (known as a jack knife) is twice as useful.
- **Shackles** are robust metal links, secured by threaded pins, for attaching ropes to rings and other rigging terminals.
- **Shears** (by Wolfcraft®) one jaw of this patent tool holds a replaceable blade, while the other acts as an anvil. It can cut a single fibre or filament and slice through any rope that will fit between its powerful jaws.
- **Sheath knife** preferable to a pocket knife for cutting rope.
- **Spike (plus shackle key)** a combination tool, indispensable if you frequently splice hawser-laid lines, untie knots and use shackles.
- **Swedish fid (small, large)** a forerunner of the gripfid, it needs the pressure of a thumb to trap the working end or strand.
- **Thimbles** round or pear-shaped liners made from metal or plastic used to protect spliced or knotted eyes from predictable abrasion and wear.
- **Wire loops (small, medium, large)** the home-made alternative for when fids, prickers and marlinspikes are too big. No knottologist should be without several of them.
- **Whipping twine** for binding cut rope ends.

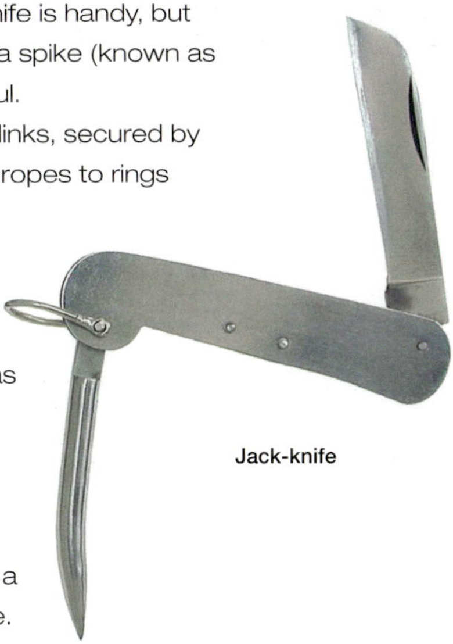

Jack-knife

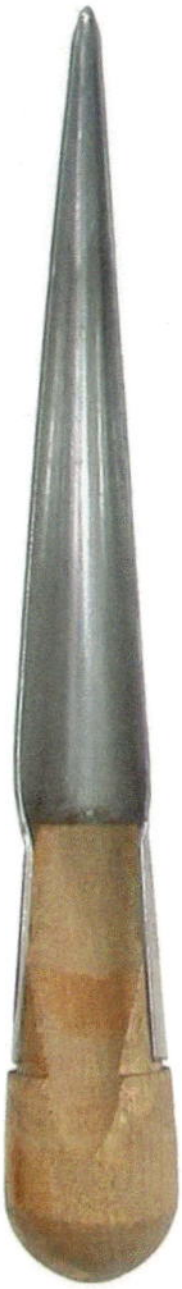

Swedish fid

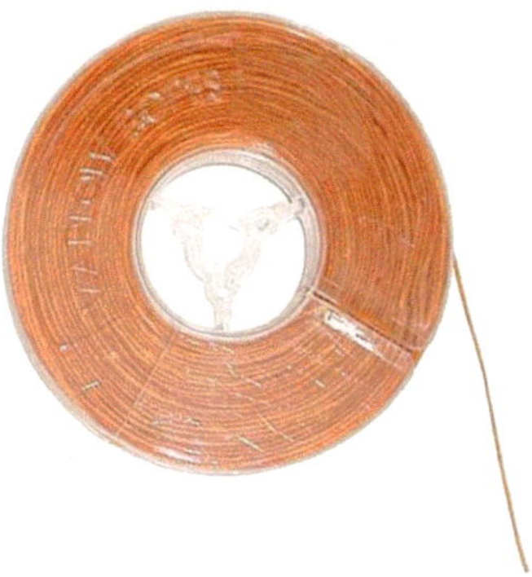

Whipping twine

want to know **more?**

Take it to the next level...

Go to...

- ▶ **Cordage facts –** pages 166–83
- ▶ **Glossary –** pages 184–5
- ▶ **Need to know more –** pages 186–8

Other sources

- ▶ **Footrope knots**
  cordage, tools, books (see pages 186–8)
- ▶ **International Guild of Knot Tyers**
  www.igkt.craft.org
- ▶ **Visit the historical ropewalk**
  for traditional ropemaking (see page 186)
- ▶ **Boat chandlers**
  for all types of cordage
- ▶ **Knotting 'bible'**
  The Ashley Book of Knots (see page 188)

boating

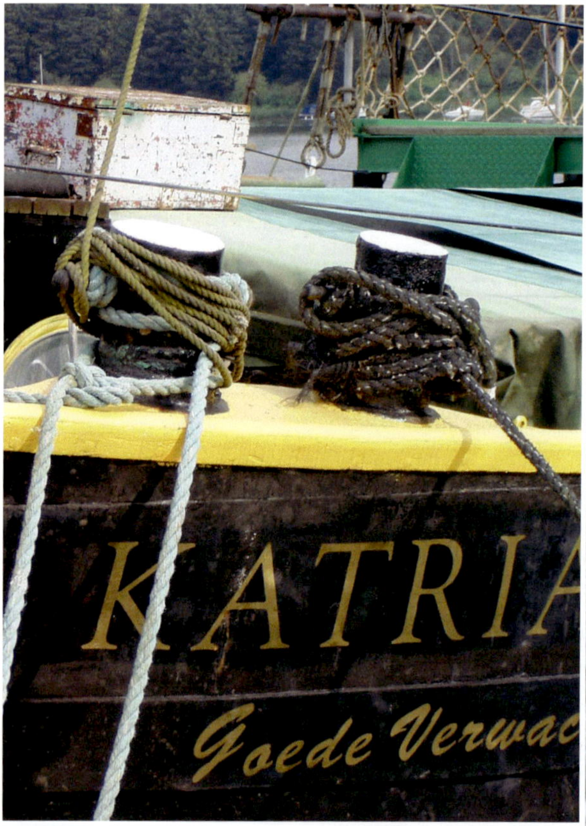

knots

Whether you are a weekend sailor or oceanic navigator, kayaker or kite surfer, jet skier or scuba diver, it is essential to know how to tie a few bends and hitches. Also, if you are transporting any kind of water craft by car or trailer; rigging and launching from a public slipway or exclusive marina; under weigh and anchored, moored or berthed; be prepared to knot and splice.

Figure eight stopper knot

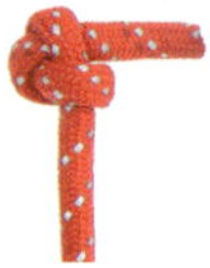

Stopper knots do as their names suggest, that is, act as 'anchors' for lengths of rope or cord. Use a figure eight stopper knot for the ends of jib-sheets that have been led through their respective fairleads, and tie one in the end of the main-sheet (or any other block-and-tackle system that you want to keep intact).

The figure eight knot was originally identified in *The Young Sea Officer's Sheet Anchor* (1908) by Darcy Lever. It is the simple progenitor of an entire family of more elaborate knots (see Life-Support Knots for two of them, namely the figure eight loop, pages 126–7, and the double figure eight loop, pages 128–9).

MUST KNOW

Easy to untie
This knot is no bulkier than an overhand knot and will not block a larger slot or hole, but you will find that it is both stronger and easier to untie than an overhand knot, so use it for those reasons.

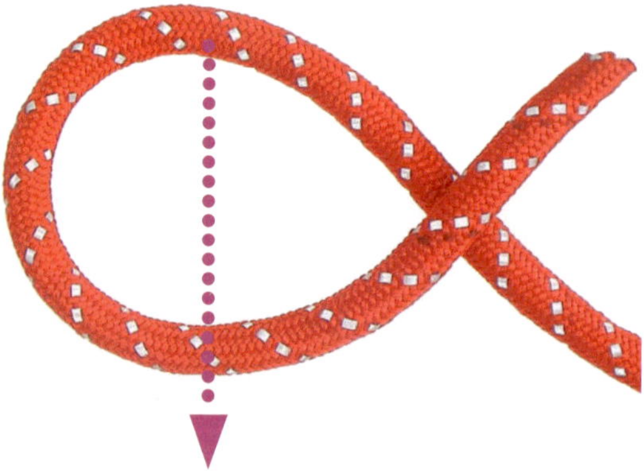

Method

Step 1

First make a simple overhand loop, placing the working end over the standing part. Then add a half twist, forming a figure of eight.

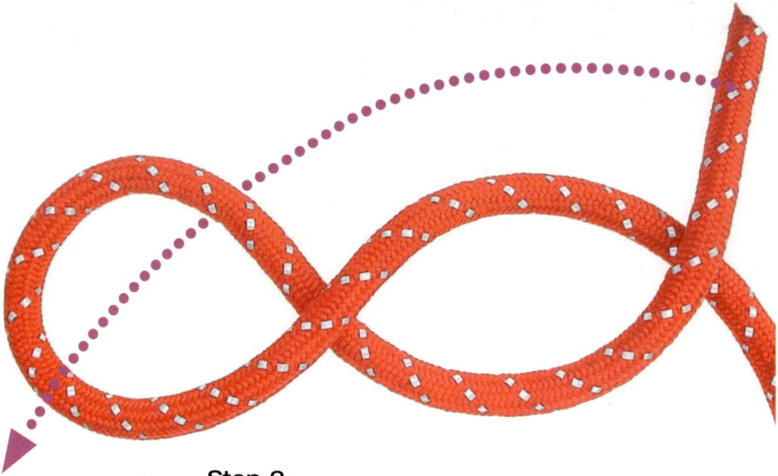

Step 2
Next tuck the working end up through the initial loop.

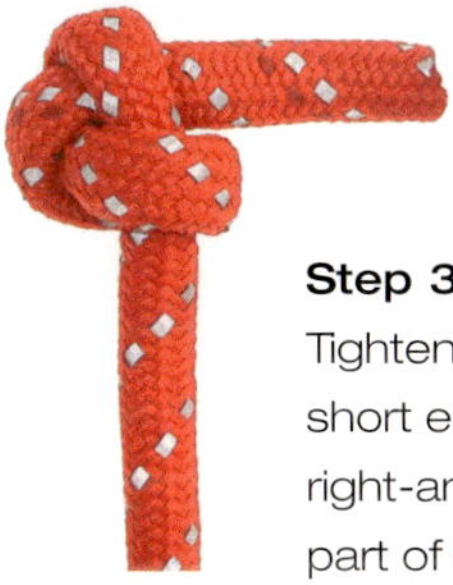

Step 3
Tighten the knot until the short end lies almost at a right-angle to the standing part of the rope.

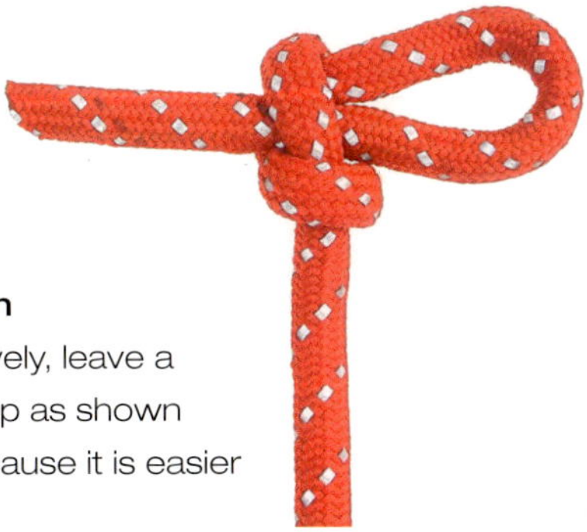

Variation
Alternatively, leave a draw-loop as shown here because it is easier to untie.

MUST KNOW

Flemish knot
An alternative label for the figure eight, still found in many books, is the Flemish knot, but its present name is a clue to its appearance.

Ashley's stopper knot

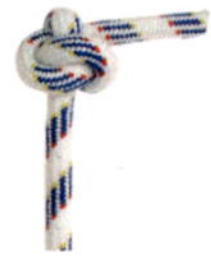

Like the figure eight stopper knot on pages 40–1, this knot can be used for a multitude of tasks when sailing. It is a bigger blocker than the figure eight and is consequently useful when a bulkier stopper is needed.

The distinctive feature of this knot is a triple crown arranged around the standing part of the rope or cord on the underside of the knot.

This stopper knot was devised sometime in the first quarter of the 20th century by the American maritime painter and illustrator Clifford Warren Ashley while he was working on a series of pictures of the oyster culture industry in Delaware Bay for *Harper's* magazine, which is why his name for this knot was the oysterman's stopper knot.

Method

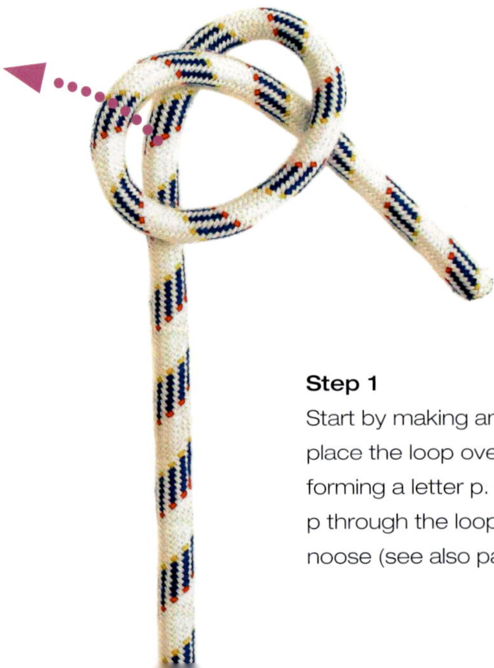

Step 1

Start by making an overhand loop. Then place the loop over the standing part, forming a letter p. Pull the top of the letter p through the loop to make a simple noose (see also page 23) and then tighten.

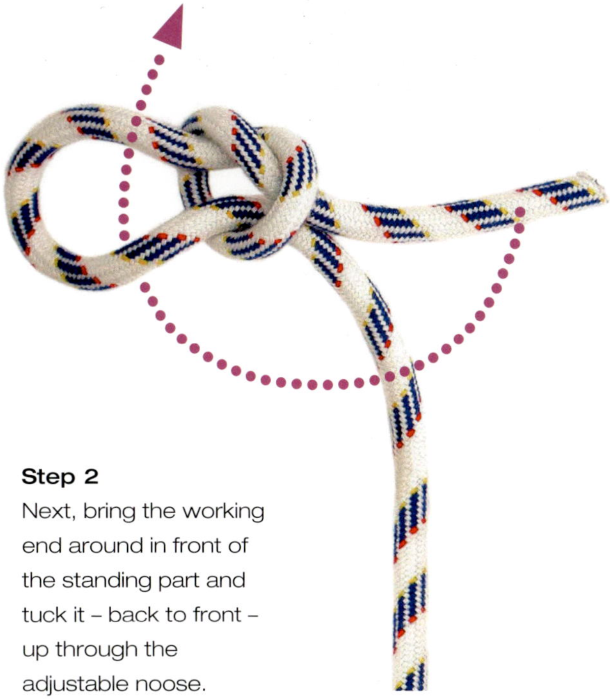

Step 2
Next, bring the working end around in front of the standing part and tuck it – back to front – up through the adjustable noose.

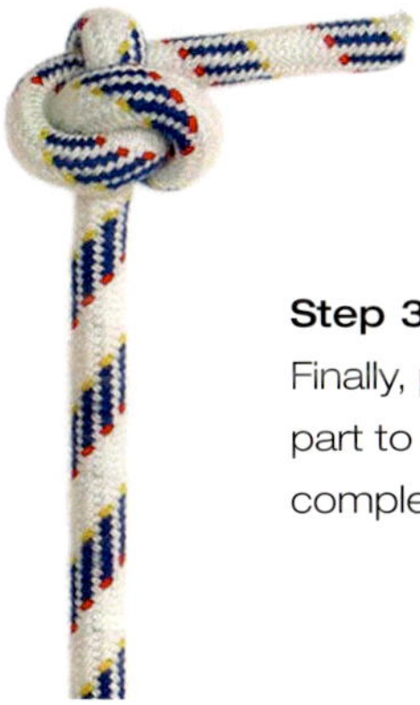

Step 3
Finally, pull the standing part to tighten the completed knot.

MUST KNOW

Knotting bible
Clifford Ashley, who devised this knot, also wrote *The Ashley Book of Knots,* which knot enthusiasts refer to as the 'knotting bible'.

Back splice (with Crown knot)

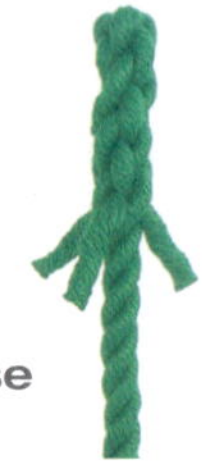

To keep a rope's end from fraying and unravelling use a back splice tied in conjunction with a crown knot.

It is more reliable than a whipping or adhesive tape and this type of round six-plait also stiffens the final few centimetres (or inches) for easy handling. Tie a crown knot first – it not only locks all three strands together, acting as first aid treatment to prevent them unravelling further, but points them in the right direction for splicing.

For the crown knot

Step 1

Begin by separating (unlaying) the strands of a hawser-laid rope for a length equal to about ten times its diameter, or a little more. Then, working counter-clockwise, fold strand (a) downwards to form a loop back on itself.

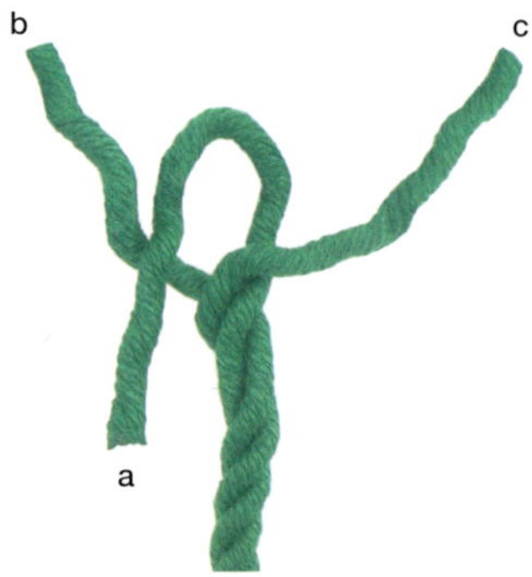

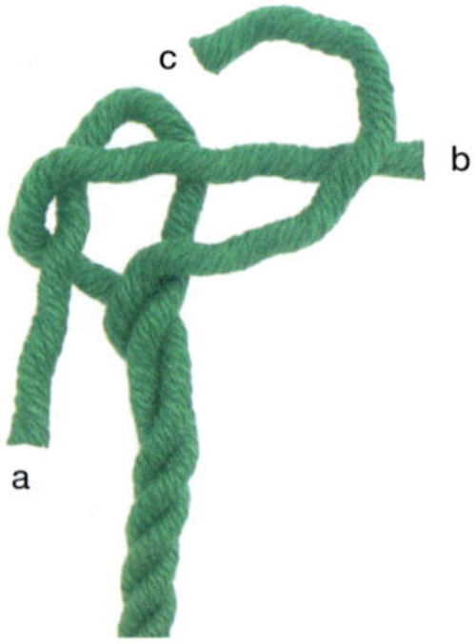

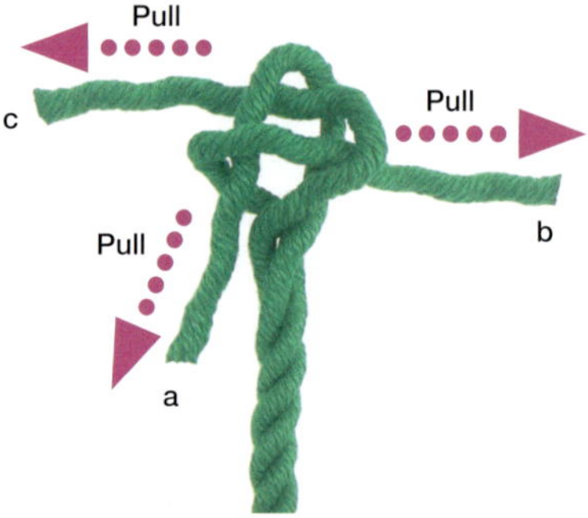

Step 2

Still working downwards, feed strand (b) across the loop and behind (c).

Step 3

Next take strand (c), feed it over (b) and through the loop. Pull all three strands evenly to tighten the knot.

For the back splice

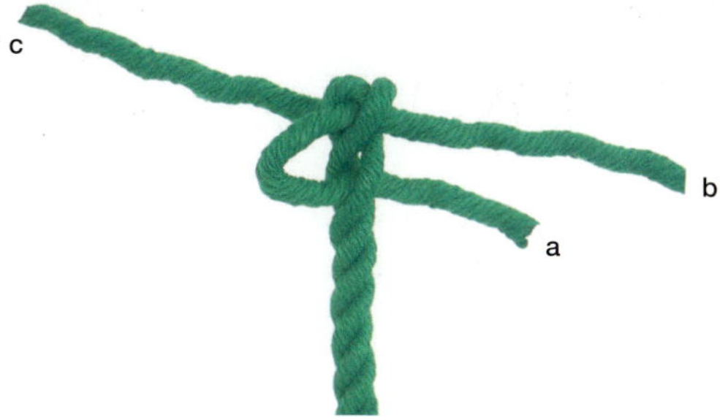

Step 4

To continue, still working counter-clockwise and downwards, take strand (a) and tuck it over and under the strands immediately below.

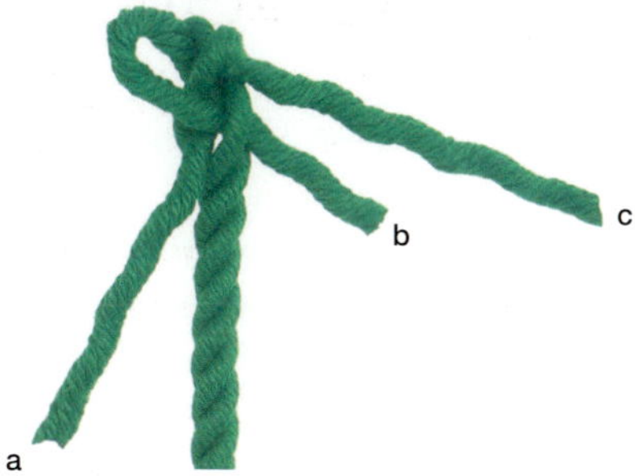

Step 5

Next, repeat the process of tucking (as in step 5) with strand (b) and thirdly with strand (c).

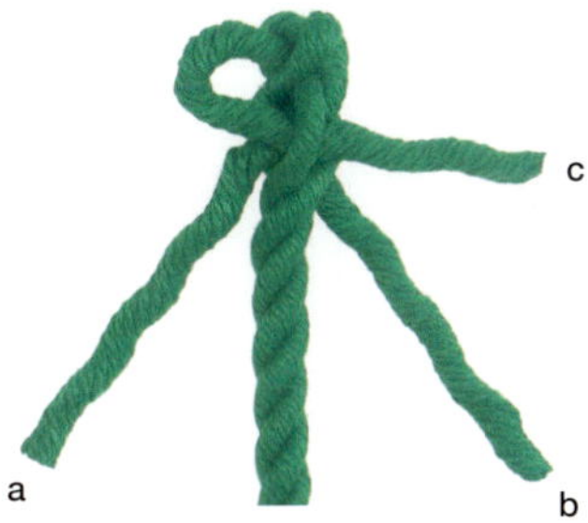

Step 6

When all three strands have been tucked once, firmly tug each one down (away from the crown knot), then up (back towards the crown knot).

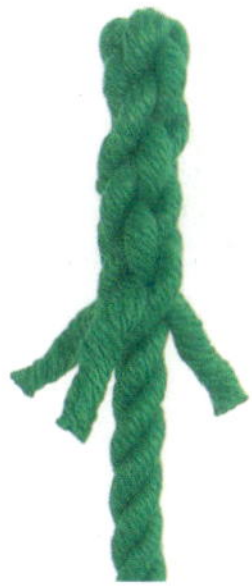

Step 7

Repeat the tucking process with each strand in turn. Tug them as before. Finally tuck a third or fourth time with each one of the three strands. Trim the ends but leave at least 15 mm (½ in) protruding, so that the last tuck does not pull out.

MUST KNOW

Fancy footwork

Roll the completed splice underfoot to achieve a neat smooth appearance. For added security and neatness, whip or tape around the cut ends. It is not absolutely essential to do this as the ends will wear with time, protruding less and less, without pulling free.

WATCH OUT!

A back splice thickens the rope's end so that it is likely to jam either entering or leaving the sheave of a block or a snugly fitting fairlead or cleat.

Sheet bend

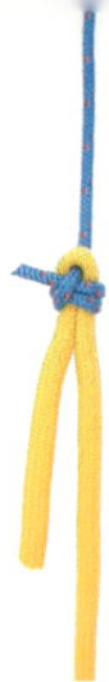

With this quick and easy bend, you can join two working ropes or cords together. A line may also be attached to a preformed permanent loop or eye in this way, when it is known as a 'becket hitch'.

If one line is noticeably thicker or harder laid (and consequently stiffer) than the other, it is advisable to create a 'double sheet bend'. This is a useful knot if you want to pick up a mooring line with a lighter heaving line from the boat.

Method

Step 1

Firstly, make a bight in one line.

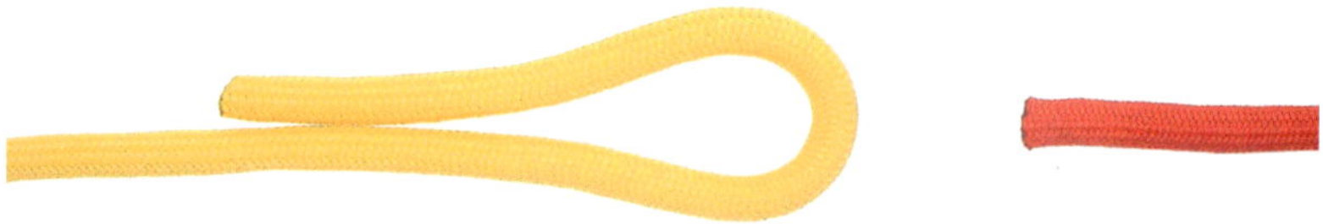

Step 2

Then tuck the working end of the other line up through the bight, before wrapping it around the back and finally tucking it beneath its own standing part.

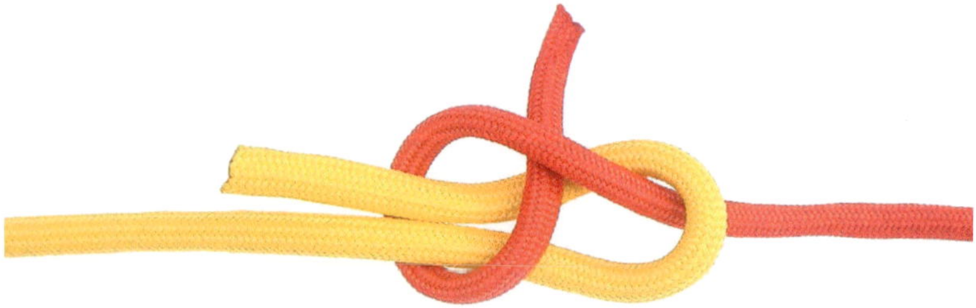

Step 3

Lastly, pull on each of the four strands in turn to tighten the knot.

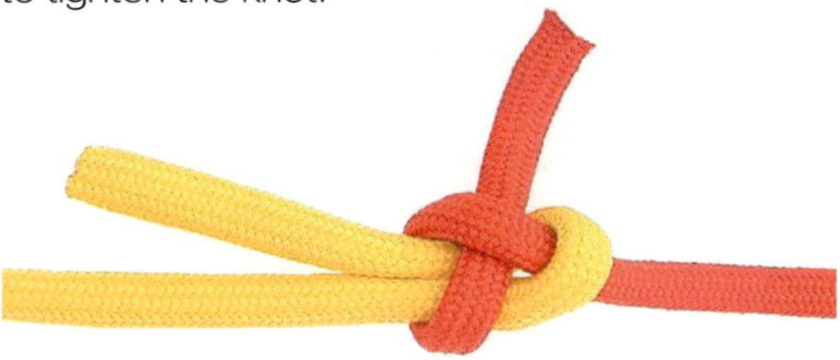

WATCH OUT!

It is recommended that you tie this bend so that both short ends emerge on the same side of the knot, because it is more secure this way.

For a double sheet bend

Step 1

Use the thicker line to form the bight and pass the working end of the thinner line through and around the bight (as in steps 1–2 opposite). Then take a second turn with the working end of the thin line before finally tucking it beneath its own standing part.

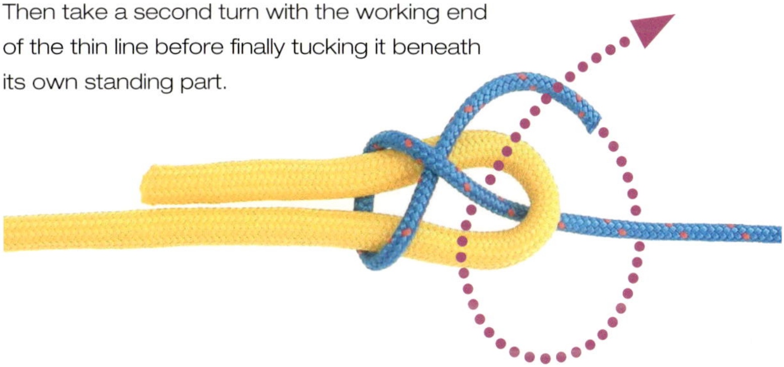

Step 2

Make the double sheet bend secure by pulling on all four strands, as above.

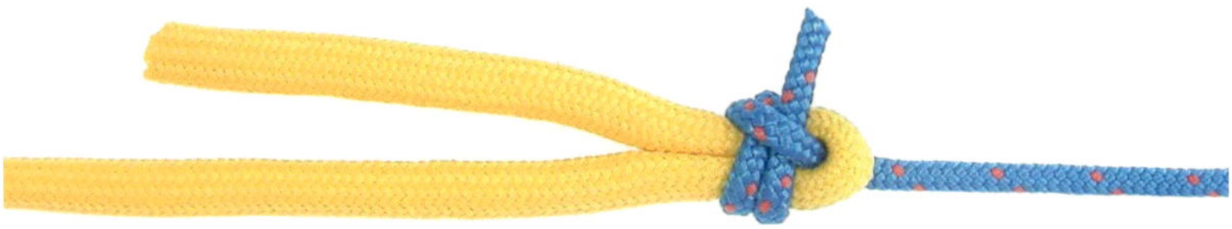

Zeppelin bend

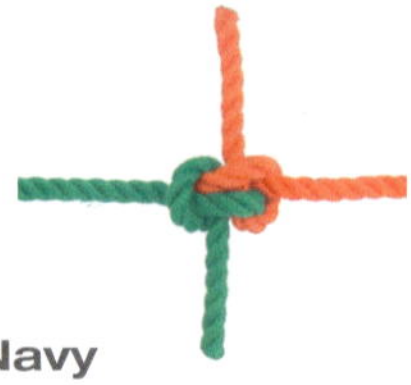

This reliable bend was employed by the US Navy to tether its lighter-than-air ships to their mooring masts from the 1930s until 1962.

You can use this strong and secure bend in rope or smaller cordage to withstand heavy loads of all kinds. A zeppelin bend can be untied by pushing and pulling on the two encircling bights until you manage to obtain some slack, when you will be able to release the ropes or cords.

Method

Step 1

Grasp both lines together with the ends pointing in the same direction, and with the right-hand working end tie a half-hitch to enclose both standing parts.

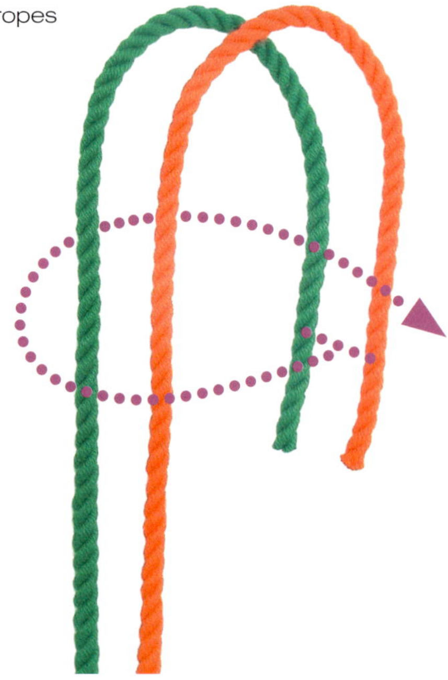

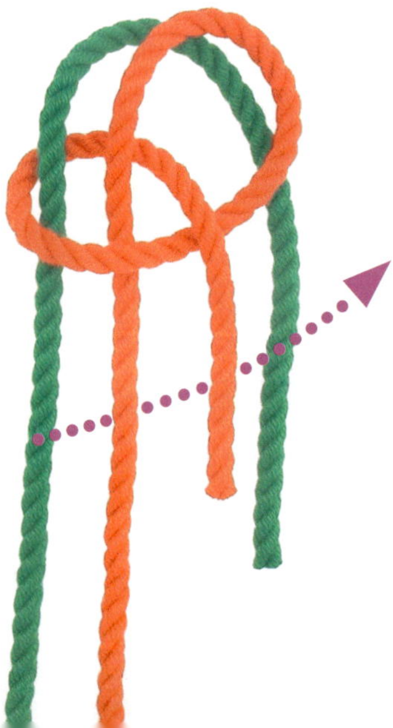

Step 2

Next, bring the left-hand standing part forward, behind the standing part and working end of the other line and in front of its own working end.

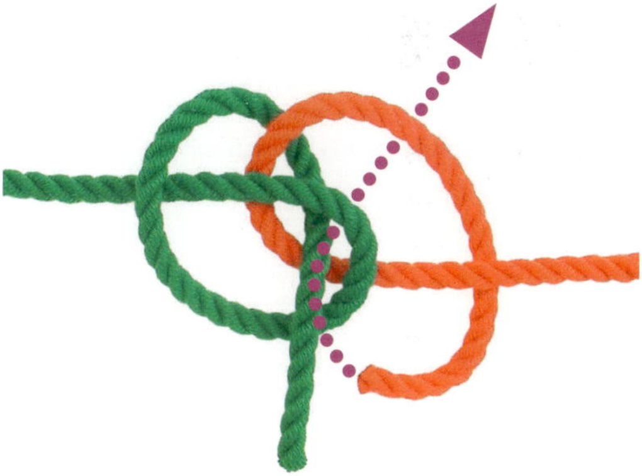

Step 3

Continue by tucking that working end first over both the other line and its own standing part and then under the other standing part and itself.

Step 4

You have now created two overhand knots with twin interlocked elbows.

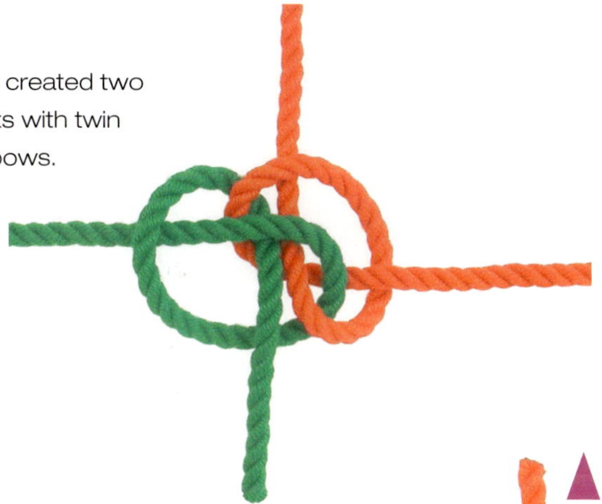

Step 5

To complete the bend tighten by pulling all four strands.

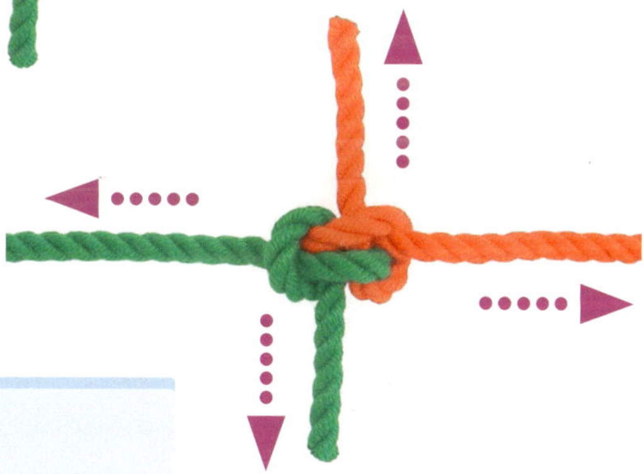

MUST KNOW

Air to water

A zeppelin bend is tough and tenacious and, although it is not often seen on boats or the quayside, it deserves to be adopted and adapted for all kinds of usage on and beside water.

Clove hitch

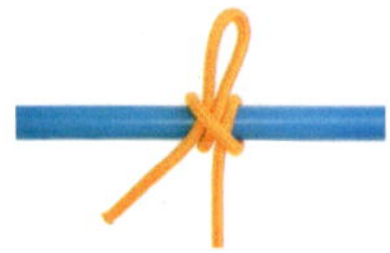

A clove hitch can be employed to secure small craft temporarily, as well as to suspend fenders. However, use this classic hitch only when the pull will be in a direction that is at a right-angle to the point of attachment.

This knot can be tied in the bight or with an end, and with or without a draw-loop for easy untying. It is helpful to learn both tying methods.

Clove hitch in the bight

Step 1

Make a couple of loops in a line – one overhand, the other underhand. Then overlap the loops.

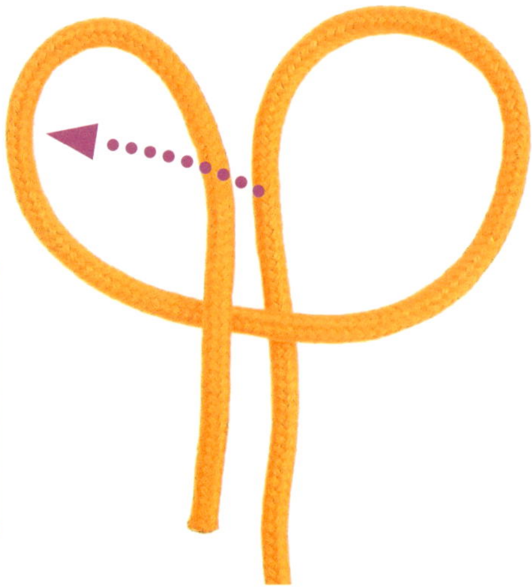

WATCH OUT!

If the load upon this hitch shifts position so as to vary the angle of pull, or it is used to tether a restless animal, it can quickly work loose and come adrift.

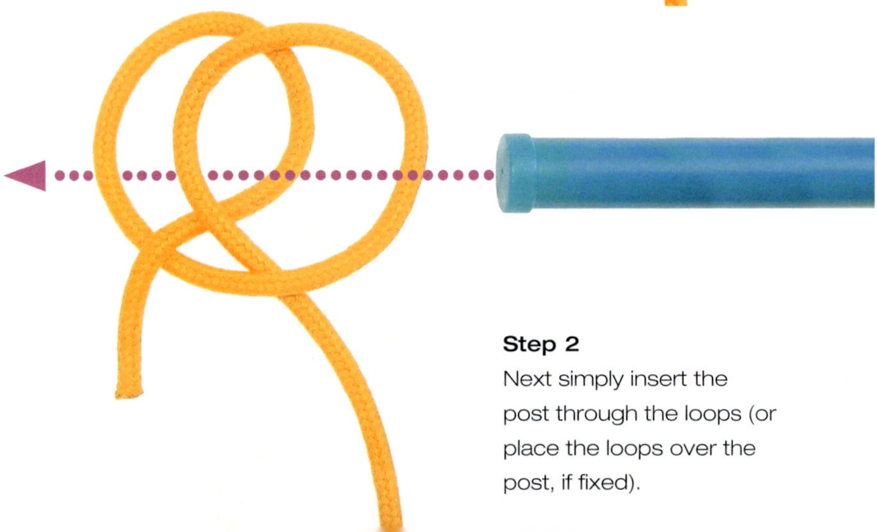

Step 2

Next simply insert the post through the loops (or place the loops over the post, if fixed).

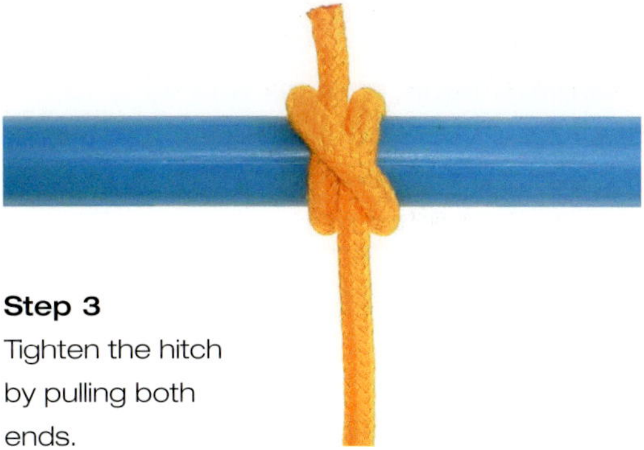

Step 3
Tighten the hitch by pulling both ends.

MUST KNOW

To the letter
When tying a clove hitch here is a useful tip. If you are making fast to a rail, ring or stanchion, wrap and tuck the working end in the shape of a letter 'N' (or its mirror image).

Clove hitch with an end

Step 1
Take the working end around the post and up across the standing part. Bring the working end around the post once again.

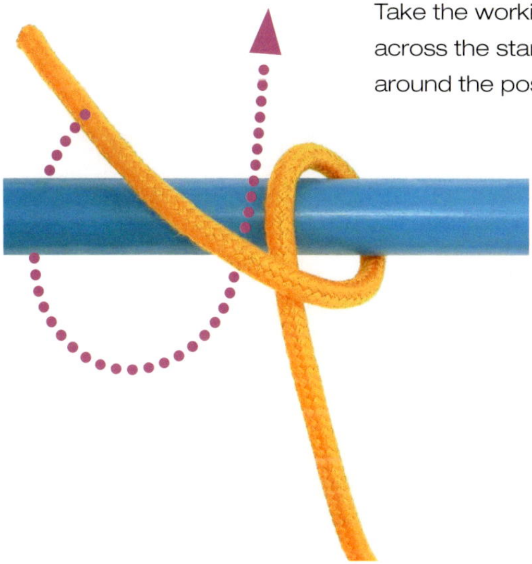

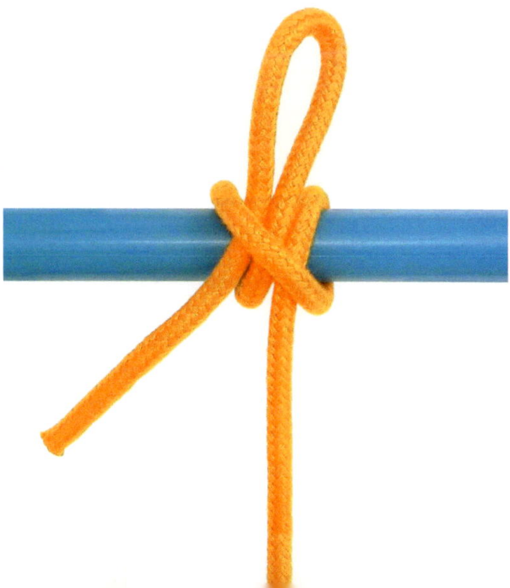

Step 2
Either tuck the end under itself (to achieve the same result as step 3 above) or form a draw loop as shown for quick release.

Rolling hitch

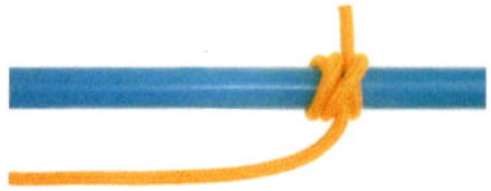

The rolling hitch, like the clove hitch, is quick and easy to execute. However, for a steady pull that is at an angle to the point of attachment, when a common clove hitch would be insecure, use this modified version of the knot.

Method

Step 1

Place the line around the post and bring the working end diagonally over the standing part. Take the working end around the post and bring it diagonally over the standing part a second time.

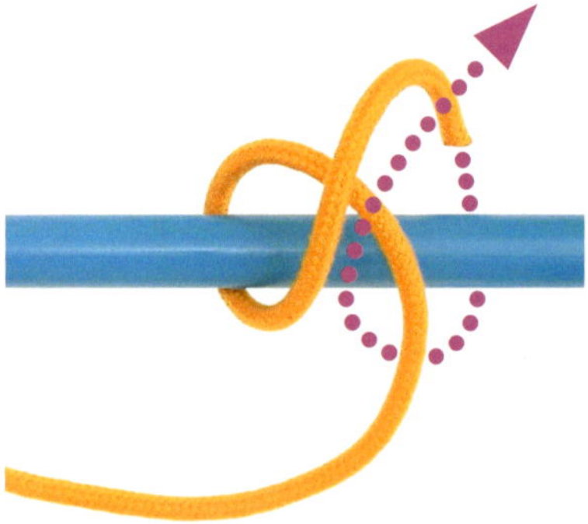

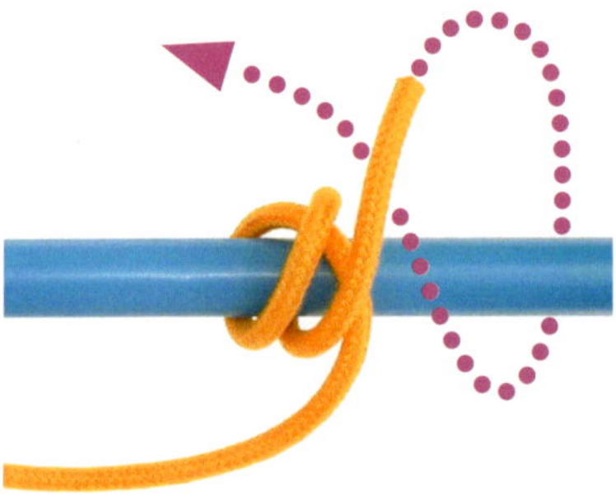

Step 2

Bring the working end around the post a third time and tuck it under the second diagonal turn, forming a half-hitch.

Step 3

Make sure that the second diagonal turn is wedged between the first turn and the standing part of the rope and tighten carefully.

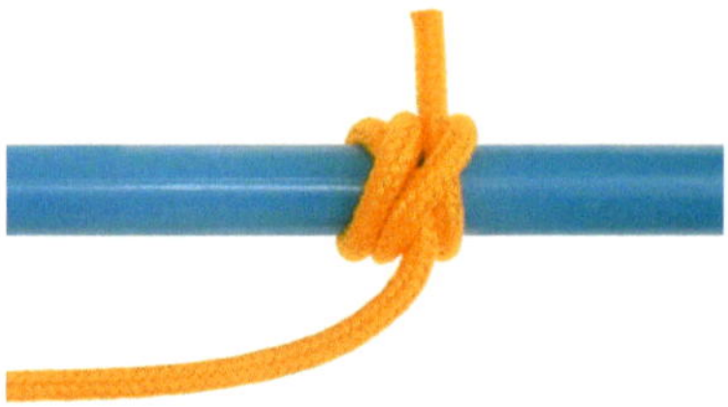

MUST KNOW

Some old seamanship manuals refer to versions of this knot as the Magnus hitch (or Magner's hitch), so do not be surprised if you find these names in such publications.

The midshipman's hitch, described on pages 60–1, is also based upon the rolling hitch – in another instance of the parsimony principle (see page 29).

Anchor bend

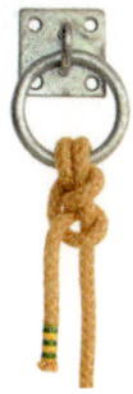

This bend can be used to secure the rope anchor warps of small boats to anchor rings. As it works well underwater, this ring hitch is particularly handy when the line is wet or slimy.

This is actually a reinforced round turn and two half-hitches (see page 110) with the first half-hitch trapped within the round turn. It is called a 'bend', although obviously it is a hitch, because sailors once talked – and some of us still do – of 'bending' a rope to a ring. Another name for it is the fisherman's bend.

WATCH OUT!

The anchor bend can be hard to untie once jammed tight, so only use it when a round turn and two half-hitches would be unreliable.

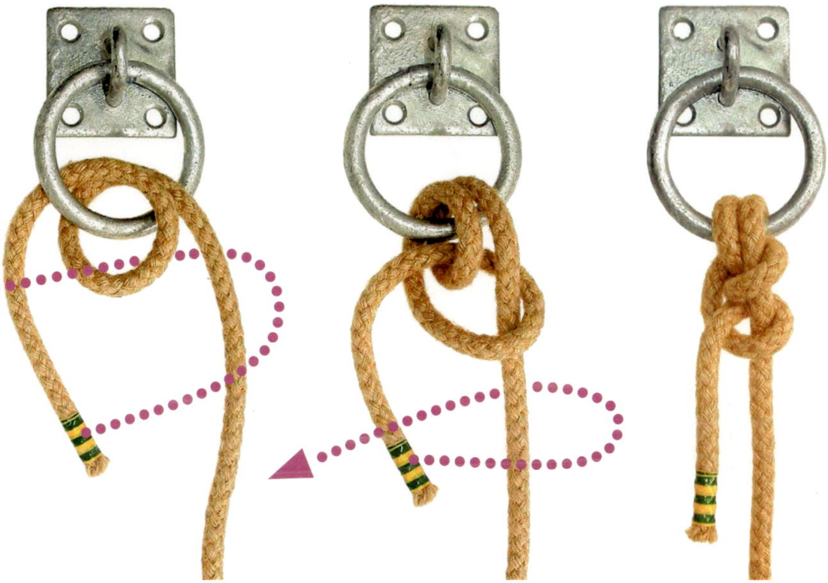

Method

Step 1

Feed the rope through the ring twice and make a round turn (or a loop). Then pass the working end around the standing part and through the loop.

Step 2

Add a half-hitch around the standing part.

Step 3

Work the hitch tight by pulling on both strands.

Bowline

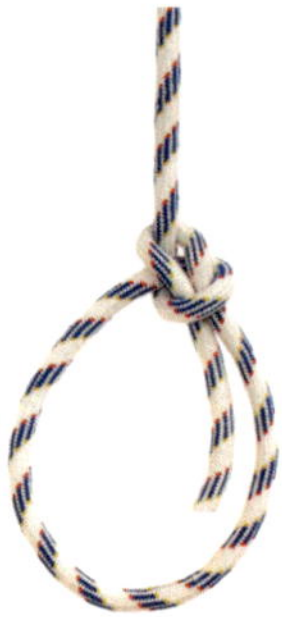

Square-rigged ships, sailing close-hauled, rigged a line to the weather side of the square-sails with this knot and led it forward, to overcome what was their least efficient aspect of sailing; which is why beating to windward was called 'sailing on a bow line' (pronounced 'boh-linn').

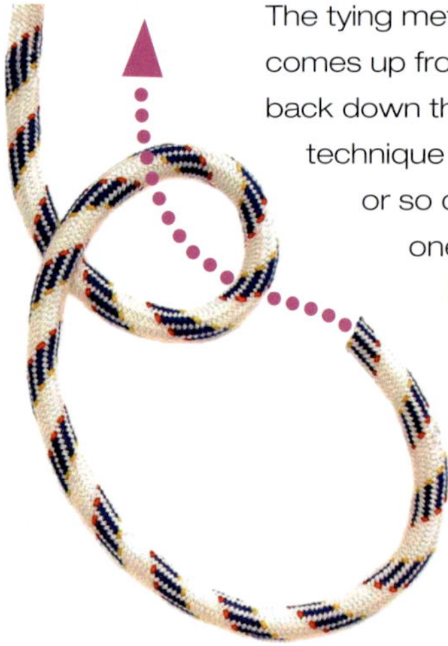

The tying method described is known as 'the rabbit comes up from its hole, goes around the tree and back down the hole'. There is another, more fluent technique called 'the sailor's method', (it is a second or so quicker, and can mostly be done with only one hand) but many people find that version less easy to learn.

Method

Step 1

First make an overhand loop and tuck the working end up through the loop, from back to front.

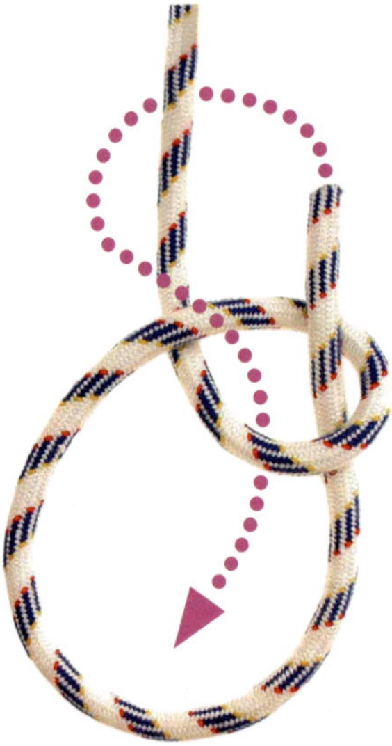

Step 2

Then pass the working end behind the standing part of the line and tuck it down through the loop once more.

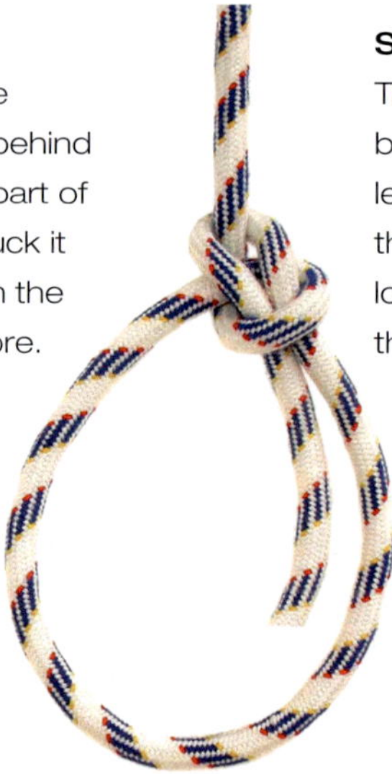

Step 3

Tighten the bowline and leave an end that is almost as long as one of the loop legs.

Water bowline

When a bowline will be towed through water or dragged over rough terrain, use a water bowline.

There are many variations of the bowline which have evolved from the basic version opposite.

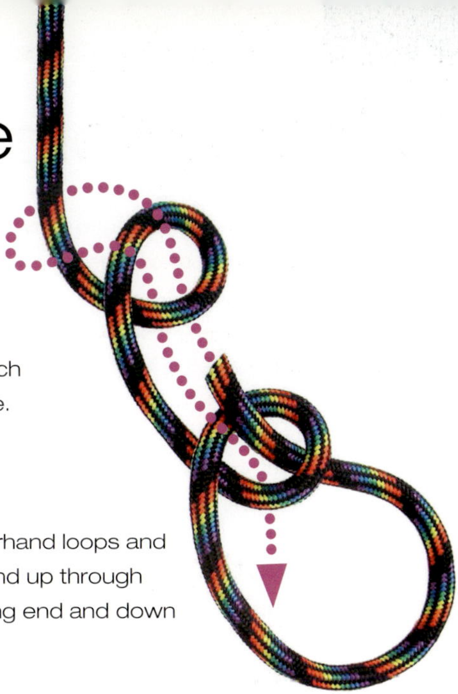

Method

Step 1

This time make two overhand loops and then tuck the working end up through both, around the standing end and down through both loops.

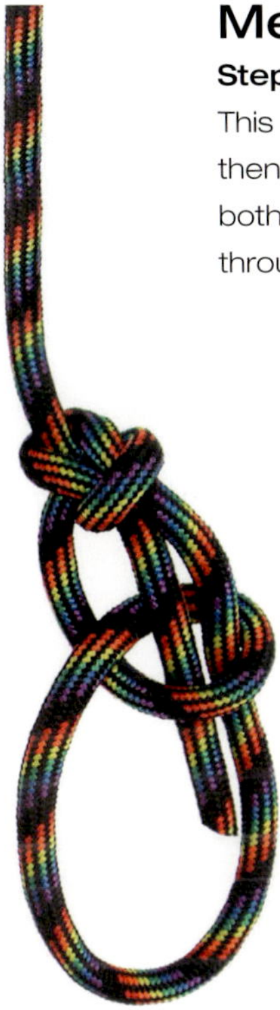

Step 2

At this point tighten the initial bowline.

Step 3

Finally pull the second half-hitch to sit snugly beneath it.

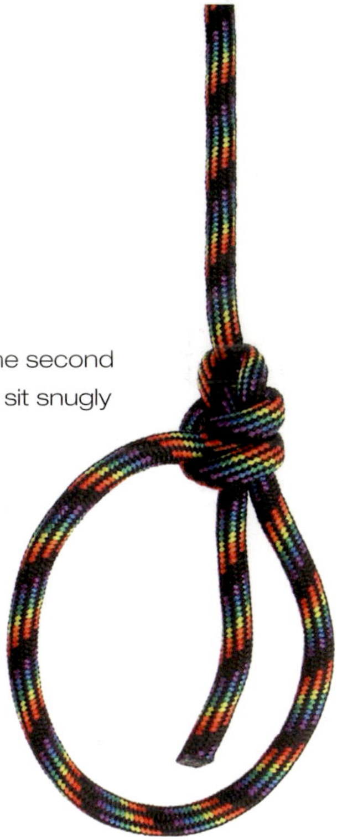

MUST KNOW

In the wet

Wet knots tend to jam, and Clifford Ashley – whose instinct and knowledge were rarely wrong – wrote that the extra half-hitch in this knot lessens the chance of it happening.

Eye splice

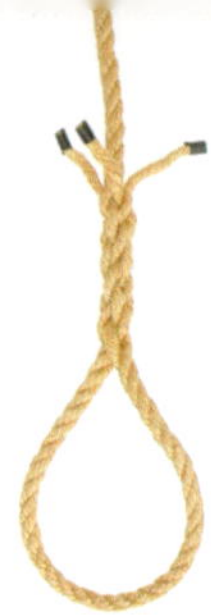

There are numerous variations of the eye splice and this example is commonly called 'the sailor's eye splice'.

While a splice is stronger and more streamlined than a knot, preserving as much as 95 per cent of a hawser-laid rope's breaking strength, knots reinforced with thimbles provide an ideal alternative (see scaffold knot pages 58–9).

Method

Step 1

First unlay the rope strands and make a counter-clockwise bight of the required size. Tuck the middle strand (a) beneath the nearest convenient laid strand.

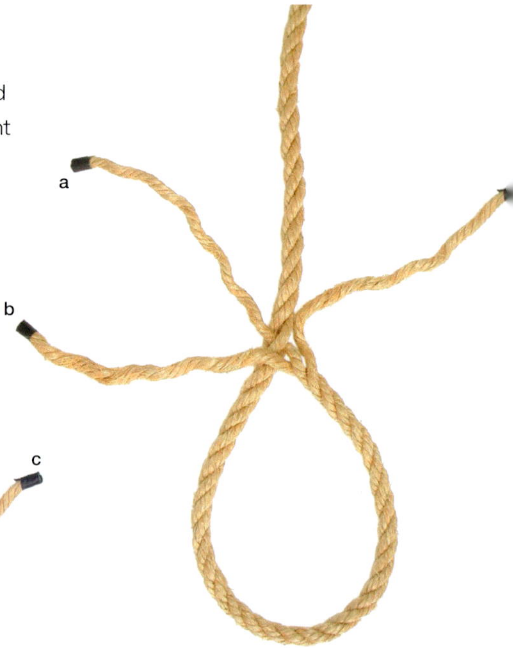

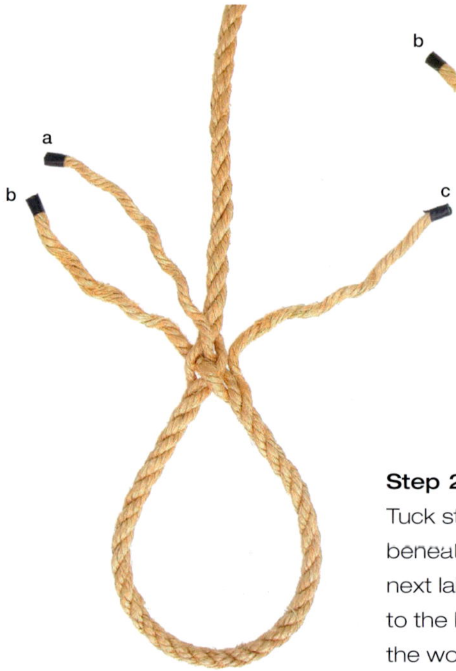

Step 2

Tuck strand (b) beneath the next laid strand to the left. Turn the work over.

Step 3

Now bring strand (c) around in a sharp turn before tucking it – in the same direction (counter-clockwise) as the other two strands – beneath the remaining unused laid strand. Pull this trio of tucks tight, so that there is a distinctive X-shape created by two strands on the front of the splice, with two strands lying parallel to one another on the reverse side of the splice. The tricky stage is now complete.

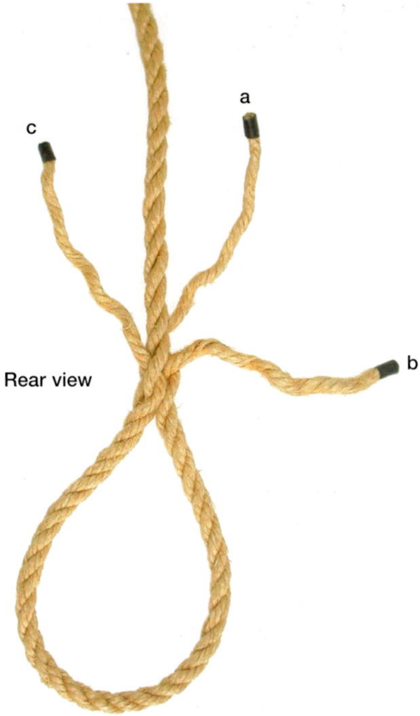

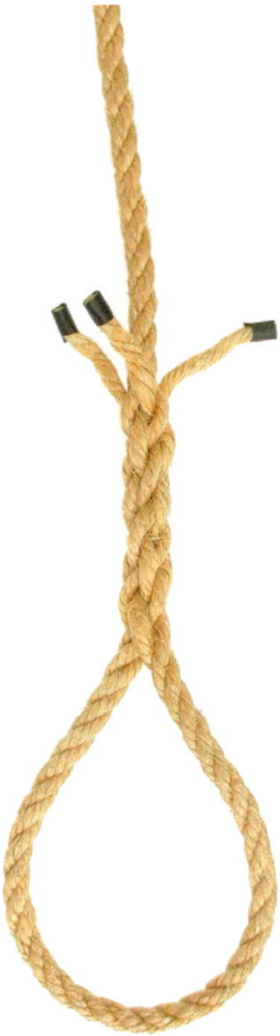

Step 4

Continue the tucking process, as described above (and on page 45) to complete the back splice.

WATCH OUT!

A load on a hawser will tighten a splice but a spinning load that turns counter-clockwise will open the lay and loosen it, so insert a swivel between the load and the eye splice. However, if the eye is lined with a metal or plastic thimble, the splice will soon stretch and lose its grip on the thimble; in which case tie the following scaffold knot.

Scaffold knot

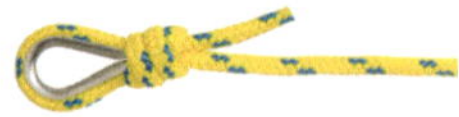

Sailors today tend to use this technique for making so-called 'hard eyes' – knots reinforced by thimbles.

This knot is generally favoured over the eye splice on pages 56–7, because the greater the load, the tighter it holds; while an eye splice, no matter how neatly made, will soon stretch and loosen its hold upon a thimble. The law of loop, hitch and bight applies (see page 29) and so this knot can be tied in the bight as well as with an end as shown here.

Method

Step 1

Firstly, make a loop in the end of a line, placing the working end over and then under the standing part, as shown. Then wrap the working end around the loop twice more. (You are effectively tying a triple overhand knot.)

MUST KNOW

Hard eyes
Thimbles can be metal or plastic and are available from boat and yacht chandlers. They protect loop or noose knots against wear and tear due to chafing.

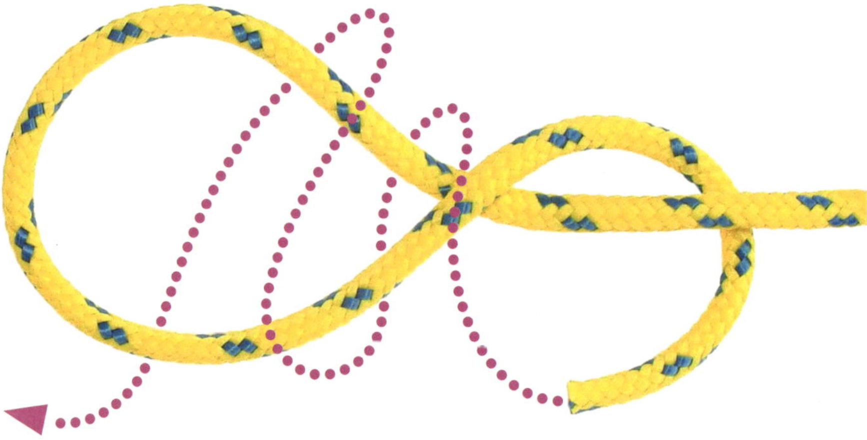

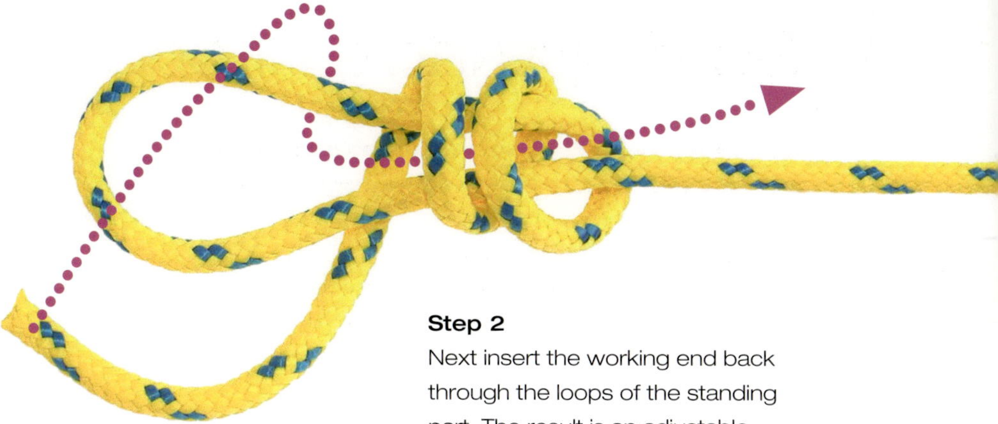

Step 2

Next insert the working end back through the loops of the standing part. The result is an adjustable sliding loop or noose of the blood knot (core-and-wrap) kind. Tighten the sliding knot at this point.

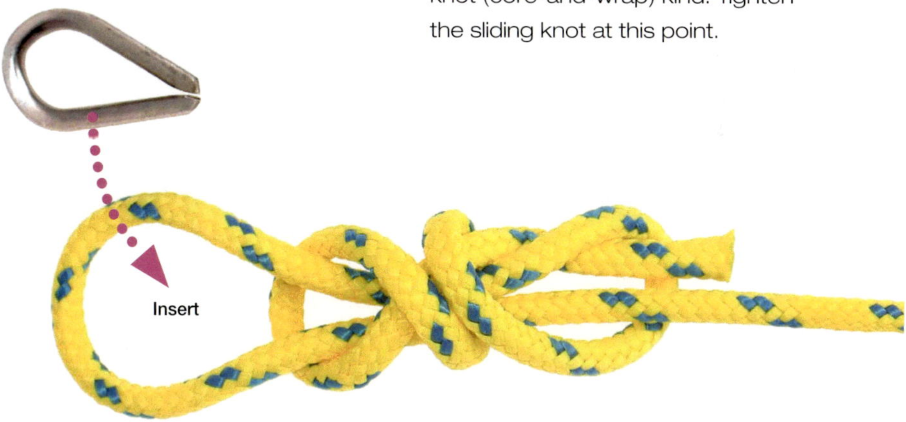

Step 3

Finally, insert the thimble into the loop and pull on the standing part to tighten the noose. This action will ensure that the thimble is held firmly in place.

WATCH OUT!

A scaffold knot can sometimes be hard to untie once it has been heavily loaded.

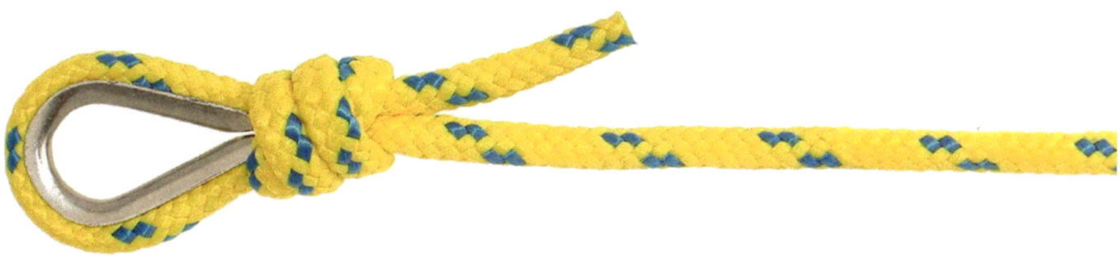

Midshipman's hitch

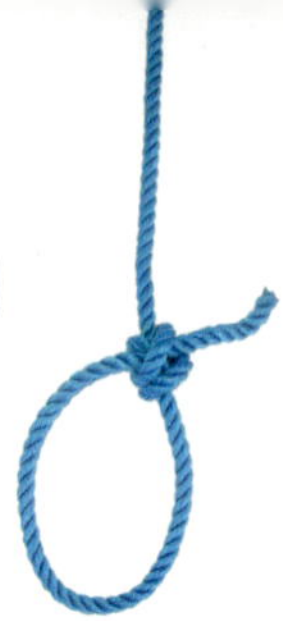

Use this hitch for salvaging flotsam and jetsam; as a makeshift tether for a crew member; or to rig a temporary awning.

This noose is one of those slide-and-grip knots (see also the Tarbuck knot pages 96–7) that can be readily adjusted by hand, but which then squeezes and holds firm under a load.

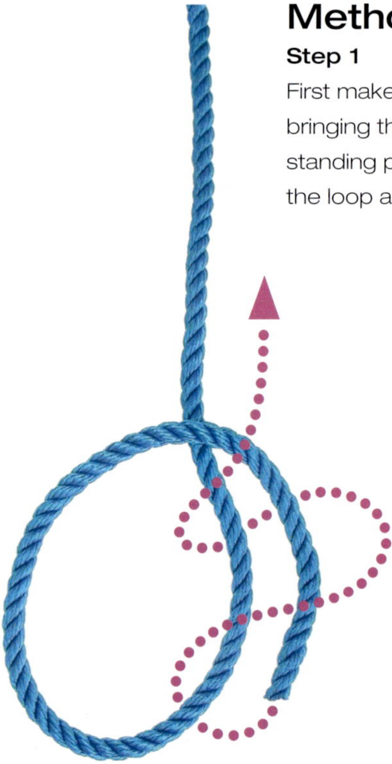

Method

Step 1

First make an overhand loop, bringing the working end over the standing part. Then wrap it through the loop and around itself twice.

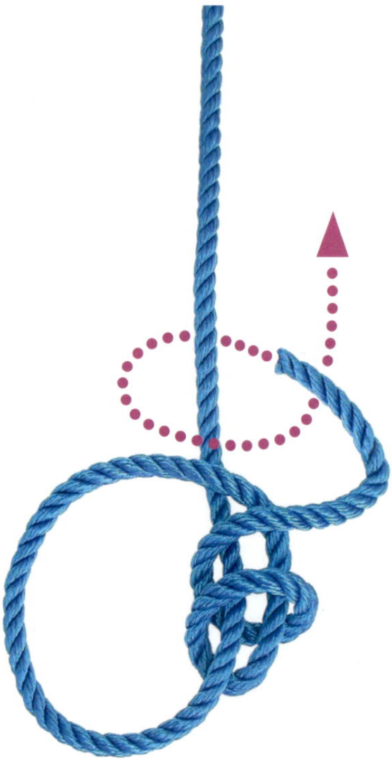

Step 2

Next pass the working end around the standing end and tuck it up under itself, making a half-hitch.

WATCH OUT!

Older seamanship manuals recommend this loop knot for hoisting a crew member aloft or hauling one from the water, but if – despite its reputation as a slide-and-grip knot – it tightened around an individual, constriction could hamper breathing.

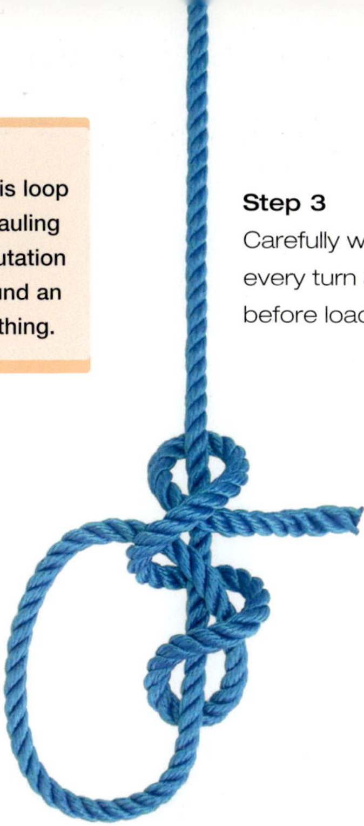

Step 3

Carefully work each and every turn and tuck tight before loading.

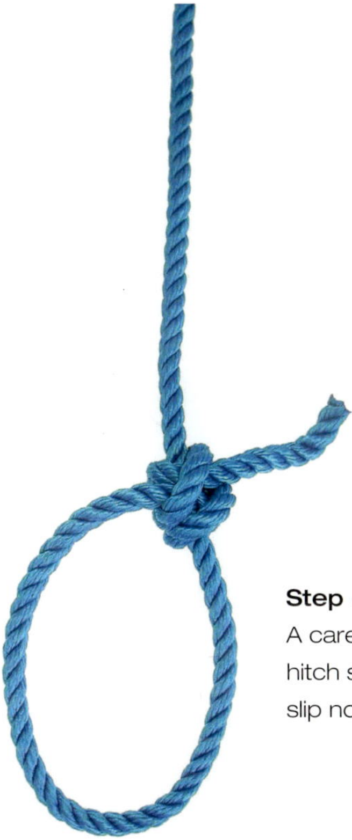

Step 4

A carefully arranged hitch should neither slip nor jam.

MUST KNOW

Dropping your hitches

The reason some loop knots are called 'hitches' is because they can be dropped repeatedly over posts and bollards without the need to untie and re-tie them. This one is also known as the tautline hitch.

want to know more?

Take it to the next level...

Go to...

- **Perfection loop –** pages 72–3
- **Constrictor knot –** pages 88–9
- **Round turn/two half hitches –** page 110

Other sources

- **Sailing schools and courses**
  contact the Royal Yachting Association
- **Ship's chandlers**
  for all ropes and cordage
- **Useful websites**
  www.sailingbooks.com
  www.boatsafe.com
- **Publication**
  The RYA Book of Knots by Peter Owen (1999), ISBN 0-7136-5898-3

fishing

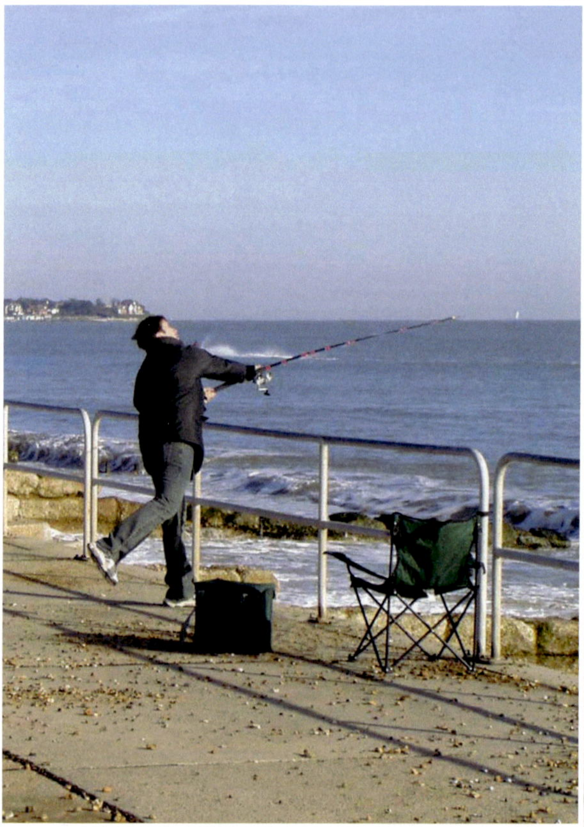

knots

Knots are the one item of tackle that anglers must make for themselves and are best learnt in small cord, before attempting to tie them in monofilaments or braided lines and leaders, which are so much thinner. Even then the fiddly task of tying knots in fishing line can be rehearsed indoors, before it is performed at dawn beside the water or out afloat upon it.

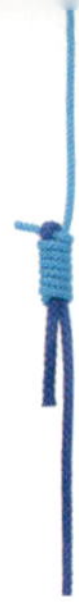

Albright knot

This reliable knot will join lines of different diameter or construction - backing line to fly line, monofilment to braid, and braid to wire.

Method

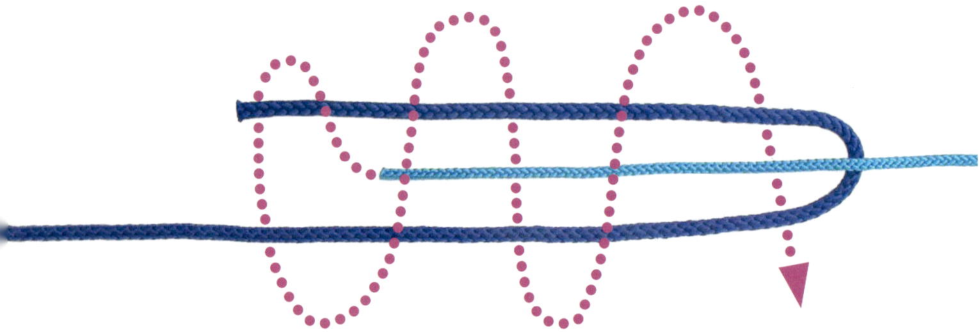

Step 1

First make a bight in the thicker line (or wire) and lay the thinner or more flexible line on top. Bring the the working (or tag) end of the thinner line behind the top leg of the bight and make a couple of snug and tight turns around both bight legs, trapping it's own standing part in the process.

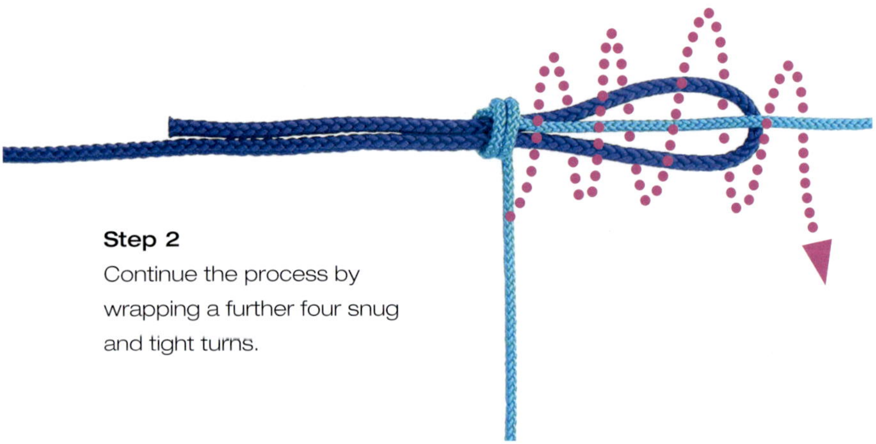

Step 2

Continue the process by wrapping a further four snug and tight turns.

MUST KNOW

Down to the wire

This knot is recommended for joining line to wire cable, nylon-coated wire and small-diameter single-strand wire leaders. When doing so, be sure to use the wire for the bight or loop, and make the wrapping turns with the more flexible line. Remember that the neater and tighter the knot, the less slippage will occur, and the stronger the knot will be.

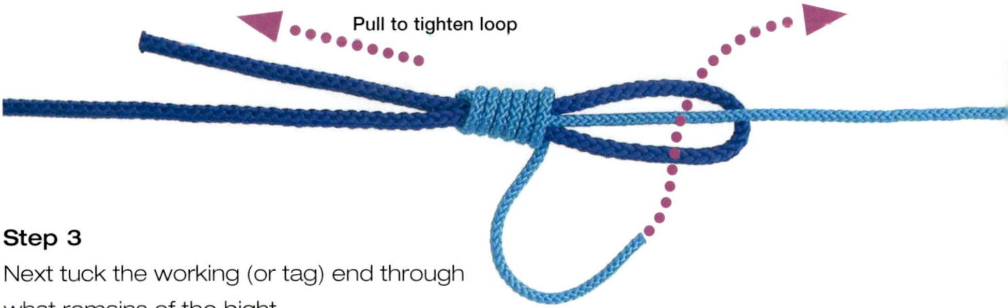

Step 3

Next tuck the working (or tag) end through what remains of the bight.

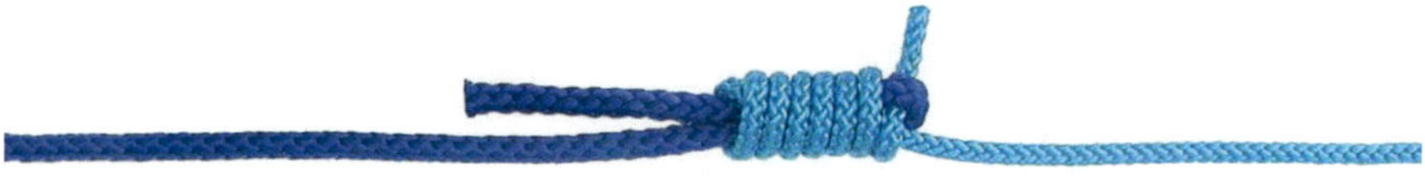

Step 4

Finally work the knot tight, so that all of the wrapping turns are tensioned equally, and either trim the working (or tag) end or tie it to the standing part of the line.

Clinch knot

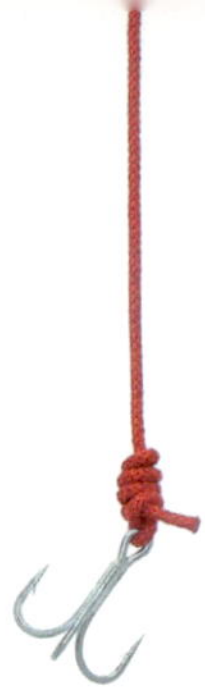

This knot is one of a family of clinch knots, each with its own distinctive features and character. It is also known as a half-blood knot. You can use it to attach line to a hook or swivel.

Use plenty of line to tie this and other fishing knots. The numerous twists will need freedom to move and override one another during the flyping process. Tighten slowly and steadily so that the wrapping turns are evenly tensioned. An irregular, lumpy knot is weaker than a neat and compact one.

Method

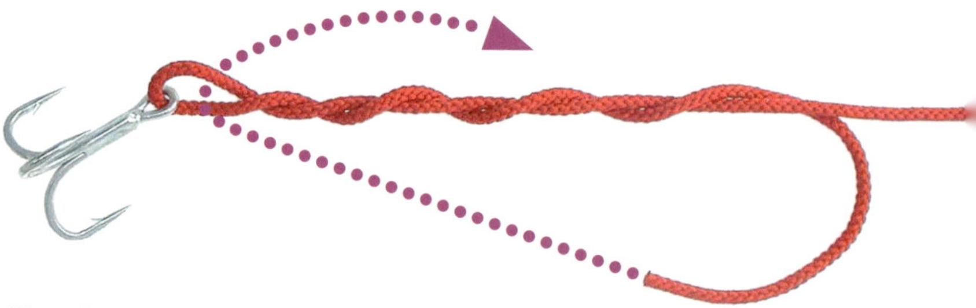

Step 1

First pass the working (or tag) end through the eye or ring and neatly wrap it five times around its standing part. Then feed the working (or tag) end back through the initial loop.

MUST KNOW

It's a wrap

Tightening is more difficult in thicker lines, so try reducing the number of wraps to three and a half turns; and, with very thin lines, tie the knot in a doubled bight of line. Either way it is reported to have a 95 per cent breaking strength.

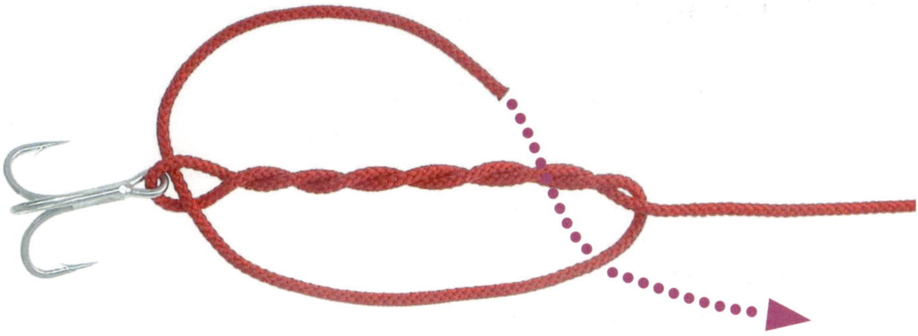

Step 2

Next pass the working (or tag) end over the standing part and tuck it under itself.

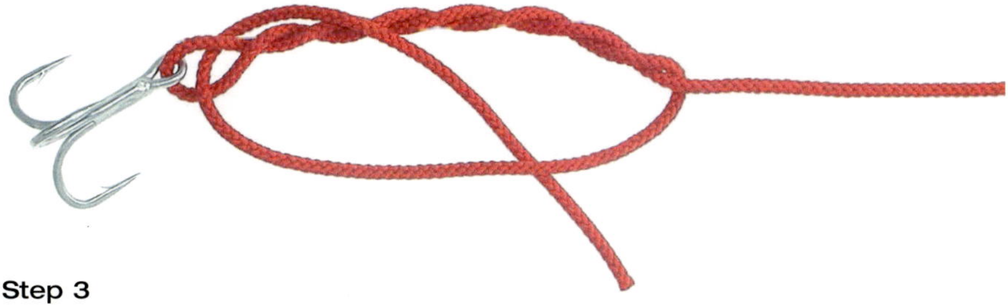

Step 3

Lastly, carefully pull both ends to flype (see Must know box, page 69) and tighten.

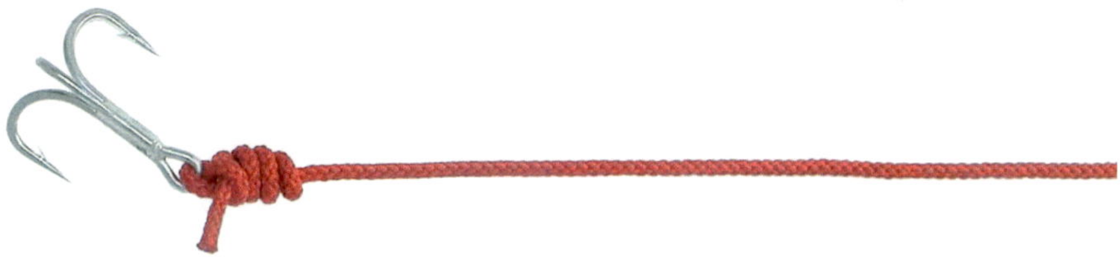

Step 4

Make sure that the wrapping turns are equally tensioned and cut off any surplus line.

Blood knot

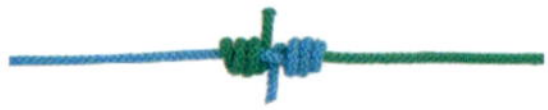

This is a very strong and secure knot of the core-and-wrap variety, which is popular with fly fishermen for joining lengths of nylon monofilament when making tapered leaders. It is also known as a barrel knot.

This knot can be troublesome to draw up tight in thicker lines, but strength test data have shown it to be close to 100 per cent efficient and it runs easily through rod guides.

To make a modified blood knot in two lines of very dissimilar diameters (and strength) simply double the end of the thinner line and use the doubled portion to tie that half of the knot.

Method

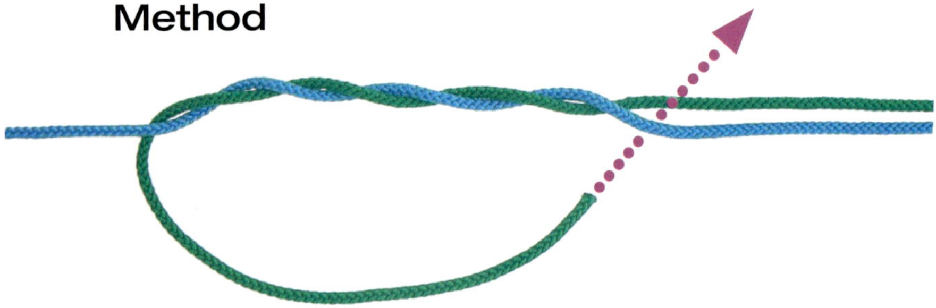

Step 1
Overlap the two lines and twist one working (or tag) end around the adjacent standing part, then bring it back and tuck it up between the two parallel strands.

MUST KNOW

Take care to:
- arrange wrapping turns so that they lie neatly beside one another;
- make more wrapping turns in thinner lines (from 3–4 turns in thick lines, to 6–7 in thin ones);
- distribute the tension evenly as the knots are tightened.

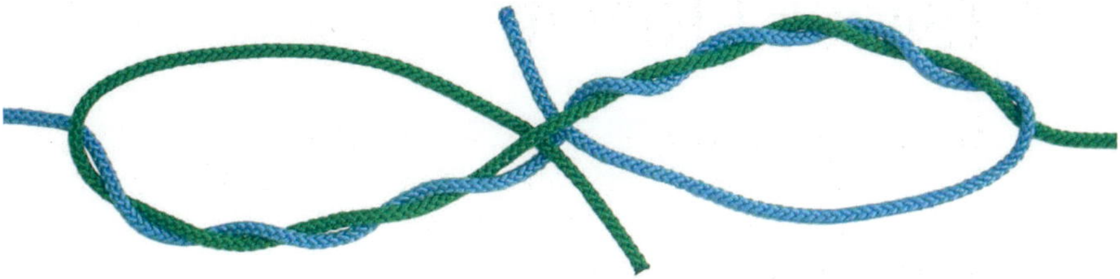

Step 2

Repeat the process with the other working (or tag) end, this time tucking the end down through the central compartment.

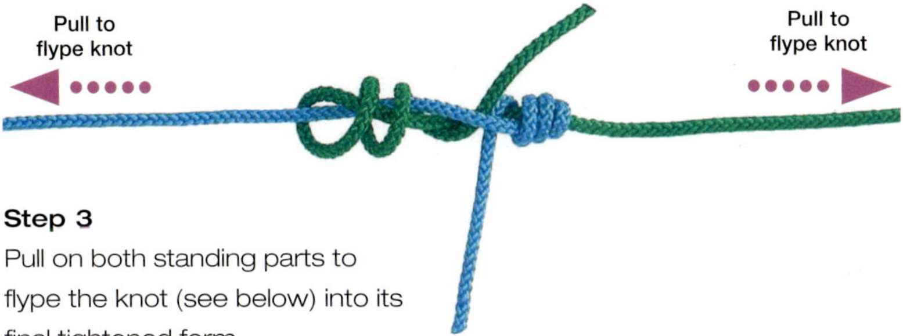

Step 3

Pull on both standing parts to flype the knot (see below) into its final tightened form.

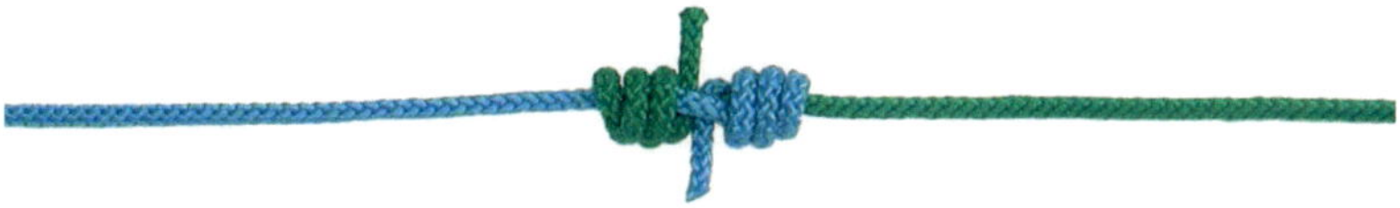

Step 4

Finally, trim both working (or tag) ends close to the knot.

MUST KNOW

Knotting jargon

Flyping is an old knotting term that became popular in the 1980s (see also page 24). Basically, to flype a knot means to turn it inside-out, similar to peeling off a sock or glove. With some knots they need to be flyped, that is, adjusted by pulling on either standing parts or ends, at a certain stage in order to achieve the final form.

Blood knot loop

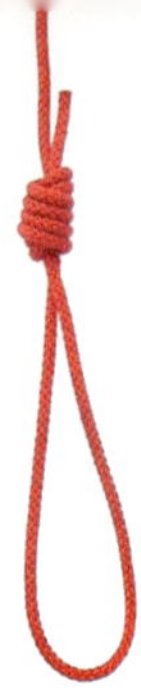

Another member of the blood knot family, this variation will help you to form a long loop quickly at the start of a tackle system. It is also known as the surgeon's loop or a spider hitch.

A blood knot loop is close to 100 per cent strong but can prove harder to tie in thick lines.

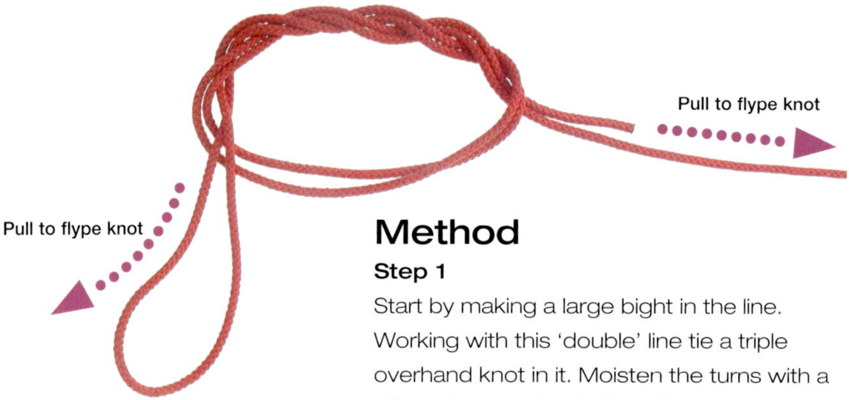

Method

Step 1

Start by making a large bight in the line. Working with this 'double' line tie a triple overhand knot in it. Moisten the turns with a little water or saliva before slowly pulling on both the loop and the two ends to tighten.

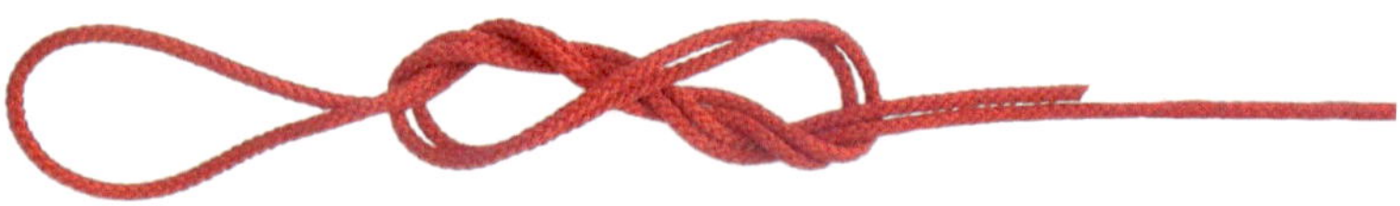

Step 2

The lower part of the knot will twist over the triple overhand knot and will flype (see page 69) into the core-and-wrap form below.

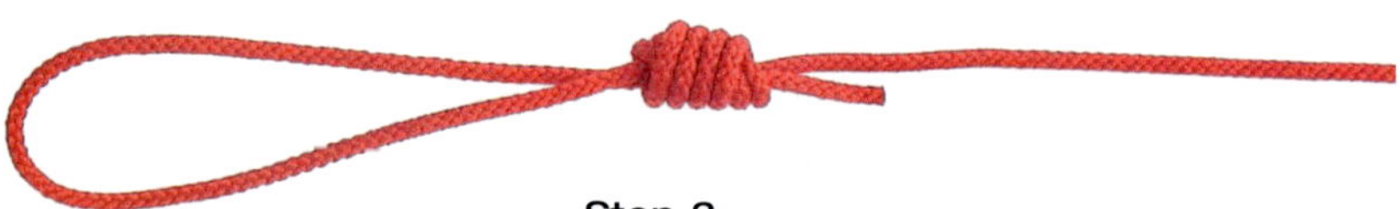

Step 3

Make sure that the turns lie neatly beside one another.

Blood loop dropper knot

Many anglers use this fixed loop to attach extra flies or droppers, as well as additional sea fishing hooks and sinker weights in a paternoster system, and to attach small jigs or quills when fishing for bait.

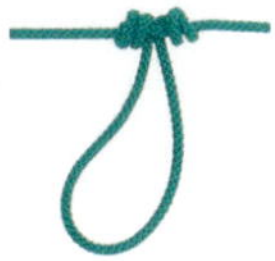

Method

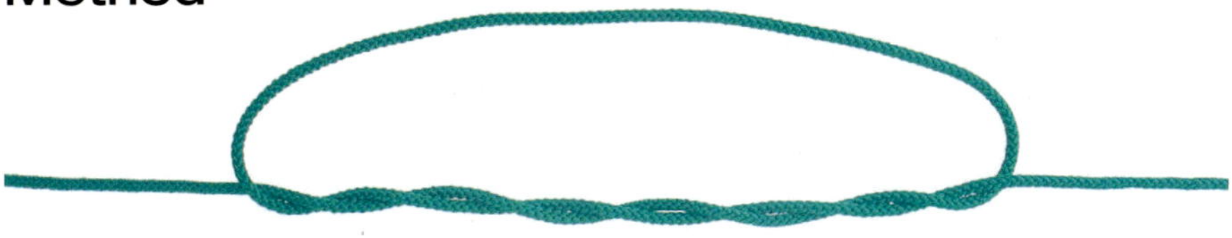

Step 1

First tie a multiple overhand knot in the standing part of the line with the working (or tag) end.

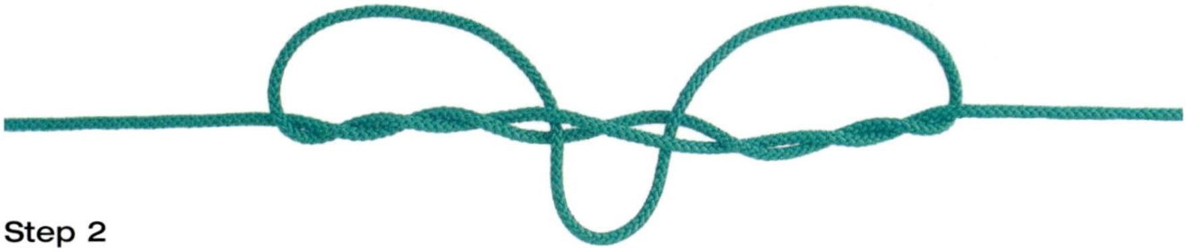

Step 2

Then locate the middle of the overhand knot (or central space) and simply pull the centre of the large loop down through it, forming another loop.

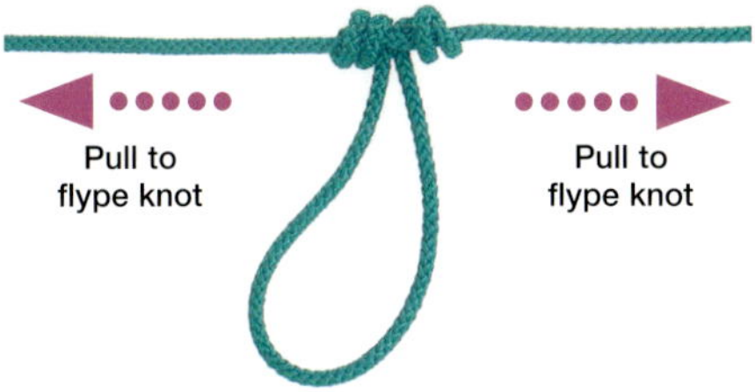

Step 3

Gently pull the ends of the knot until it flypes into the characteristic core-and-wrap form of a blood knot (see pages 68–9) and then tighten firmly.

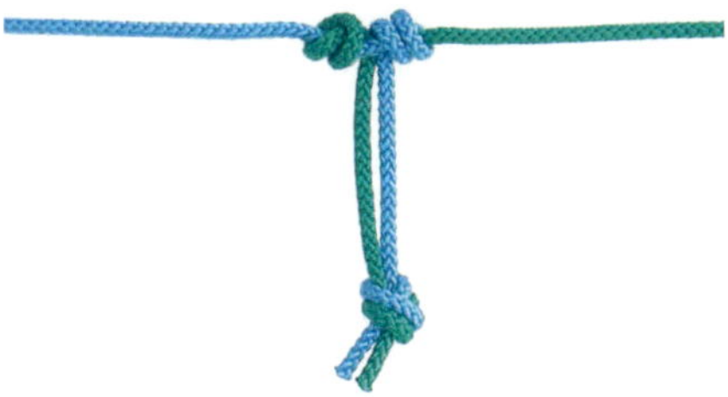

Variation

This knot may also be tied by joining two separate lines with a blood knot and then tying the two working (tag) ends together with an overhand knot.

Perfection loop

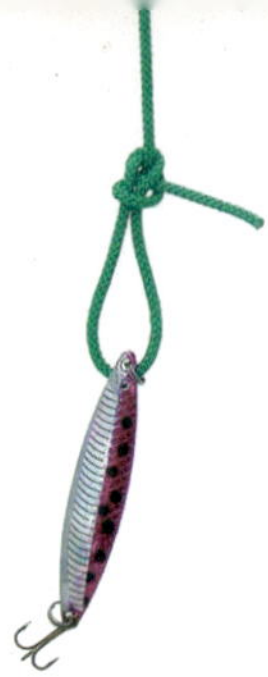

To assemble a tackle rig in any kind of line or leader – from slender monofilament to large rope – use this classic loop This age-old knot is also known as an angler's loop.

A perfection loop can also be tied in the bight, when it will have to be attached to the requisite eye or ring by means of a ring hitch (see pages 108–9). It is believed by some to date from the days of English angling author Izaac Walton (1593–1683) and fishing lines of horsehair, gut and silk. However, it also functions well in synthetics.

MUST KNOW

A useful tip; hook the loop around a pair of fishing pliers or any other round object, even a nail, in order to pull it really tight.

Method

Step 1

Begin by tying an overhand knot, leaving a fairly long working (or tag) end. Then tuck the end through the ring or eye and back through the initial knot.

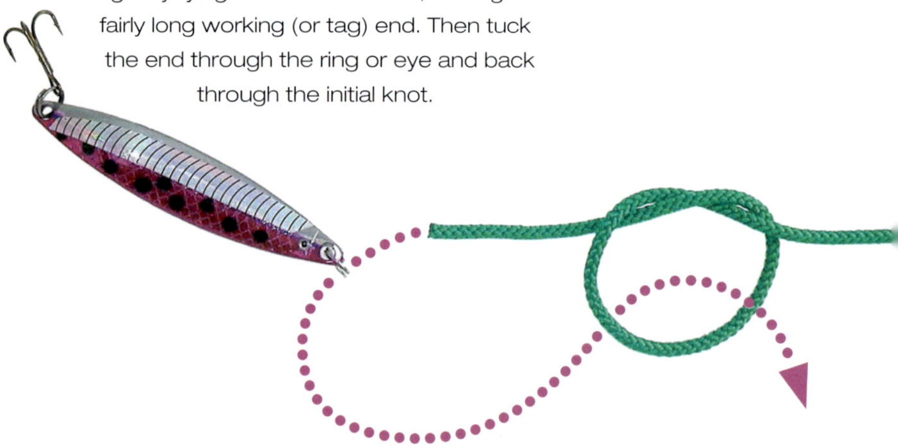

WATCH OUT!

The tag (working) end projects sideways from the knot and – unlike the blood knot loop – will create a disturbance underwater.

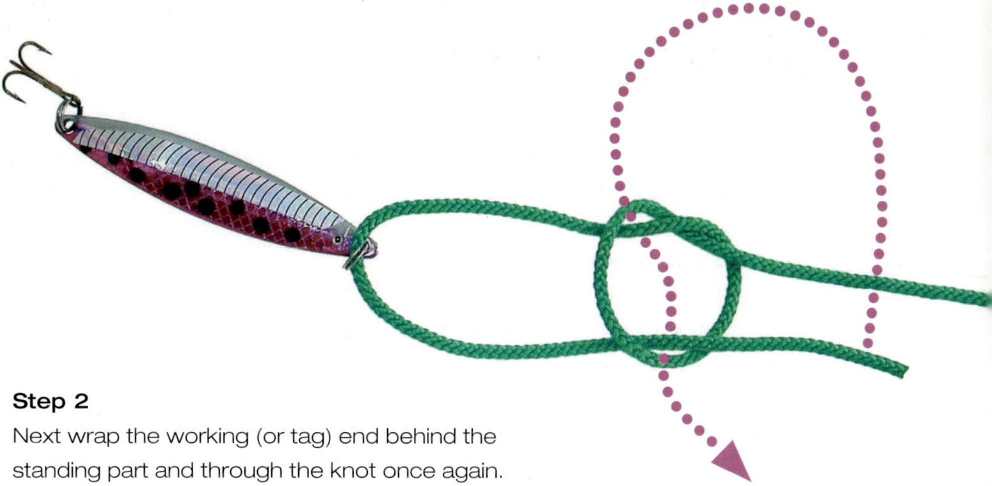

Step 2

Next wrap the working (or tag) end behind the standing part and through the knot once again.

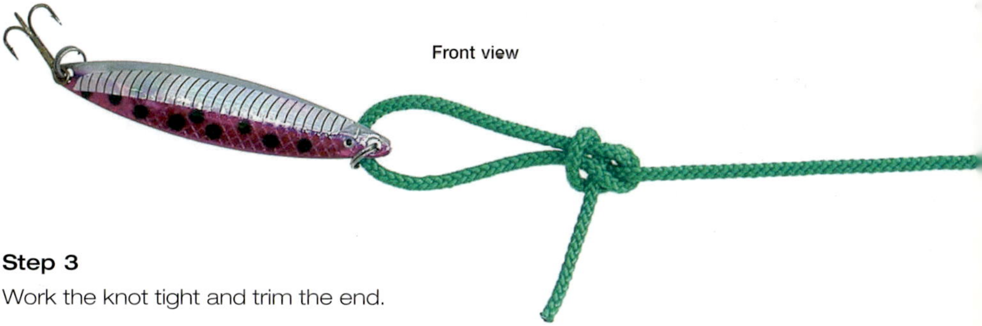

Step 3

Work the knot tight and trim the end.

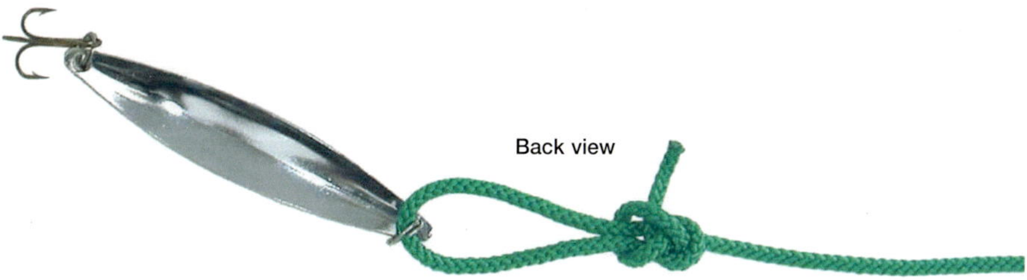

Double check

Like all knots, if not tied correctly the perfection loop will slip and fail. Check front and back faces of this knot, which are both clearly recognizable, before using it.

Tube knot

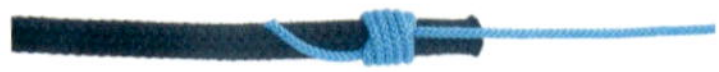

A tube or nail knot joins a fly to the butt section of the leader. There are several variations of this knot, devised to overcome or short-cut the awkwardness that some people find in tying the orthodox version.

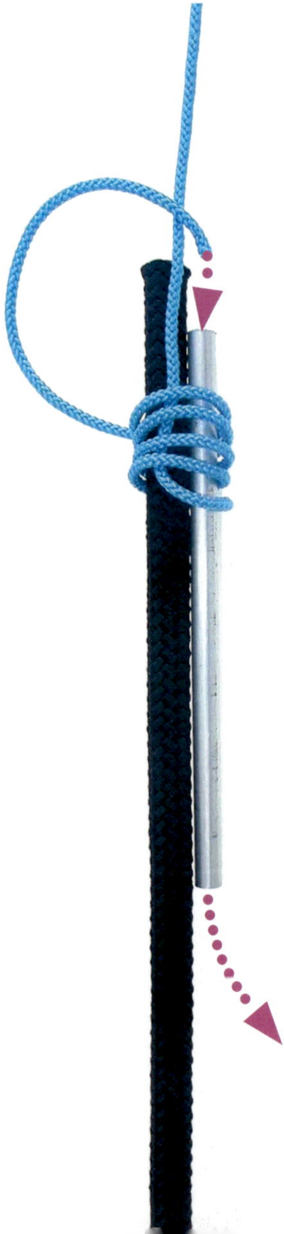

Tying this knot requires a short length of small diameter tubing, which could be a drinking straw, a medical cannula, or even the hollow body of a ballpoint pen.

The noted American fly fisherman Joe Brooks is said to have discovered this knot in Argentina, where it was tied with the aid of a horseshoe nail, which is why it is also widely known as the nail knot.

Method

Step 1

Place the fly line and leader line next to one another. Add the tube and with the working (or tag) end of the leader line, make at least five consecutive wrapping turns to enclose both lines plus the tube. Then pass the working (or tag) end of the leader line through the tube.

MUST KNOW

The virtue of patience

Whatever tying method you finally choose, make sure that you tighten your knot patiently and, only when the final form is inevitable, finish with a couple of sharp tugs. When working with fishing line you will need that extra bit of patience as it is particularly fiddly.

MUST KNOW

The name game

This is identical in construction, but not in the way it is tied, to snelling on page 81 (the parsimony principle on page 29 yet again), and another instance of how tying something a different way, for another purpose, can lead to a different name.

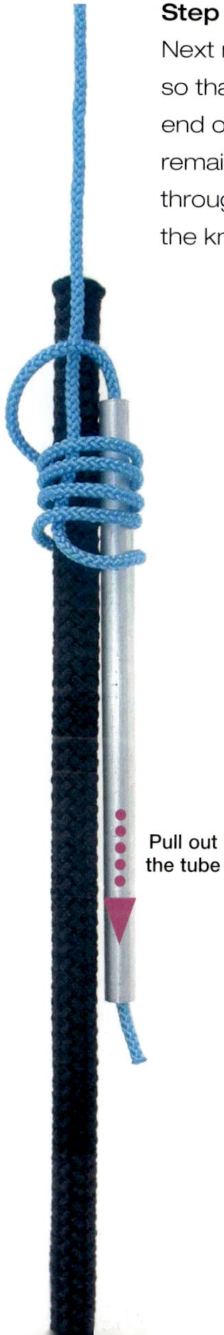

Step 2

Next remove the tube so that the working end of the leader line remains threaded through the turns in the knot.

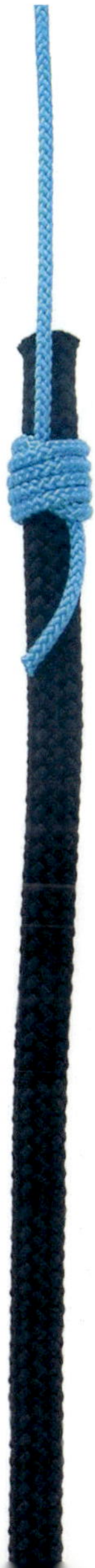

Step 3

Make sure that the wrapping turns bed down beside one another, before tugging both ends to tighten. Trim both ends and consider strengthening the knot by coating it with a rubber-based cement.

Offshore swivel knot

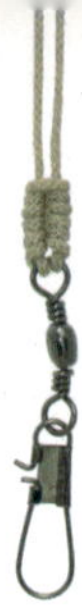

The offshore swivel knot is used in big-game fishing to attach long loops to heavy-duty swivels, as well as to the eyes of hooks and lures.

It is said to have been developed by deep-sea tuna fishermen who needed a knot to absorb the enormous and damaging shocks created by the strikes of such big fish. Outside of angling an offshore swivel knot is known as a cat's paw and is used as a crane hook sling by dockside and construction workers.

Method

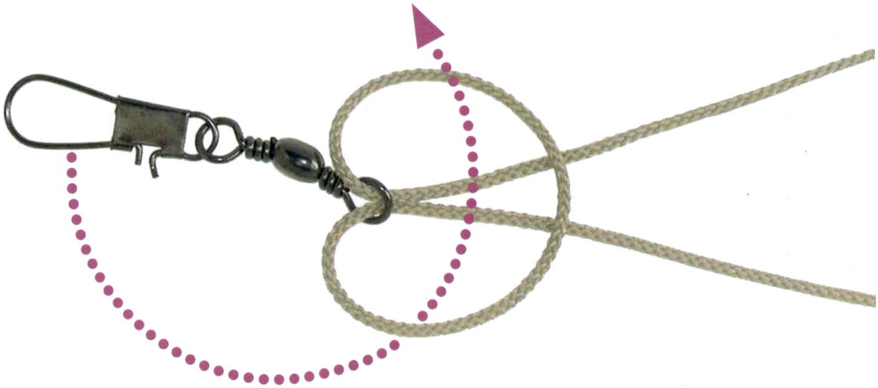

Step 1

Tuck the loop end of a long knotted line through the eye or ring and bring it back to lie on top of the two standing parts of the line. Then pass the hook or swivel through the central space.

MUST KNOW

Strong bow

This unusual knot is exceptionally strong and, if one leg of the long loop breaks, the knot itself is likely to remain intact (preserving tackle and possibly a catch).

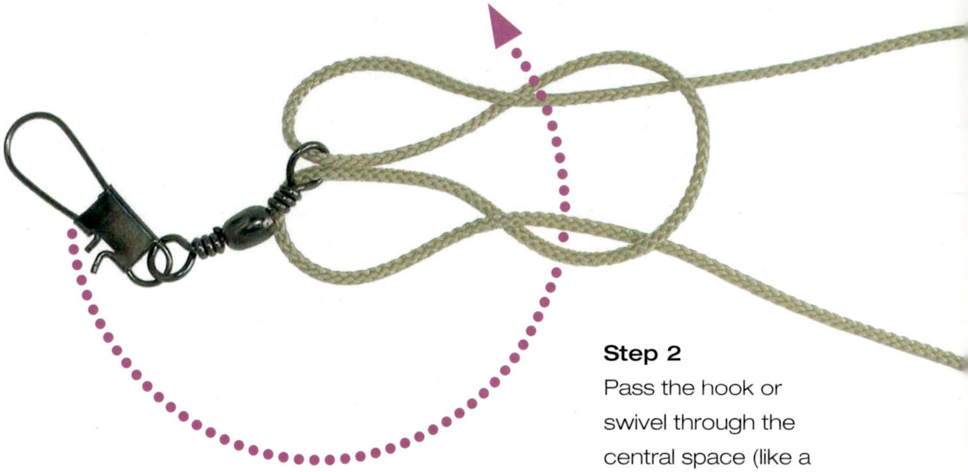

Step 2
Pass the hook or swivel through the central space (like a backward somersault) a second time.

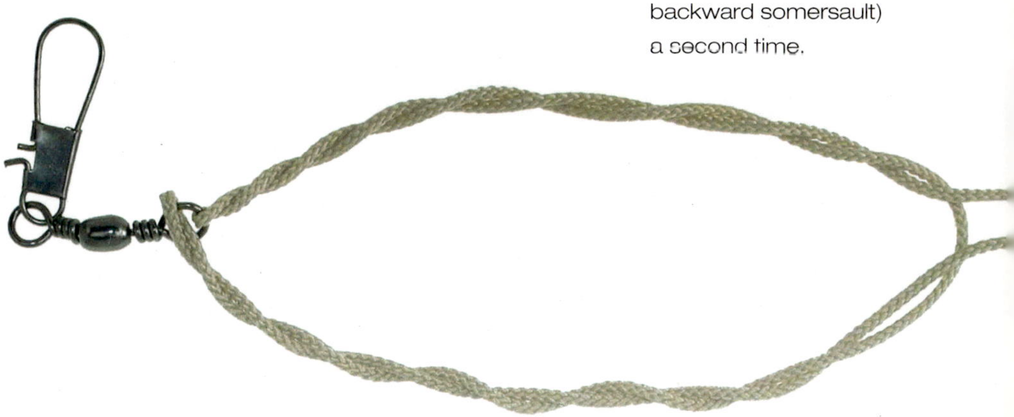

Step 3
Repeat the process in step 2 six to eight times in order to achieve the required twin twists.

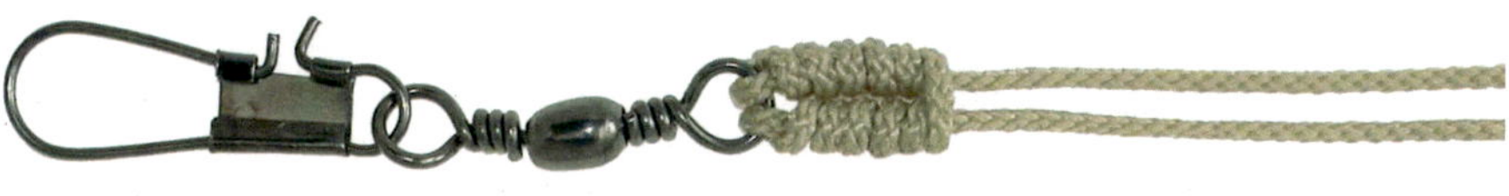

Step 4
Lastly, moisten the line with water or saliva and alternately pull and push to tighten the turns of the knot.

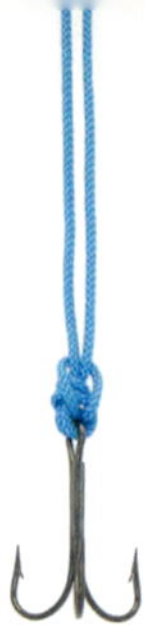

Palomar knot

This is a strong but simple knot for attaching hooks, lures, swivels or sinkers, and is easily tied in the most difficult conditions.

The palomar requires a doubled length of line and will consume more of a fly-fishing leader than most other knots. It is best tied in large single hooks or connectors, rather than a triple hook (as shown) which can be troublesome to pass through the bight.

Method

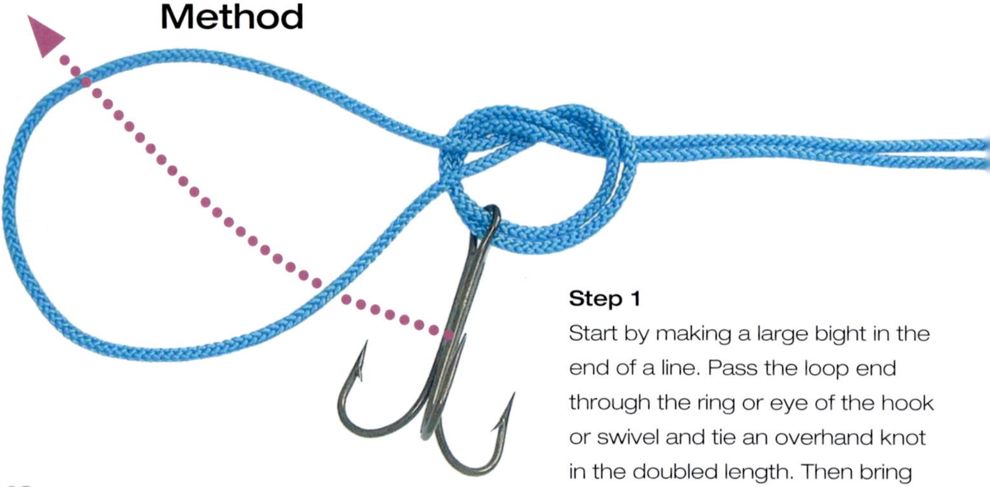

Step 1
Start by making a large bight in the end of a line. Pass the loop end through the ring or eye of the hook or swivel and tie an overhand knot in the doubled length. Then bring the hook or swivel through the bight or loop of the knot.

MUST KNOW

One hundred per cent
The palomar is a strong knot with nearly 100 per cent breaking strength if it is carefully tied and tightened, because of the double section of line passing around the ring or eye.

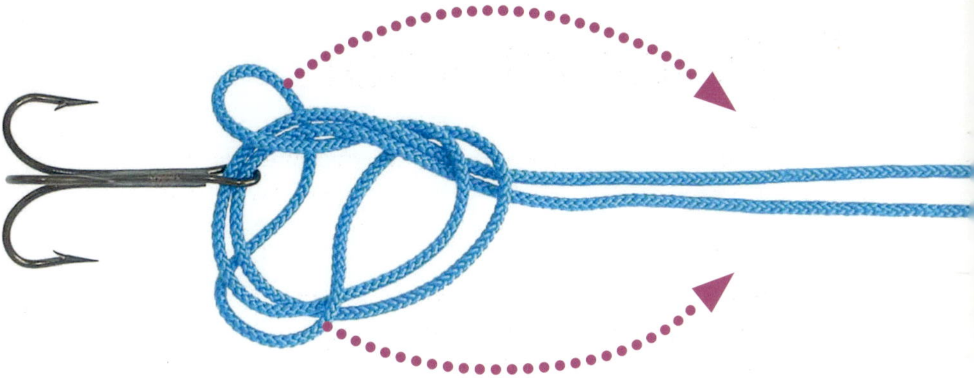

Step 2
Next, bring the initial loop down around the standing part of the line.

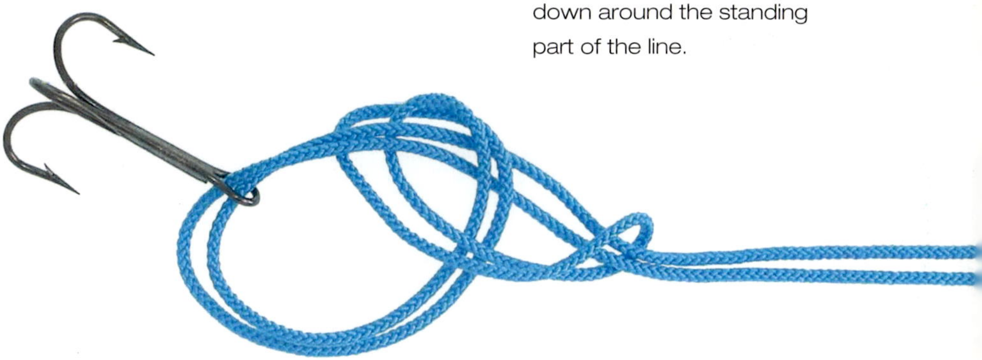

Step 3
Tighten carefully by pulling both ends together.

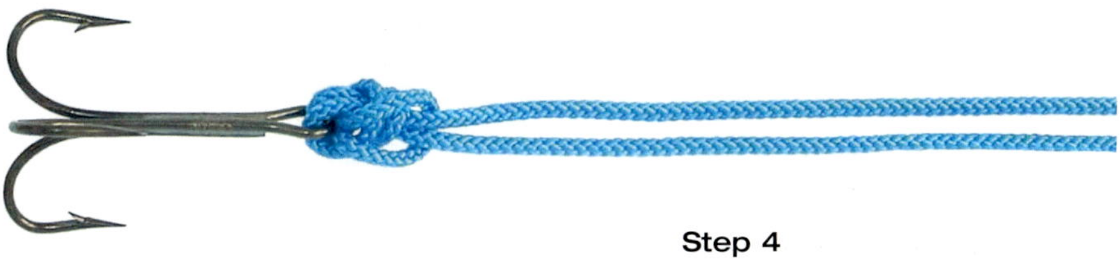

Step 4
Check that the overhand knot sits snugly around the eye, and the retaining bight or loop is around the doubled standing part of the line.

Berkley braid knot

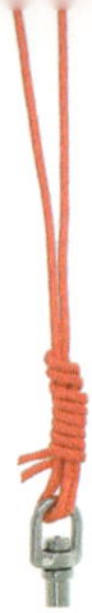

This knot was promoted, if not devised, by the Berkley Tackle Company to tie their so-called 'super-braids' to hooks, flies and lures and should be used accordingly.

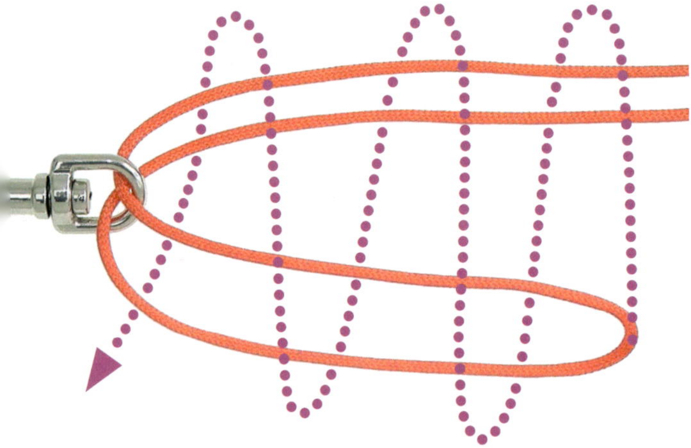

Method

Step 1

Double the end of a line and pass the end of the bight through the eye of the hook or other item of hardware. Bring it back alongside both of its standing parts. Working with the end of the bight, wrap a series of four or five turns around all four strands in the direction of the hook.

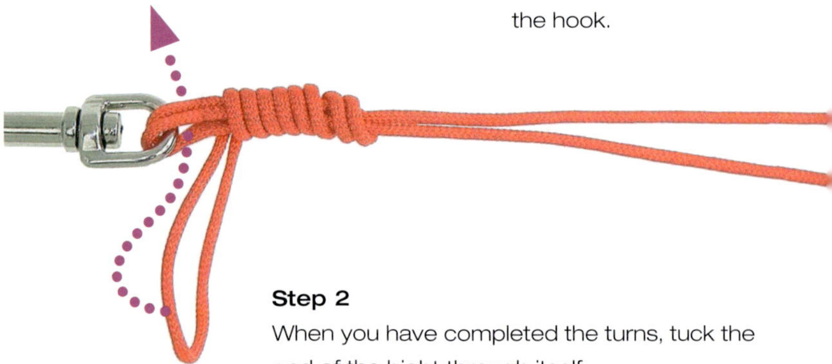

Step 2

When you have completed the turns, tuck the end of the bight through itself.

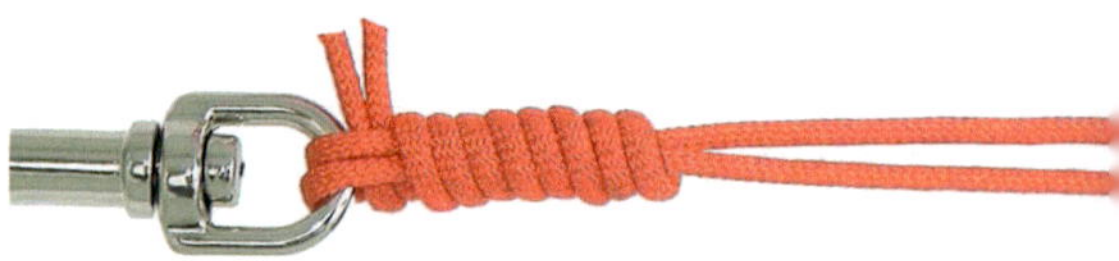

Step 3

Tighten with care and trim off the resulting end loop to create twin working (tag) ends.

MUST KNOW

Efficiency

This knot sacrifices only 10 per cent of the line's unknotted breaking strength; in other words, it is 90 per cent efficient.

Snelling

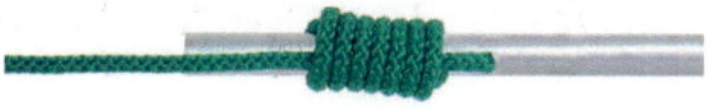

This technique is often used by sports fishermen. Snelling a lead to the shank of a hook, with either an upturned or a downturned eye, creates a straight pull that is claimed to be 100 per cent strong.

Method

Step 1

Place the line alongside the shank of the hook (or pass it through the eye of a hook) and make a large loop. Using the loop – not the end of the line – create a series of wrapping turns, enclosing and trapping the working (or tag) end alongside the shank of the hook.

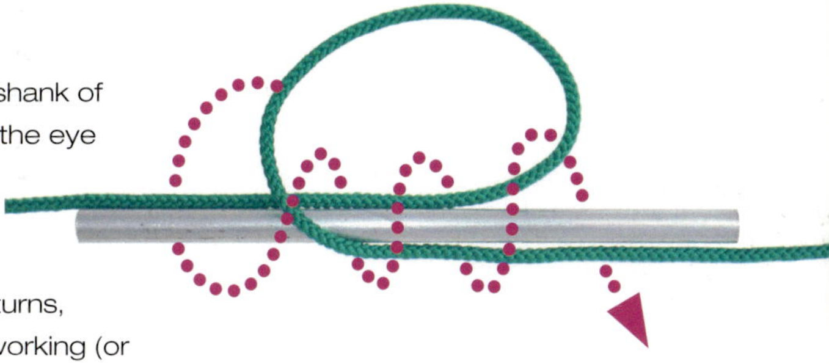

MUST KNOW

A good hooker

Snelling is very secure and has been extensively used to attach fishing lines to spade-ended hooks which lack eyes. There are several other versions of snelling, all of which are closely related (by the parsimony principle, see page 29) to nail or tube knots and whippings.

Step 2

Make at least five to six snug and tight wrapping turns.

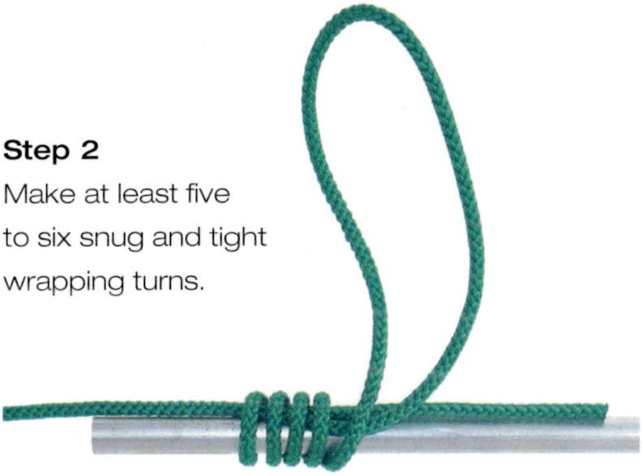

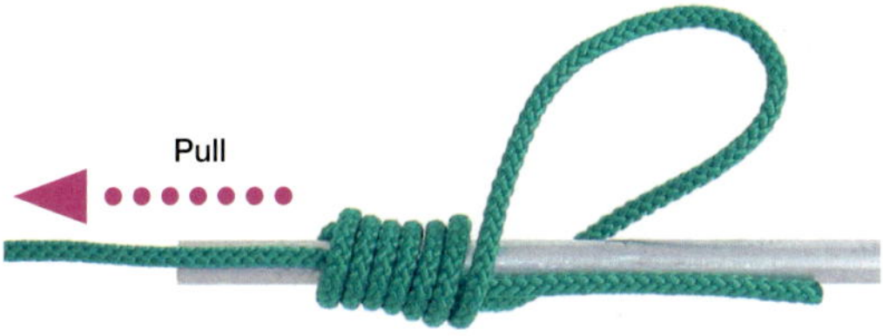

Step 3

Pull on the standing end to eliminate the initial loop. Work the rest of the turns with your fingers.

Step 4

Once tightened, trim the working (or tag) end.

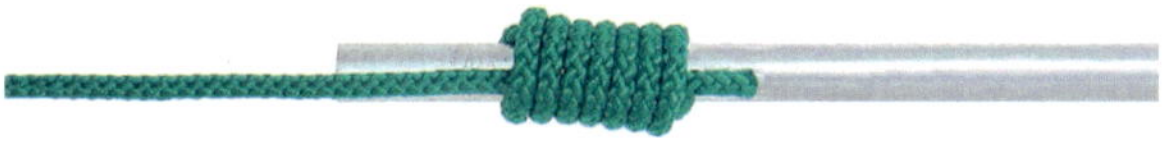

Lock knot

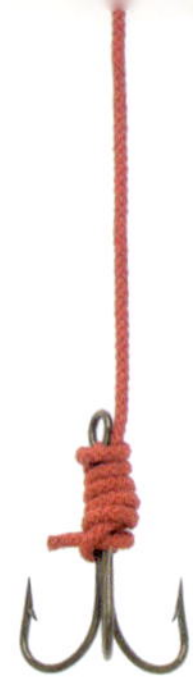

This knot was purposely designed to attach monofilament to flat-eyed hooks, rather than to those with upturned or downturned eyes, while maintaining a pull in line with the shank.

It originated in France where it is called *noeud* (knot) *serrure* (lock). While it is never safe to be dogmatic where knot history and lore are concerned, the lock or *serrure* knot appears to be a relative newcomer to the knotting scene as few angling manuals feature it.

Method

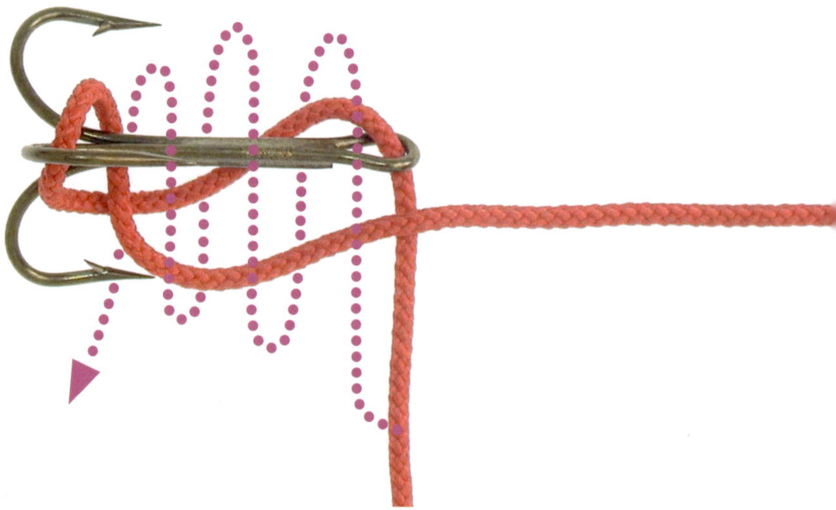

Step 1

Begin by holding the standing part of the line alongside the shank of the hook, then create a loop around the shank and take the working (or tag) end back to tuck down through the hook's eye. Working away from the eye, make four to six wrapping turns over the hook and standing part with the working (or tag) end.

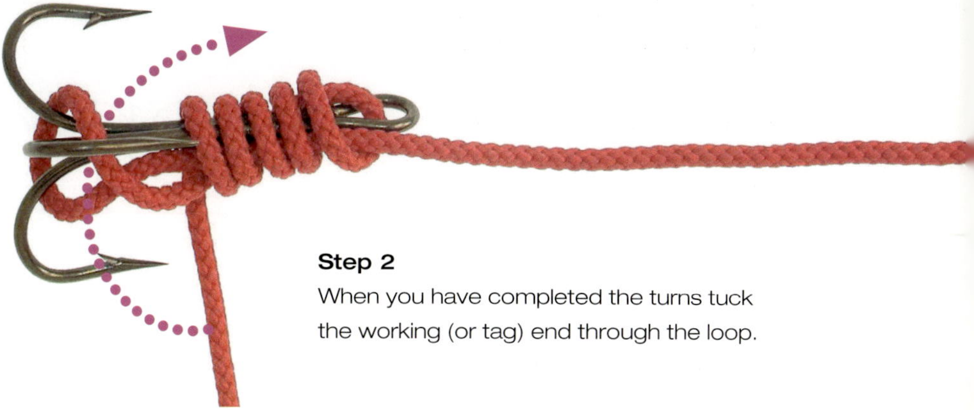

Step 2

When you have completed the turns tuck the working (or tag) end through the loop.

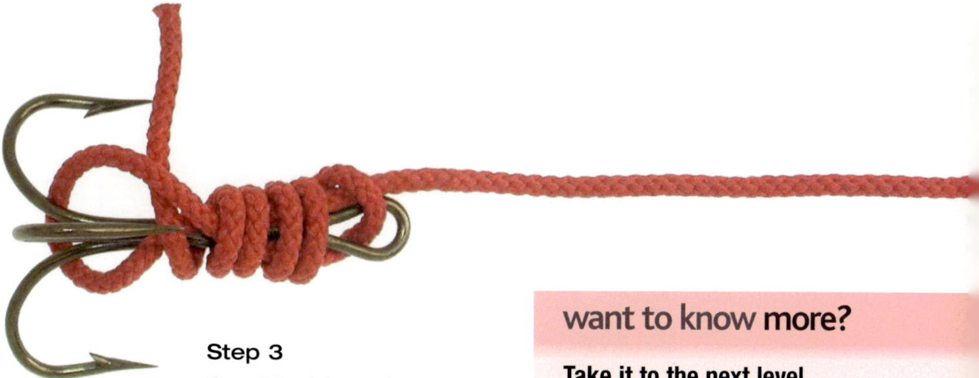

Step 3

Carefully tighten the knot so that it jams behind the hook's eye.

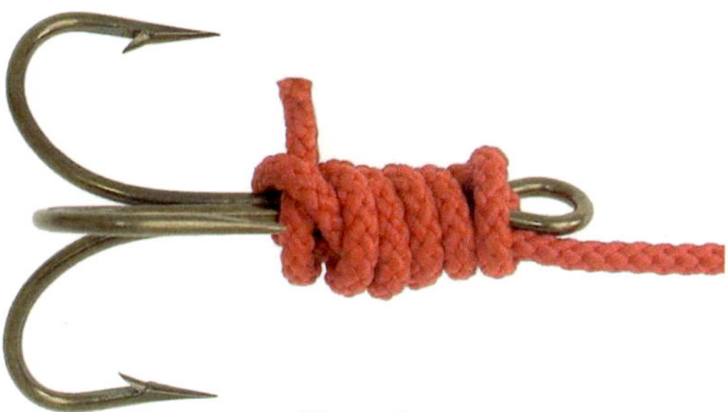

Step 4

Finally, trim the working (or tag) end.

want to know more?

Take it to the next level...

Go to...

- ▶ **Ashley's stopper knot –** pages 42–3
- ▶ **Bowline in the bight –** page 133
- ▶ **Knute hitch –** page 106

Other sources

- ▶ **Angling associations and clubs**
  see Yellow pages or local directories
- ▶ **Internet**
  www.aandfishingtackle.co.uk
  www.brook-fishing.com/knots
- ▶ **The International Guild of Knot Tyers**
  see pages 187–8 for further information
- ▶ **Publications**
  Tying Strong Fishing Knots by Bill Herzog (1995), ISBN 1-57188-022-4

home and

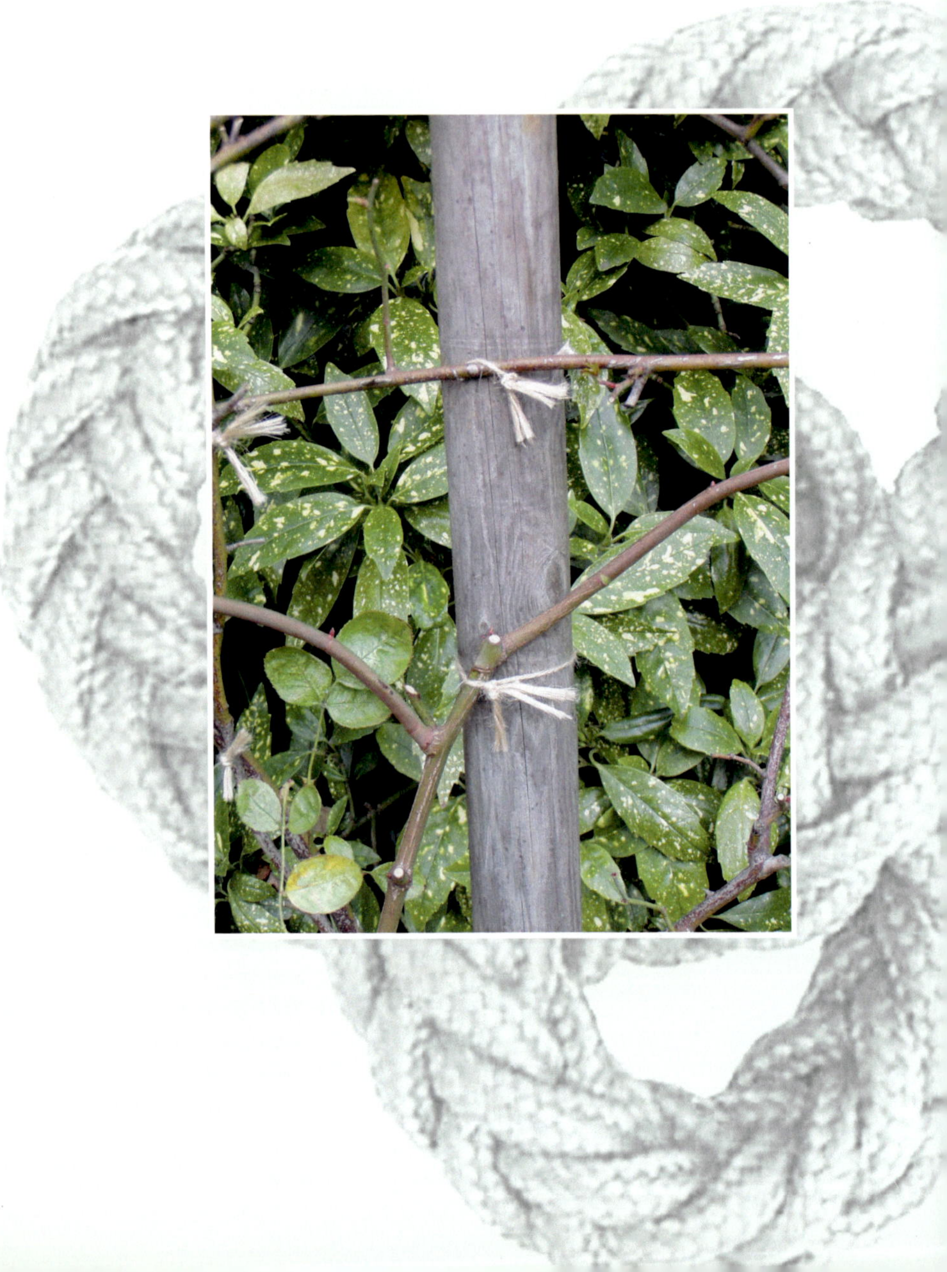

hobbies

Indoors and outdoors, in the garage or garden, there is a need to tie things up (or to tie them down) with rope, cord or string. Home-makers, hobbyists and DIY devotees often need a 'third hand' or a 'sky hook' to overcome an awkward job and the assortment of knots that follows will all serve as tireless workmates.

Strangle knot

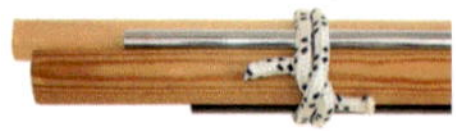

The strangle knot is merely a double overhand knot with something inserted through its middle.

Some prefer this to the constrictor knot on page 88, but the only practical difference is that the constrictor – unlike this knot – can, in accordance with the law of loop, hitch and bight, be tied in the bight (see page 29).

Use this binding to seize and hold anything from a cut rope's ends to a roll of carpet, or even rolled-up posters and prints.

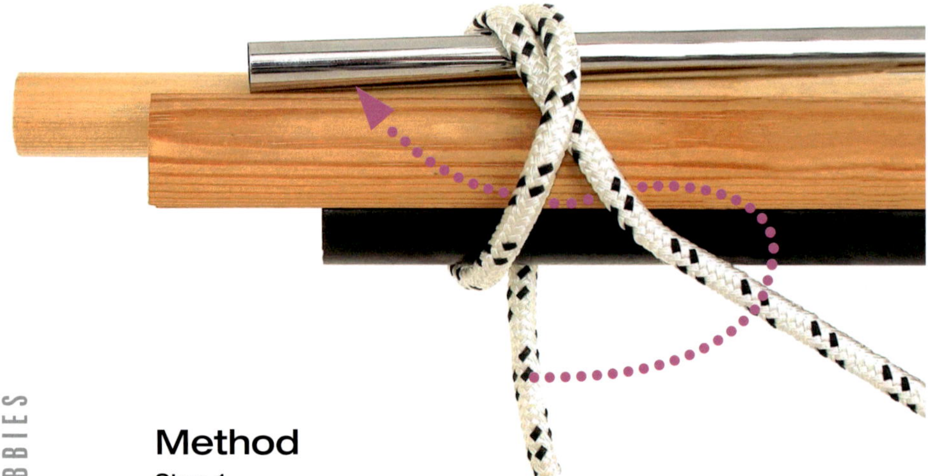

Method

Step 1

Take the working end around the object(s) to be held and then bring it diagonally across the standing part and over the object(s)once again. This is how you would begin to tie a clove hitch with an end (see pages 50–1).

WATCH OUT!

The strangle knot, like the constrictor, is a binding knot, which should not be employed as a hitch, (see page 16) because it jams and would be very difficult to untie.

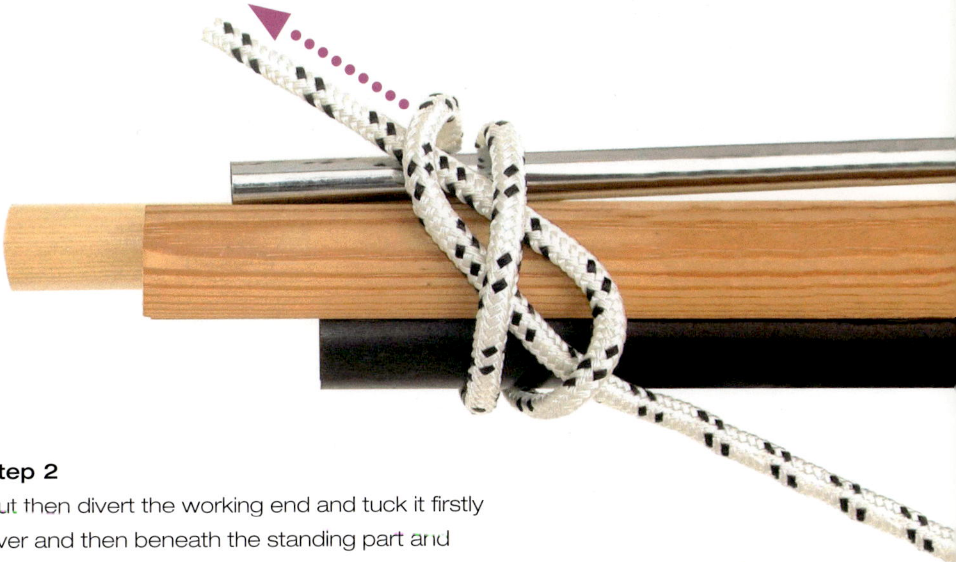

Step 2

But then divert the working end and tuck it firstly over and then beneath the standing part and the diagonal crossing.

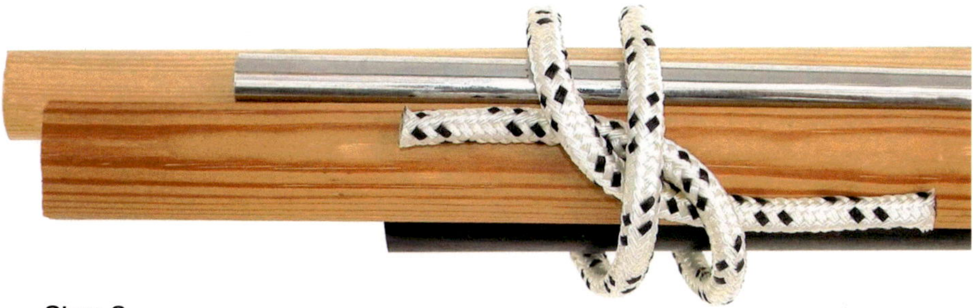

Step 3

Tighten the knot carefully.

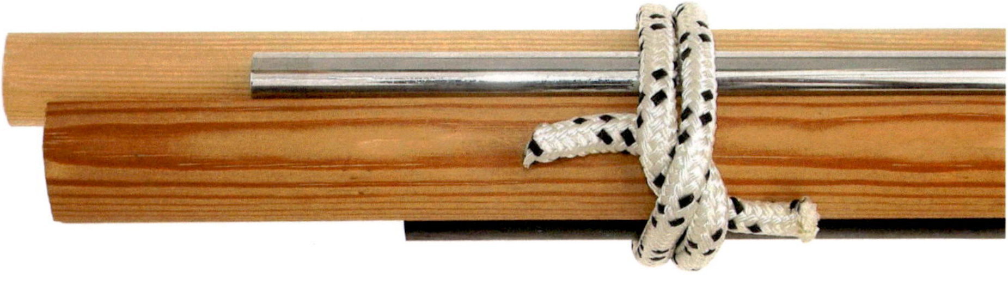

Step 4

Finally, trim the ends short.

Constrictor knot

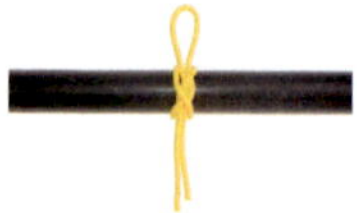

An alternative to the strangle knot (see pages 86–7), the constrictor knot can be applied as a semi-permanent binding to prevent a rope's end fraying and unravelling.

You can also use it to reinforce garden trellises weakened by the weight of climbing plants or even simply to attach a pencil to a clipboard. Tie the knot with an end when the end of the object to be seized is inaccessible and in the bight when it is accessible.

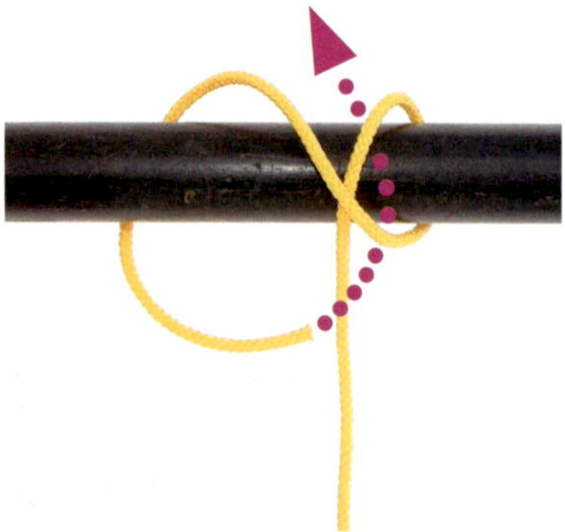

Tied with an end

Step 1

Start by taking the working end over the fixed part to form a cross (like tying a clove hitch, see pages 50–1). Then place the working end over the standing part and tuck it beneath the two knot parts (or the cross in the cord).

Step 2

The resulting knot needs to be tightened. Pull strongly on both the working and standing end.

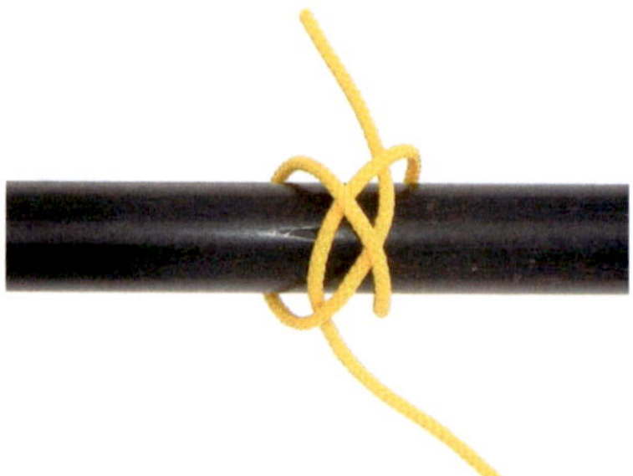

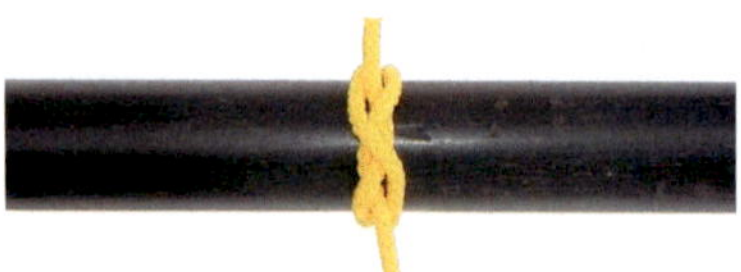

Step 3

Lastly, trim the ends fairly short.

Variation

Alternatively, you can leave a draw-loop for quick release.

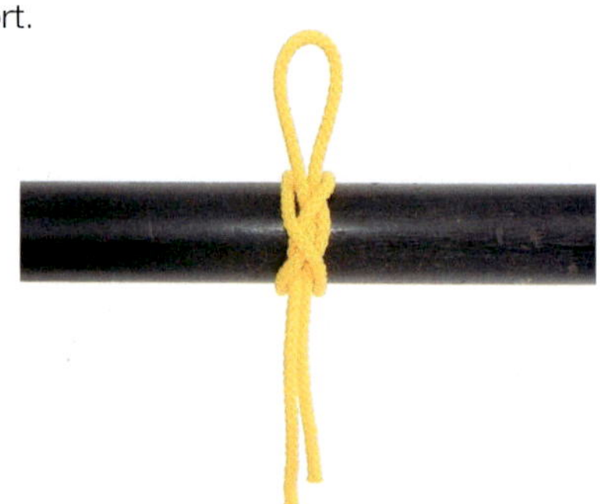

Tied in the bight

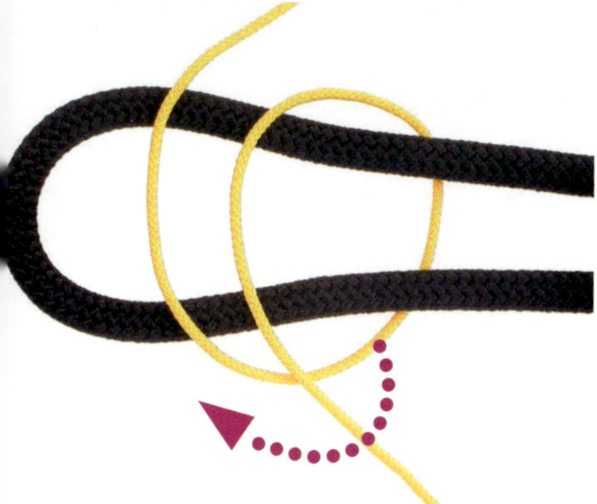

Step 1

Pass a loop (as shown) over the end of the item to be seized. Then pull out a bight from the back of the turn.

MUST KNOW

Hard to untie

For optimum grip use hard-laid cord around something softer (such as a rope); but, around an unyielding surface, like a metal rail or pipe, tie the constrictor in soft and stretchy stuff. Either way it will seize solidly.

A constrictor can be difficult to untie, so use a knife to sever just the overlaying diagonal knot part – taking care not to nick or scar the underlying material – and the knot will fall away in two dead curly segments.

Step 2

Make a half-twist and pass the resulting loop over the end of the fixed item.

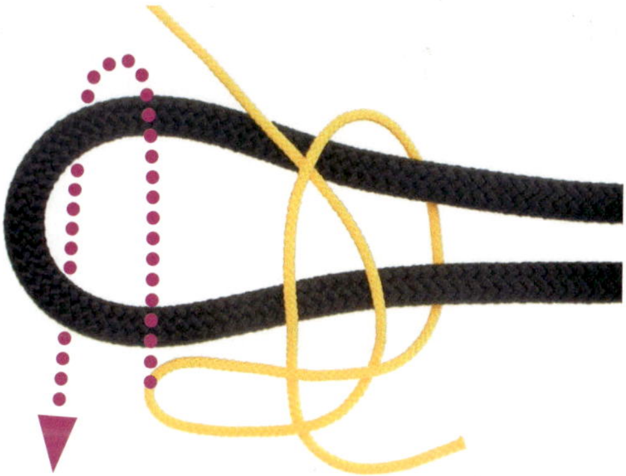

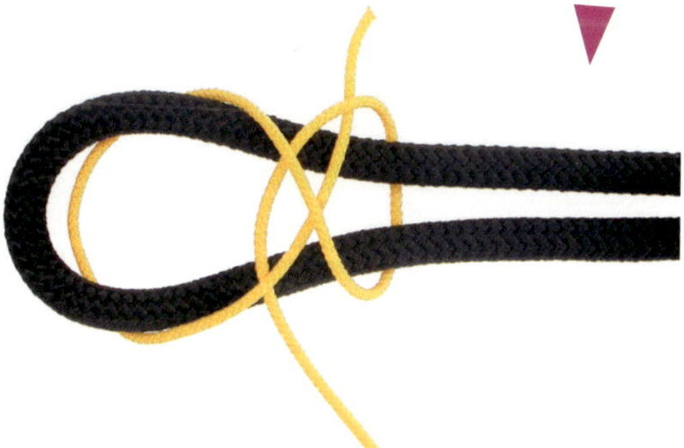

Step 3

Shape the knot and pull it tight.

Step 4

Trim both the ends quite short.

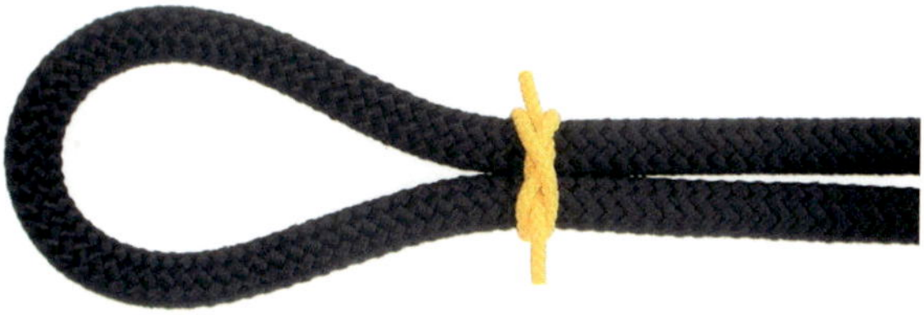

Boa knot

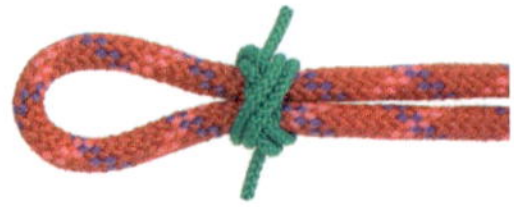

Try this bulkier binding, using thin twine or thread, instead of the strangle knot or the constrictor knot.

The boa knot combines the forms and functions of both these knots but can be too bulky for thicker cords. It was devised for use by handicraft workers, to bind the ends of plaits or braids that were then cut off close to the knot.

Method

Step 1

First make a couple of clockwise loops in a length of cord. Then impart a 180 degree half twist to the resulting mini-coil (forming an elongated figure of eight).

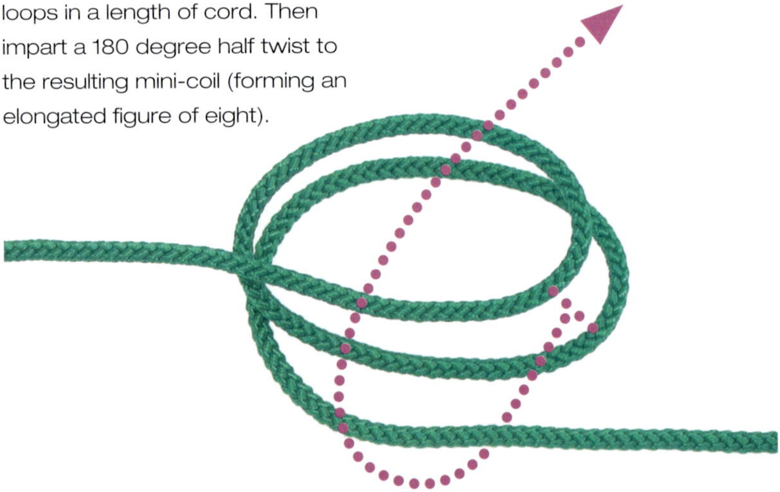

MUST KNOW

Tying for the lead

This knot was devised and publicized by the eminent weaver and craft author Peter Collingwood in the 1990s, although it later transpired that at least two other knot tyers – namely John Halifax (UK) and Heinz Prohaska (Austria) had also discovered this innovative seizing for themselves and had been using it for at least a decade. The history of knotting is often like that.

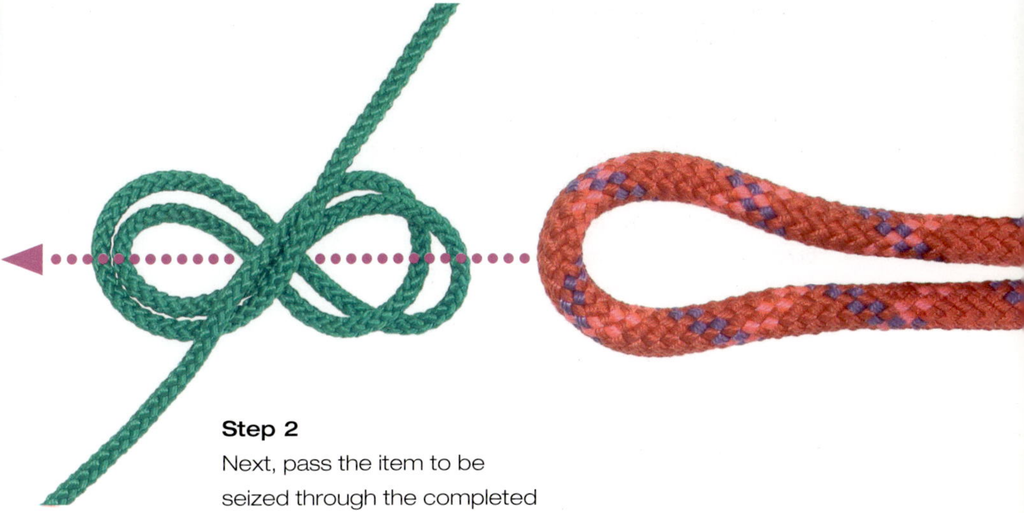

Step 2

Next, pass the item to be seized through the completed layout or alternatively, when possible, slip the binding over the end of the item.

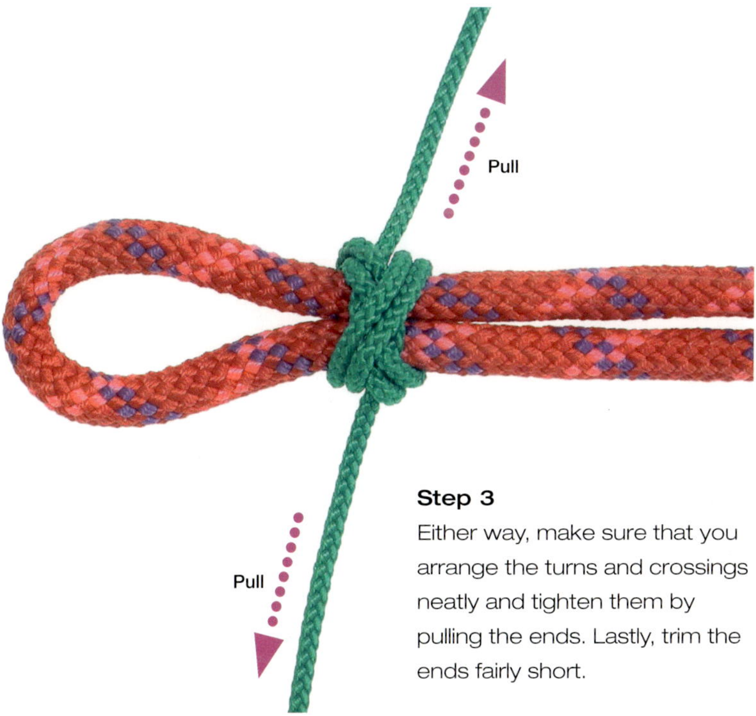

Step 3

Either way, make sure that you arrange the turns and crossings neatly and tighten them by pulling the ends. Lastly, trim the ends fairly short.

Short splice

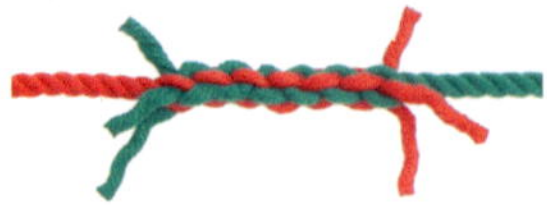

Numerous short splices have been devised by sailors, sail-makers and riggers, but this is the best known and a most efficient way of joining two ropes of equal thickness.

Method

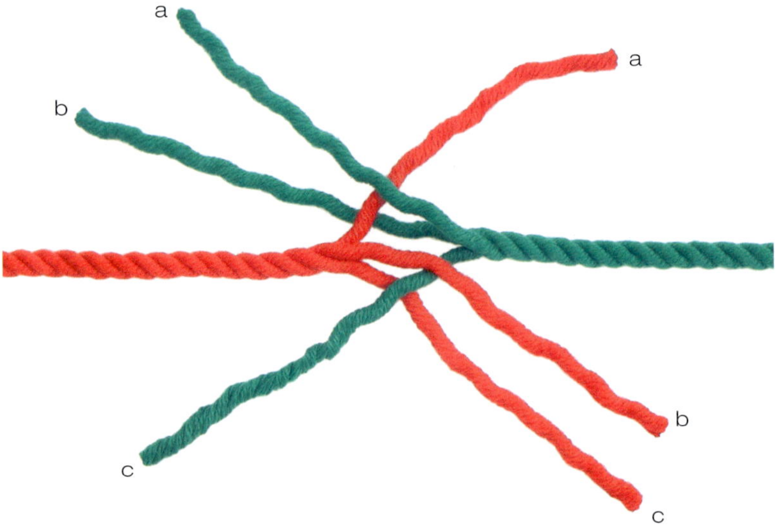

Step 1

Undo the strands of both ropes to a length of, say, 10 to 15 times the diameter of the actual rope. Then place red strand (a) over green stand (b) and under green strand (a). Next, place red strand (b) over green strand (c). Lastly, place red strand (c) under green stand (c). The aim is to interlock the strands.

WATCH OUT!

This splice thickens the rope and may prevent it passing through the eye of a block, fairlead or other item of rigging hardware.

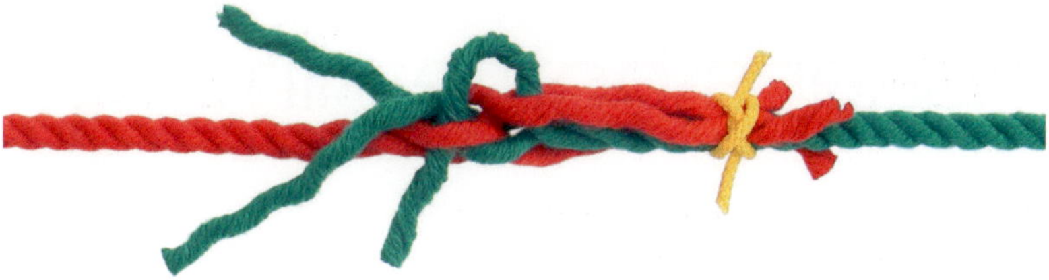

Step 2

Push the ropes together and temporarily tape the three red strands to the green rope, or seize them with a strangle knot or a constrictor knot (see pages 86-7 and 88–9). Turn the rope clockwise and using the back splice method (see page 45), that is, over one strand and under one strand, begin to splice the green strands onto the red rope.

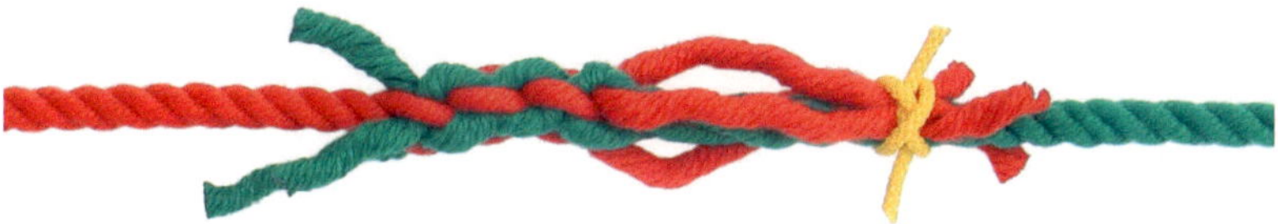

Step 3

Continue splicing the green strands onto the red rope. Do this three to five times, and make sure that you tighten the splice after each turn.

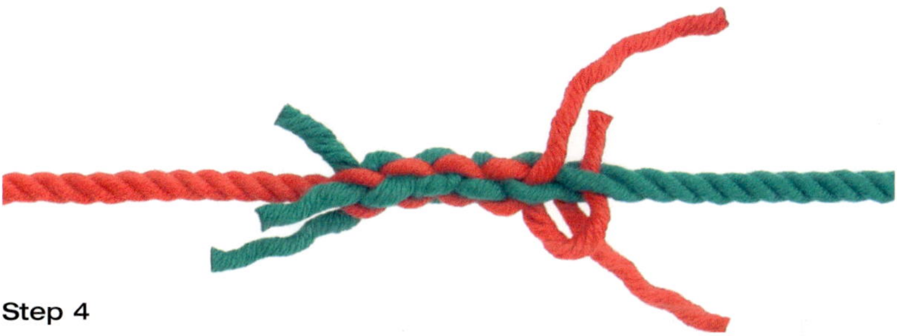

Step 4

Next, untie the three unused red strands and splice these into the green rope in the opposite direction.

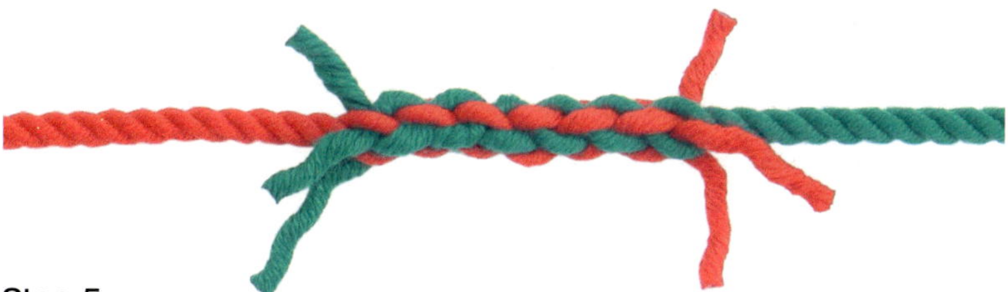

Step 5

It is not essential to whip or tape over the cut ends of the six tucked strands, as they will wear down with time, but do so in order to prevent them from snagging obstructions when the joined ropes are in use.

Asher's bottle sling

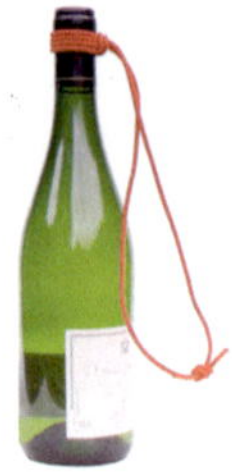

Carrying a vessel full of liquid - whether it is a jeroboam of champagne, drinking water or battery acid - is easier and safer using this sling, devised by Dr Harry Asher and first published in 1986.

In addition, such a container can be heavy and on a hot day condensation can make the outer surface slippery. By employing this device your task will be made simpler. It is also an excellent method of suspending a bottle of your favourite summer beverage in a cold stream until it is to be consumed.

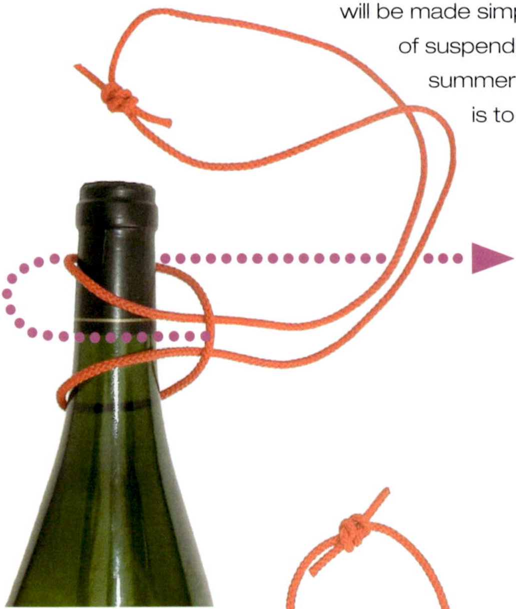

Method

Step 1

To make a neat carrying handle for bottle, jar or jug, first tie or splice a length of cord into an endless sling (circular piece of cord). Tie a ring hitch by wrapping the cord around the neck of the container, and feeding one end of the loop underneath the other. Then pull out a bight and wrap it around a second time.

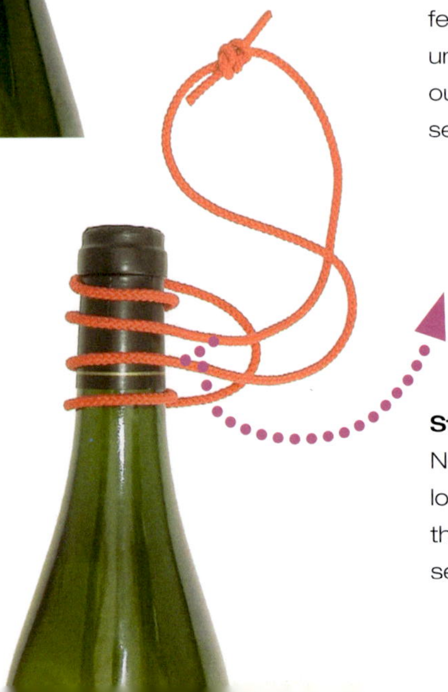

Step 2

Next tuck the bight under the loop once again. (Tightened, this would be a Prusik knot, see page 124.)

Step 3
However, for the Asher sling, pull out an extra bight and impart a 180 degree half-twist.

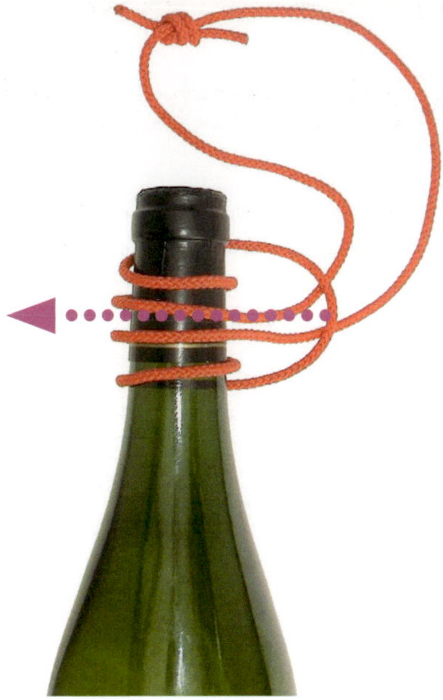

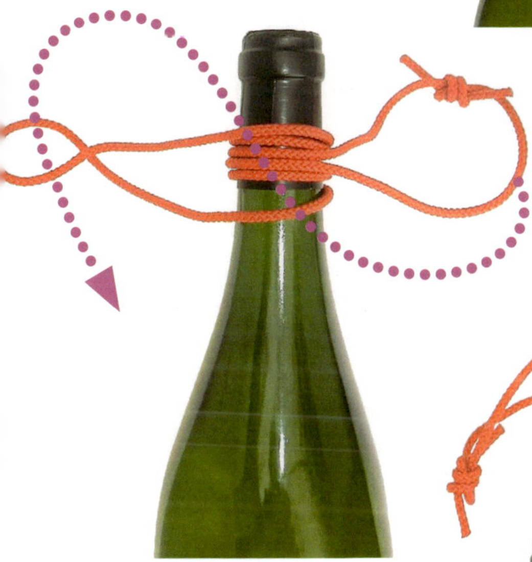

Step 4
Tuck the main bight up through the newly formed loop.

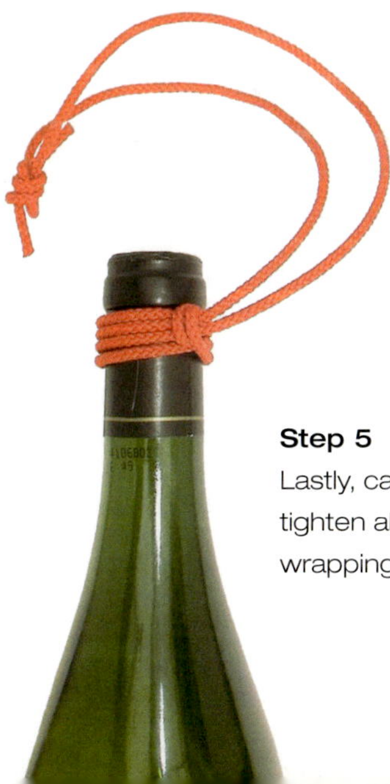

WATCH OUT!

This sling cannot be relied upon to jam and remain tight. Each time it is used, re-tighten all of its wrapping turns.

Step 5
Lastly, carefully tighten all of the wrapping turns.

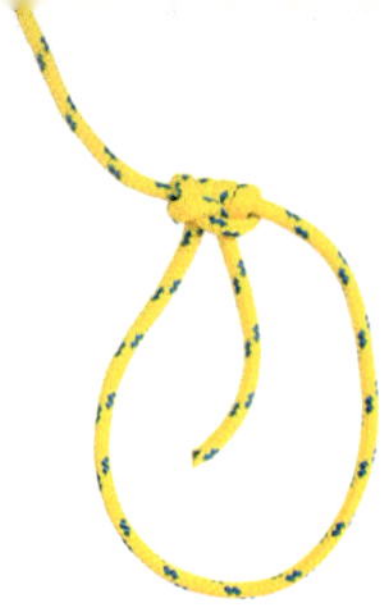

Tarbuck knot

For guy-lines and other ropes that require periodic alteration of their tension for whatever reason, use this knot.

This is another slide-and-grip noose, like the midshipman's hitch (see pages 60–1), that can be adjusted by hand to the required size but which seizes and holds firm when loaded.

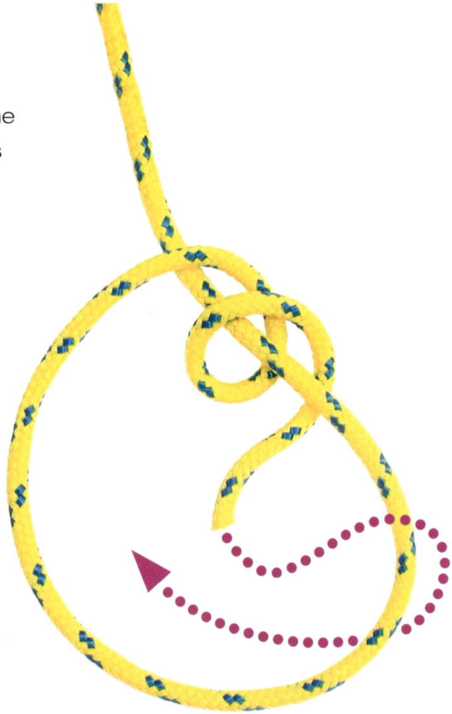

Method

Step 1

First make an overhand loop and then take two-and-a-half turns around the standing part with the working end.

MUST KNOW

Squeezed out

This knot was known and used by tree surgeons in Wisconsin, USA, in the 1940s, where it was simply referred to as 'the squeeze knot'. It was rediscovered and made briefly popular with 1950s climbers in the UK by Ken Tarbuck for use in nylon ropes. However, it was soon found to be unsuitable for sheath-and-core (kernmantel) construction cordage, as the knot damaged the outer covering. Consequently, it is now not recommended as a life-support knot.

Step 2

Complete the third turn and then bring the working end across the standing part and make another turn.

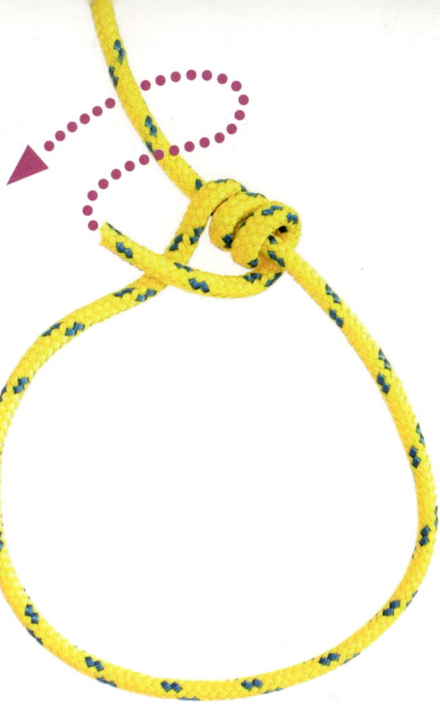

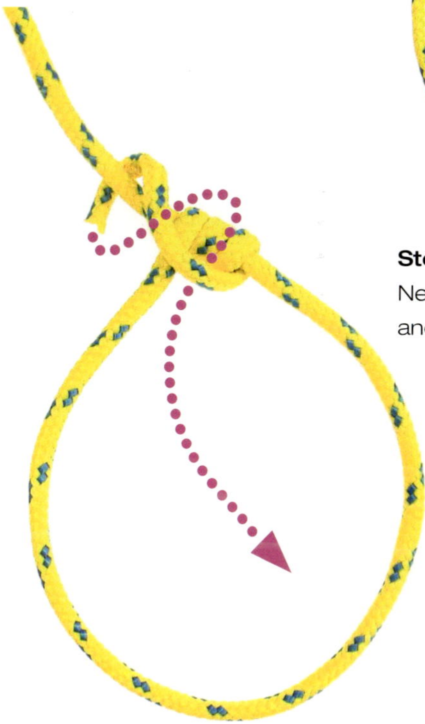

Step 3

Next tuck the working end over and beneath itself.

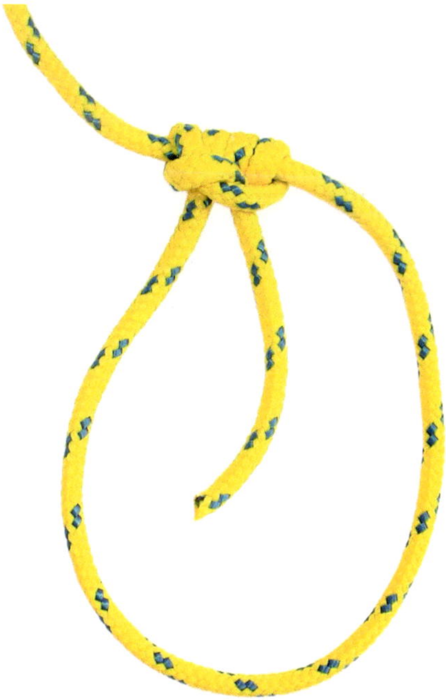

Step 4

Tighten the knot meticulously, making sure that the turns sit neatly next to one another.

Sheepshank

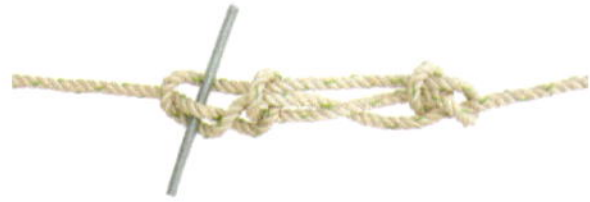

This underrated knot will temporarily shorten any rope that is too expensive to cut. It can also be used to bridge a damaged and weakened section of rope.

Method

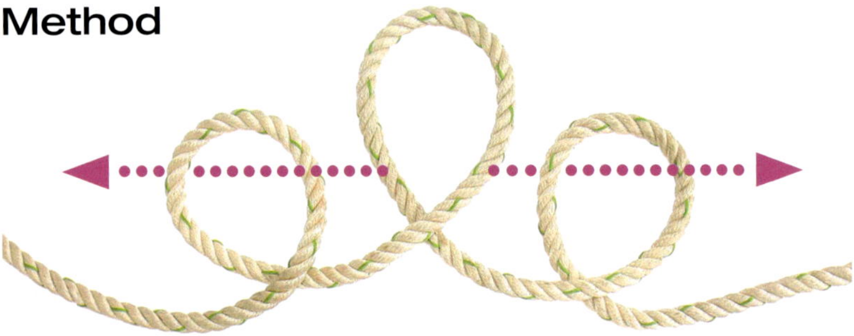

Step 1

Make a trio of loops (two clockwise, the third counter-clockwise) with the middle one larger than the outer two. Pull each leg (side) of the central large loop out through its adjacent smaller loop.

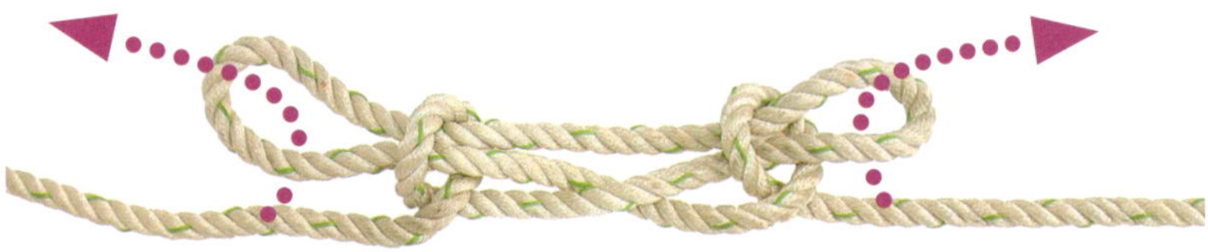

Step 2

To prevent it coming undone, tuck an end through each bight – as long as the line is short enough to make this an easy option.

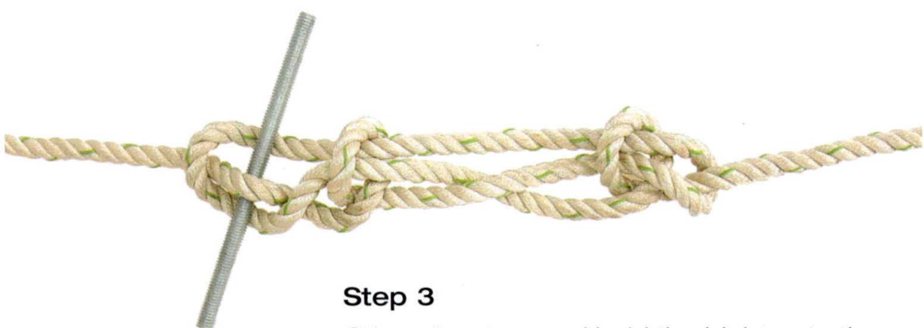

Step 3

Otherwise, trap and hold the bight onto the standing part with an improvised toggle.

Braid knot

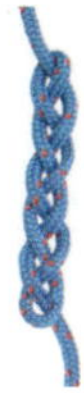

This fancy trick knot will serve as a decorative shortening for a tie-belt, such as a dressing-gown cord, and as ornamentation for a lanyard attached to a referee's whistle.

A braid knot is a very handy one to know because it will also enable you to make a handle for a heavy parcel or item of luggage.

Method

Step 1

Form a long loop with the working end resting over the standing part in a downward direction. Using both sides of the loop and one section of line, begin to make a three-strand plait. Bring the left-hand side over the working end.

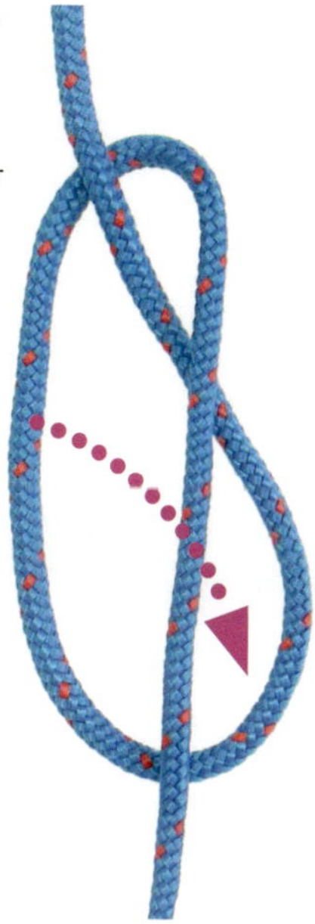

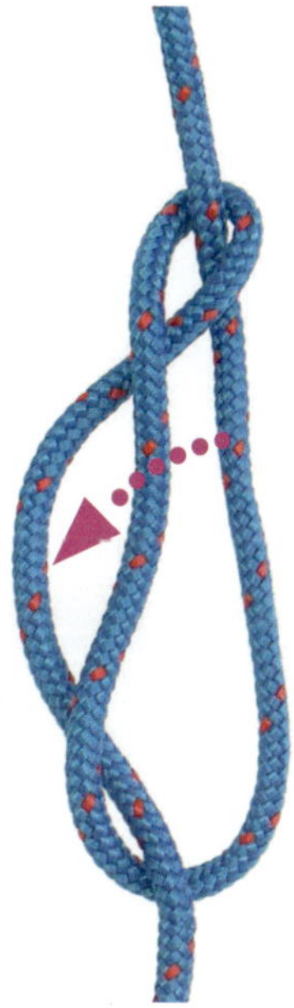

Step 2

Next bring the right-hand side over the middle cord.

Step 3

Then pass the left-hand cord over the middle cord. Continue with the sequence, making sure that you work the plait tight from time to time. You will need to disentangle the free end from the bottom of the loop whenever it tangles and interferes with the plaiting process.

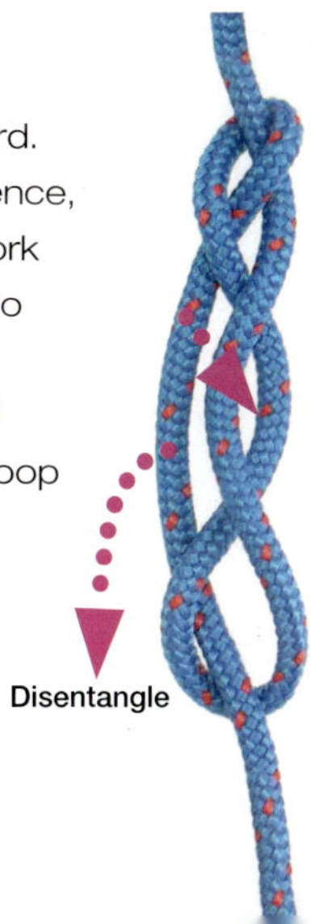

Step 4

When the required length has been created, make a final locking tuck down through what little remains of the initial loop. No tightening should be necessary.

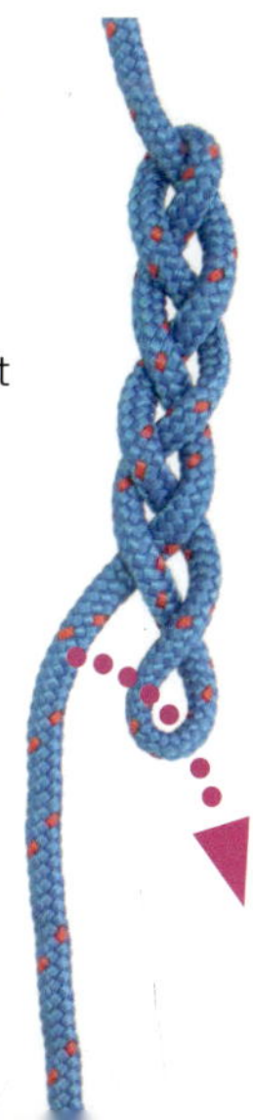

Lapp knot

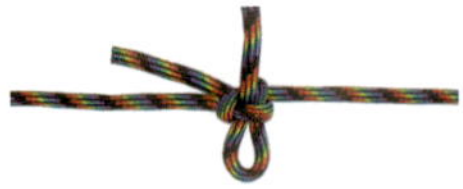

The Lapp knot is used to tether reindeer in the Arctic – hence its name – but it will also act as a cost-free substitute for a buckle, snap-hook or any other item of hardware on a lanyard or leash.

This is a quick-release knot (one of the few knots that comes apart with just one tug) and can be used for a tie-belt, whether it is a knife lanyard or an improvised safety harness.

Method

Step 1

First make a bight in one end of the line. Then place the working end on top of it and pass it beneath the two legs of the bight.

MUST KNOW

Single pulling power

Most so-called 'slipped' knots (those with a draw-loop) are easy to untie, but do not readily release whoever or whatever they are securing. They often have extra turns or tucks to be undone. The Lapp knot, however, melts away with a single pull.

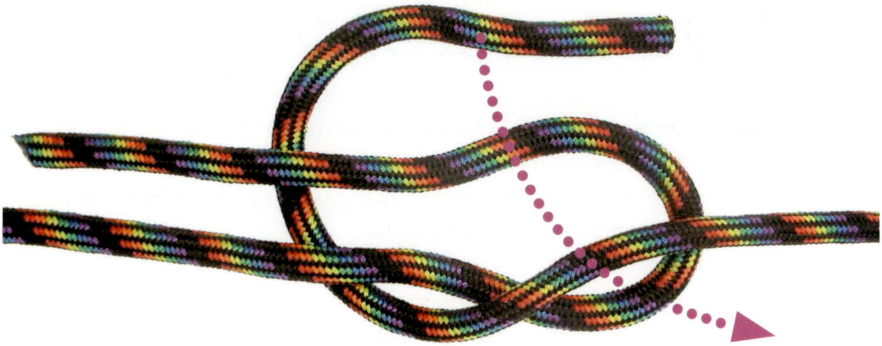

Step 2

Next pull out a bight and bring it downwards, over the top of the first bight and in between its own standing part and the lower leg of the first bight.

Step 3

Tighten the knot carefully so that the working end is surrounded by a three-strand crown of knot parts.

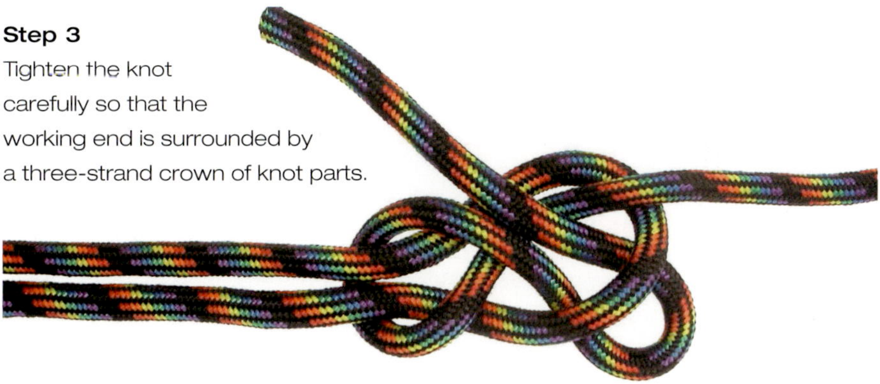

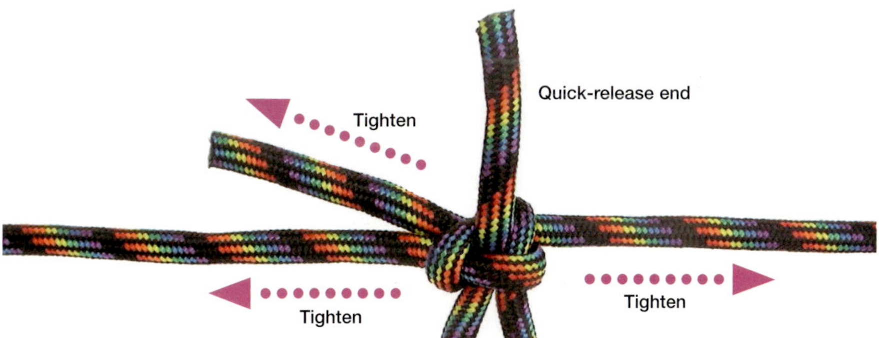

Step 4

To release this knot, give a firm tug on the working end that conveniently projects upwards.

Harness bend

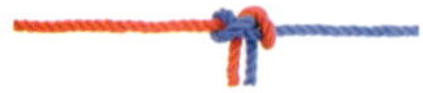

The harness bend is a legacy from our rural and agricultural past, as its name implies, but it can be tied in most hi-tech cordage materials as well as the crudest of string and leather or rawhide thongs.

At one time it was known as the drawing bend, referring to when it was used to attach horses to carts or carriages so as to pull (or draw) them. It was also called the parcel bend, implying a humbler employment in domestic string. Use it whenever two pieces of twine or cord need to be joined to make a single length. The harness bend is the basis for the reever bend (see page 118).

Method

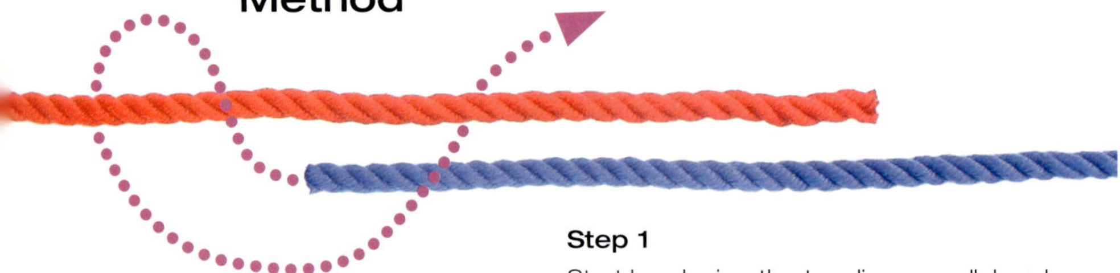

Step 1

Start by placing the two lines parallel and close together, with the working ends pointing in opposite directions. Then wrap the blue working end around the red line, bring it over itself and tuck it under the other line.

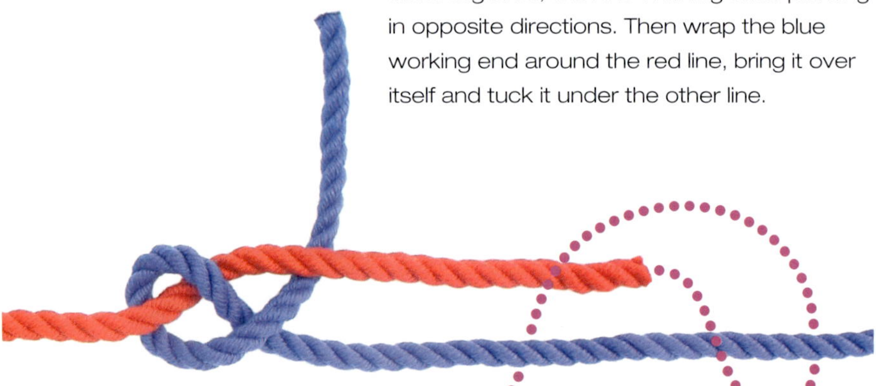

Step 2

Repeat the above process with the working end of the red line.

Step 3

To complete the harness bend, simply adjust the two working ends, following the direction of the arrows (the blue rope moves down and to the right and the red rope moves to the left).

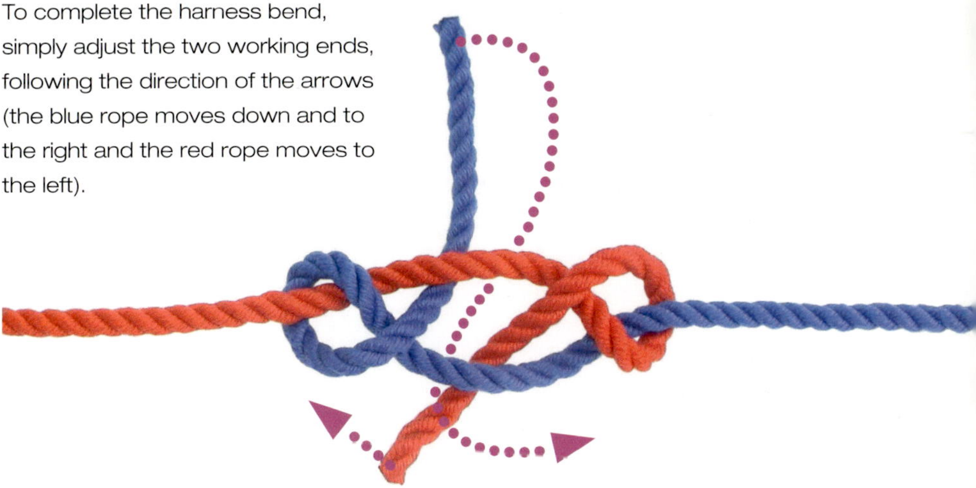

Step 4

Make sure that you have this configuration before tightening the bend.

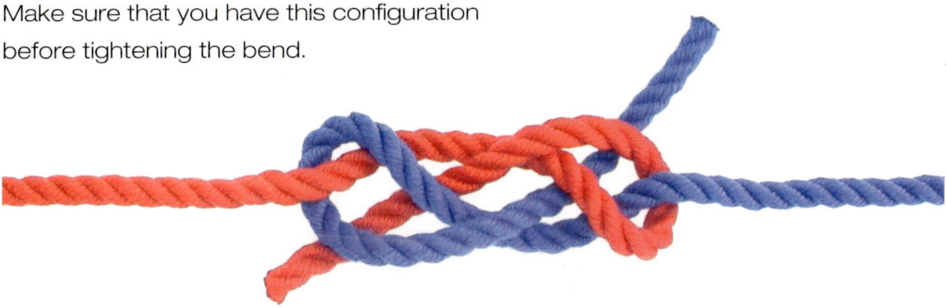

Step 5

Work the knot tight by pulling on both working ends and standing parts in turn.

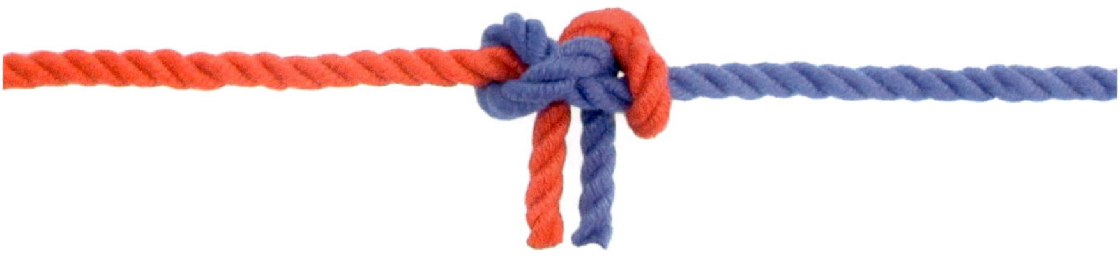

Fisherman's knot

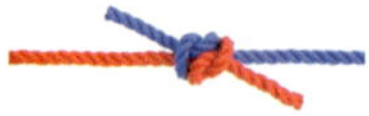

This adaptable knot can be tied in string, cord or rope, for every imaginable purpose, when two lengths of line must be joined to make a single longer piece.

Use it to unite short lengths of string to tie up a parcel, or to join rope and other cordage used in outdoor pursuits. However, it is best to employ rope of the same diameter.

Method

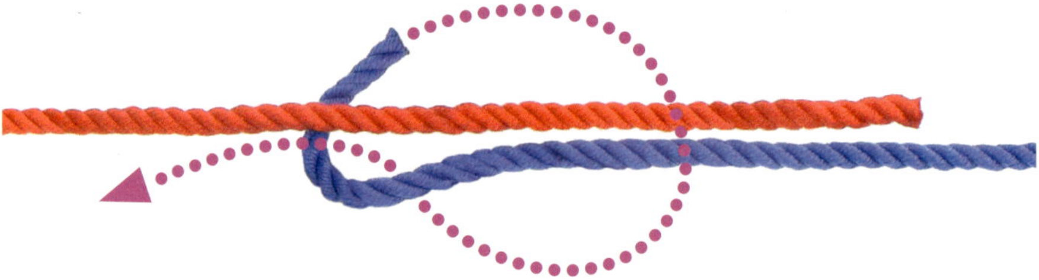

Step 1
Lay the two lines to be joined close together, parallel, with the working ends pointing in opposite directions. With the working end of the blue line tie an overhand knot around the adjacent red line.

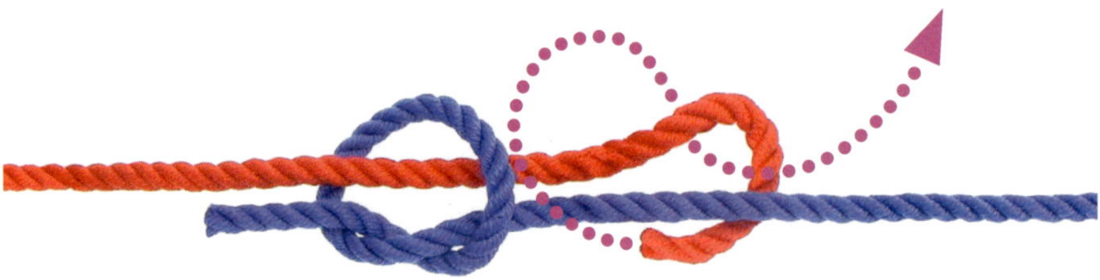

Step 2
Then, with the working end of the top red line, tie another overhand knot of identical handedness (both either S-laid, or both Z-laid, see page 15) around the lower blue line.

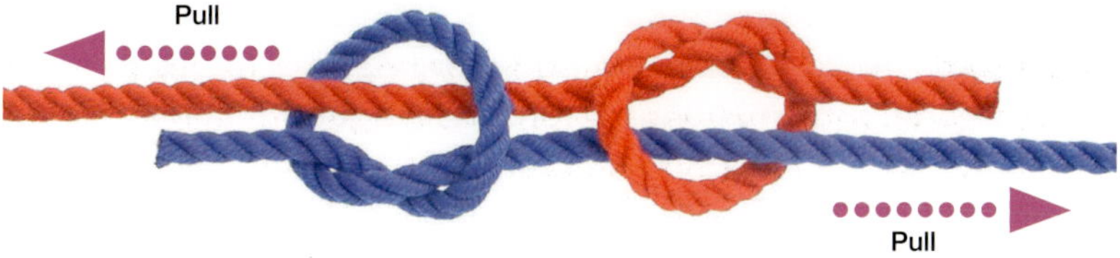

Step 3

Pull the two working ends to tighten the individual knots and then pull on the standing parts to bring them together.

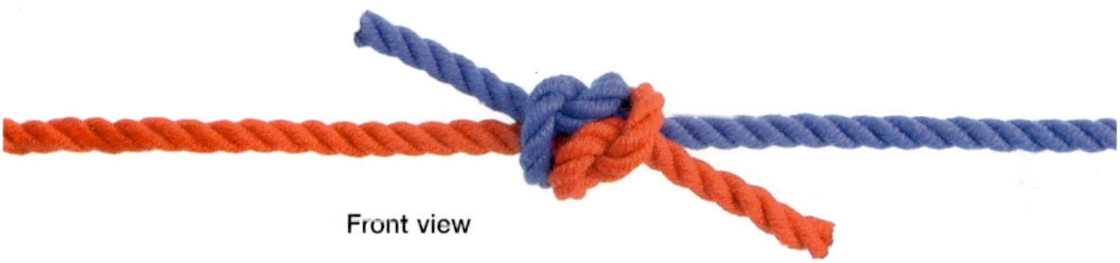

Front view

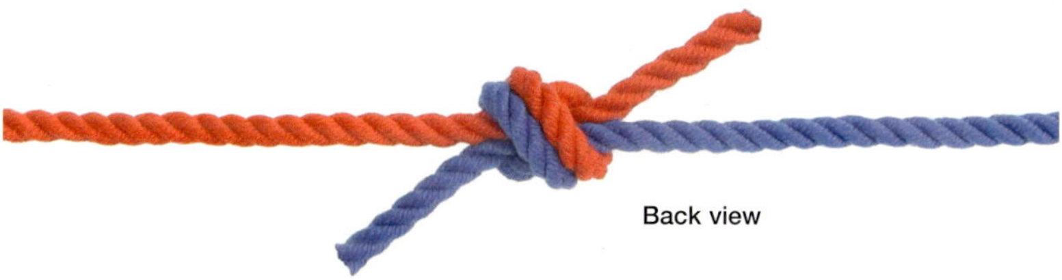

Back view

MUST KNOW

Single handed

Some knot tyers deliberately make this knot with overhands of opposite handedness (one S-laid, the other Z-laid – see page 15), influenced no doubt by the many knotting manuals which describe and illustrate the knot that way, and then insist it is the correct thing to do. There was, however, a report of test data in *The Alpine Journal* (no. 40, 1928) which concluded that concordant knots (that is, those of the same handedness) were stronger. In any case, this version is neater and – in accordance with Budworth's rule – elegance in a knot is always preferable.

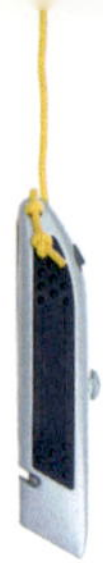

Knute hitch

This simplest of hitches can be used to attach a tool to a lanyard, retain the inactive end of a heaving line to the thrower's belt, or make a halyard fast to a dinghy sail.

Pronounced 'canute', this previously undistinguished knot appears to have been named in 1990 by the American rigger and writer Brion Toss.

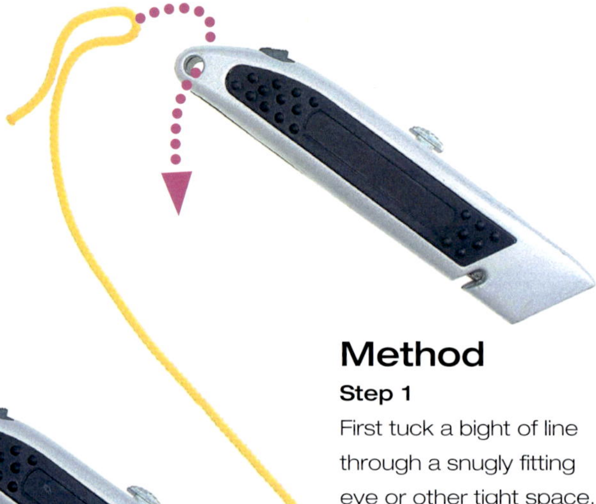

Method

Step 1

First tuck a bight of line through a snugly fitting eye or other tight space.

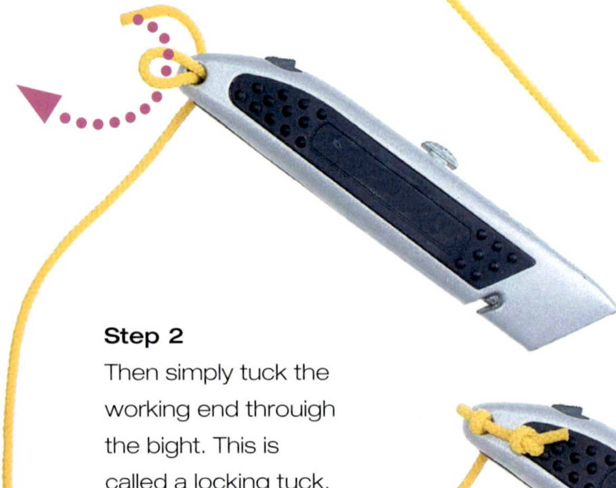

Step 2

Then simply tuck the working end through the bight. This is called a locking tuck.

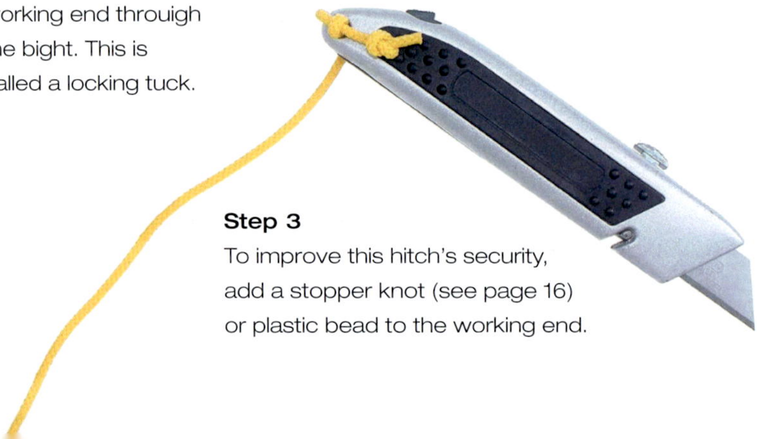

Step 3

To improve this hitch's security, add a stopper knot (see page 16) or plastic bead to the working end.

Pedigree cow hitch

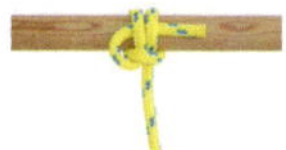

A variation of the common cow hitch, this knot is a general purpose hitch that can be used to attach a rope to a rail, ring or post.

Method

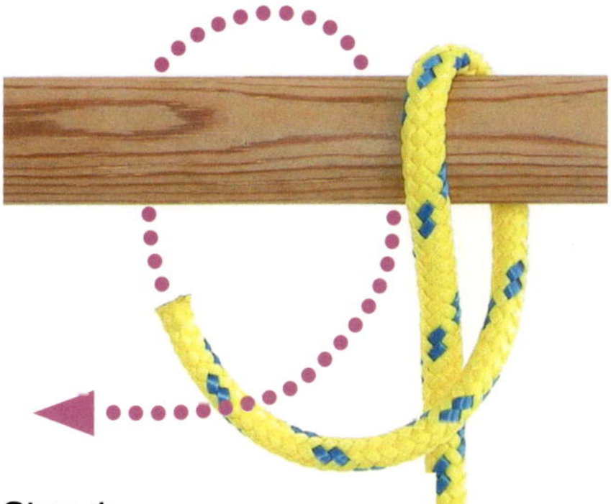

Step 1

Place the working end over the post and across its own standing part. Repeat the process a second time.

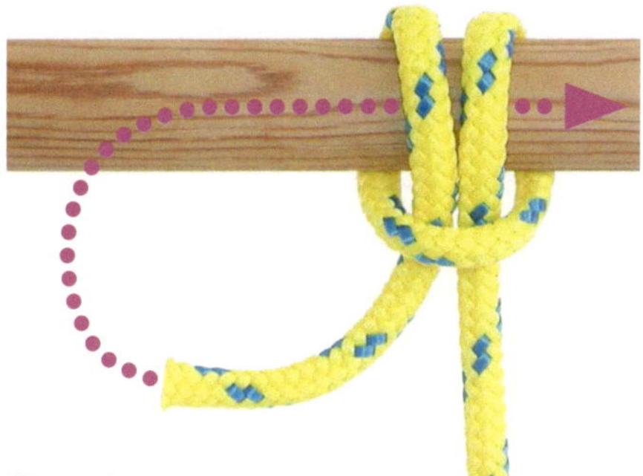

Step 2

(This is a basic cow hitch.) Next take the working end and tuck it beneath the two parts that encircle the post.

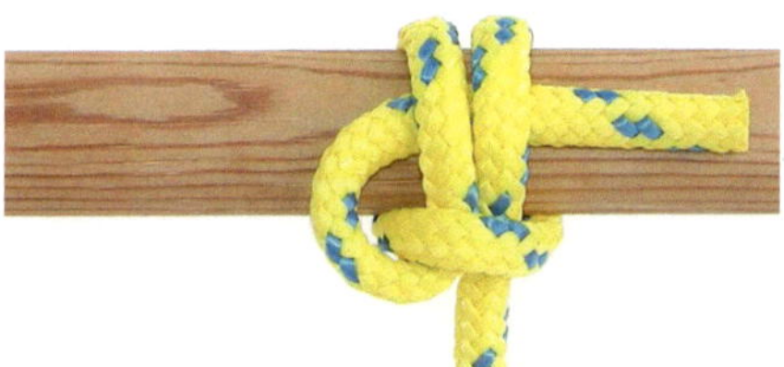

Step 3

Pull the working end and standing part to secure the hitch.

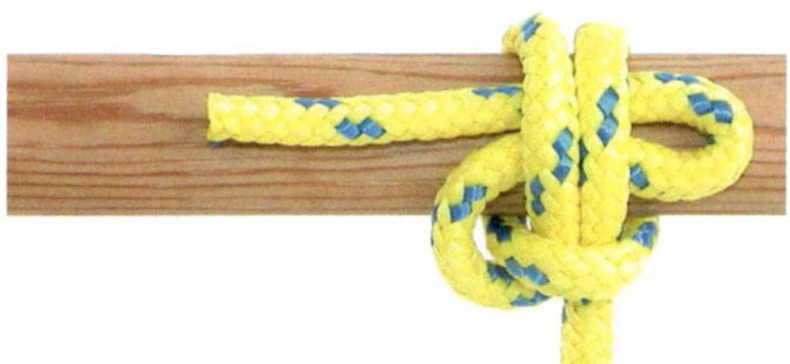

Variation

For quick release, form a draw-loop beneath the two knot parts.

MUST KNOW

Hitch in time

A cow hitch takes the load on the standing part of the line alone and has always been deemed unreliable; until, that is, it was rehabilitated (by the simple modification of tucking the end), named as the pedigree cow hitch and widely publicized in 1986 by research scientist, Dr Harry Asher.

Ring hitch

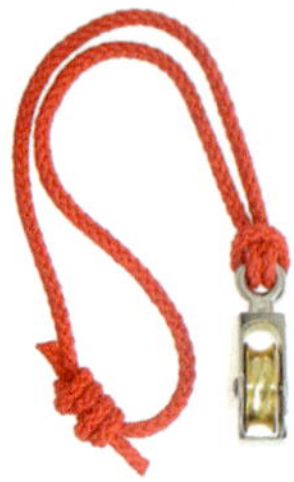

When an endless sling has to be bent to a ring, and the ring is attached to something much bigger than the loop (say a building or a prize bull), a ring hitch provides a solution.

It is also most useful for attaching labels to parcels or luggage.

This cordage configuration is often referred to as a lark's head or sometimes, wrongly, a cow hitch (see also the pedigree cow hitch on page 107).

Method

Step 1

Tuck one end of the endless sling through the ring. Then bring this back through itself.

Step 2

Slide the resulting hitch up tight beneath the ring.

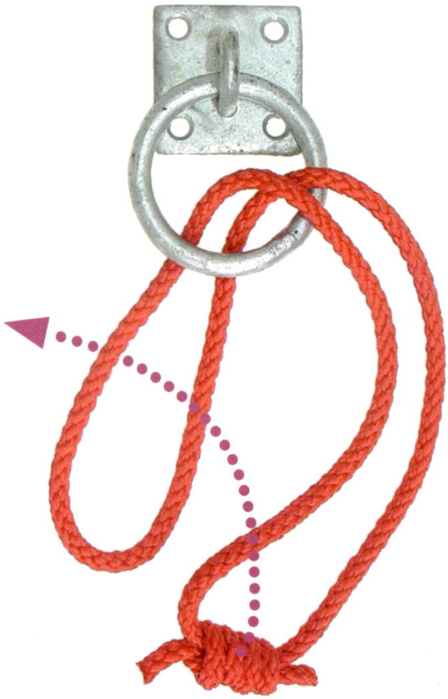

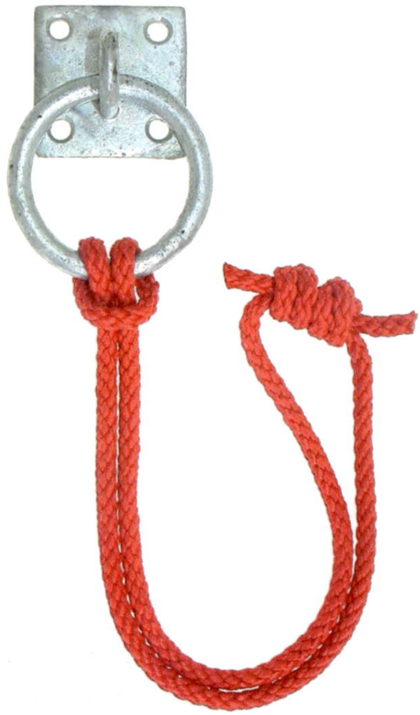

Method for small objects

Step 1

To attach a stop watch or whistle to a lanyard that is smaller than the loop, first pass the loop through the ring or eye of the item, then simply pass the object through the loop.

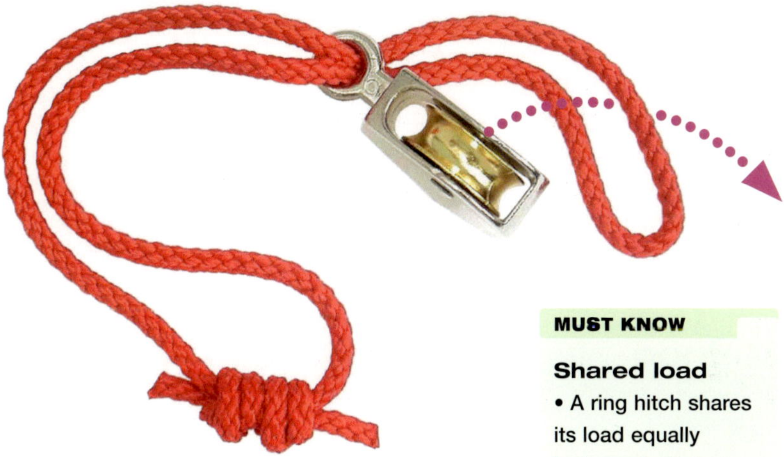

MUST KNOW

Shared load

- A ring hitch shares its load equally between both loop legs.
- To make sure that it will hold, exert equal pressure on both parts of the rope.

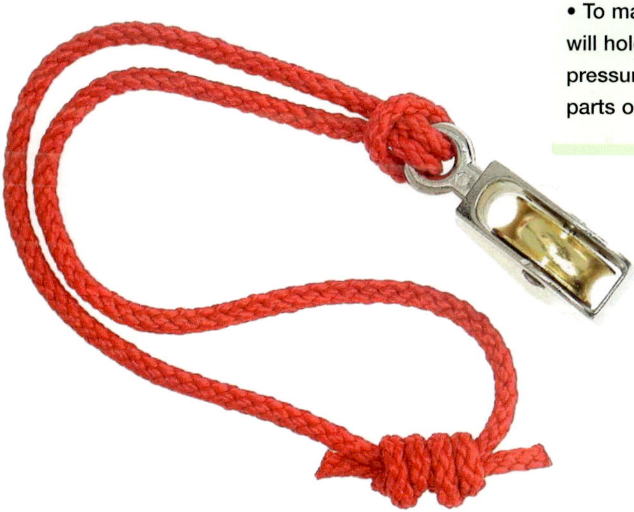

Step 2

Pull the loop to tighten and secure the object. To remove the object simply reverse steps 1 and 2.

Round turn and two half-hitches

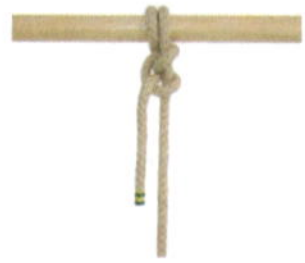

This is an extremely simple and quick knot to tie that will withstand intermittent tugging or pulling from several directions.

It is used to moor boats, tether animals, tow vehicles or suspend anything from anything, as the load can be held (or braked) by the friction generated within the round turn, before adding the two half-hitches. When releasing the knot, the half-hitches can be untied while control of the load is maintained through the round turn.

MUST KNOW

Related knot

A round turn and two half-hitches is closely related to the anchor bend (see page 53). The difference is that the first half-hitch is tied below, not through, the turn.

Method

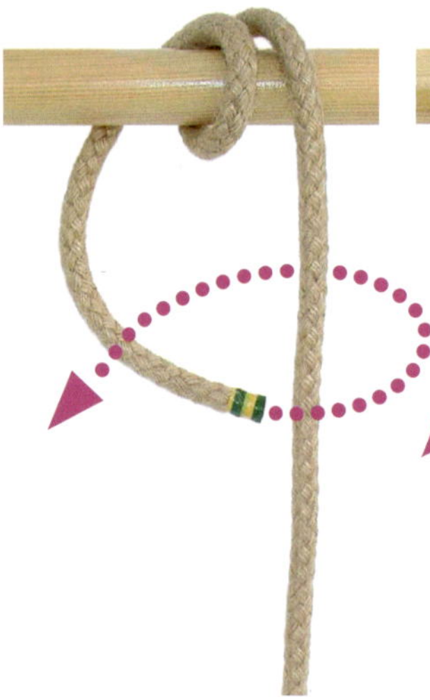

Step 1

Take the working end around the post twice to form the round turn. Then pass it around the standing part.

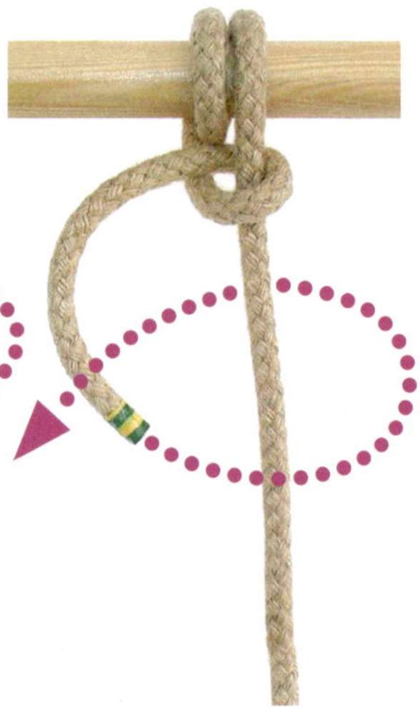

Step 2

Make this first half-hitch taut. Then repeat the process again to form the second half-hitch.

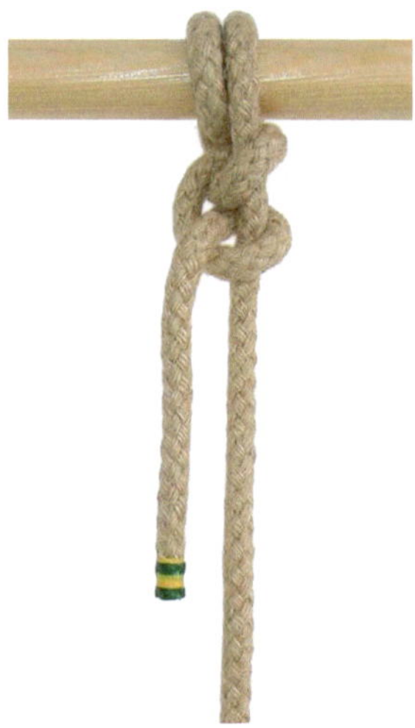

Step 3

Lastly, work both hitches snug and tight.

Highwayman's hitch

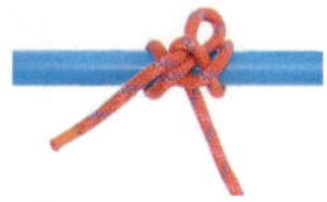

This remarkable hitch will anchor a doubled rope in such a way that it can be released at a distance or very quickly with one hand.

Method

Step 1

Make a bight in the line and place it behind the rail or other point of attachment. Using what will be the standing part of the rope, insert a second bight through the first one.

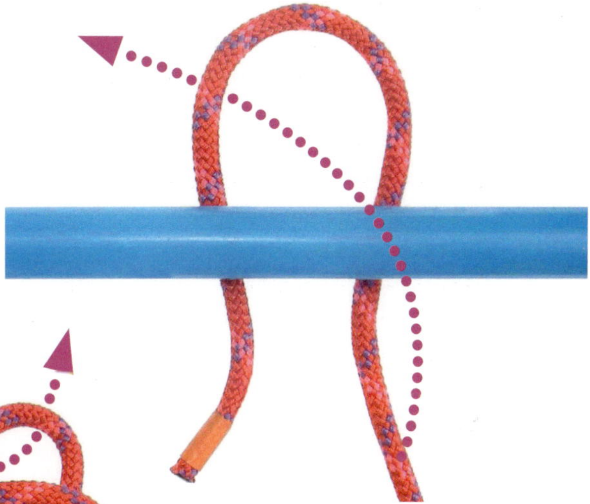

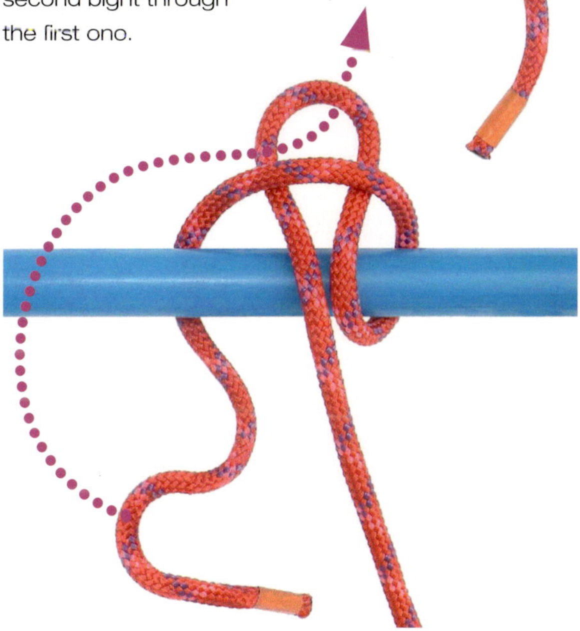

Step 2

Now insert a third (locking) bight through the second bight with the working end, leaving a draw-loop.

Step 3

Take care to load only the standing part. Pull the draw-loop end to release the knot.

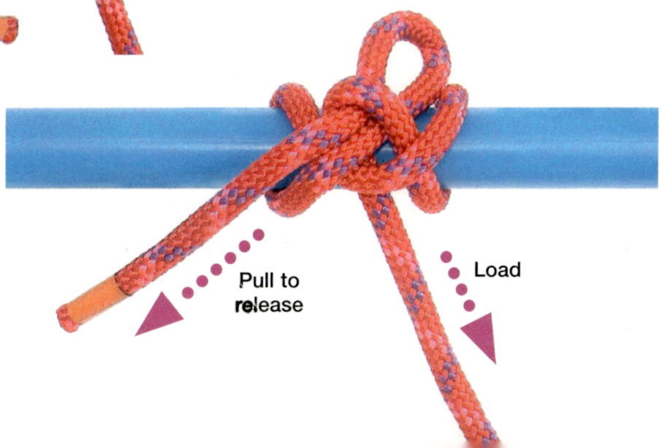

Killick hitch

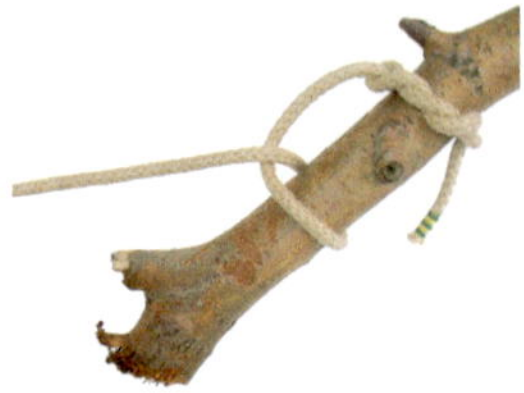

The killick hitch works particularly well on rough objects but can be prone to slipping on smoother items.

It is most useful if you need to drag a fallen tree trunk or log over land and tow it through water, or even to hoist plastic roof guttering or drainpipes.

Method

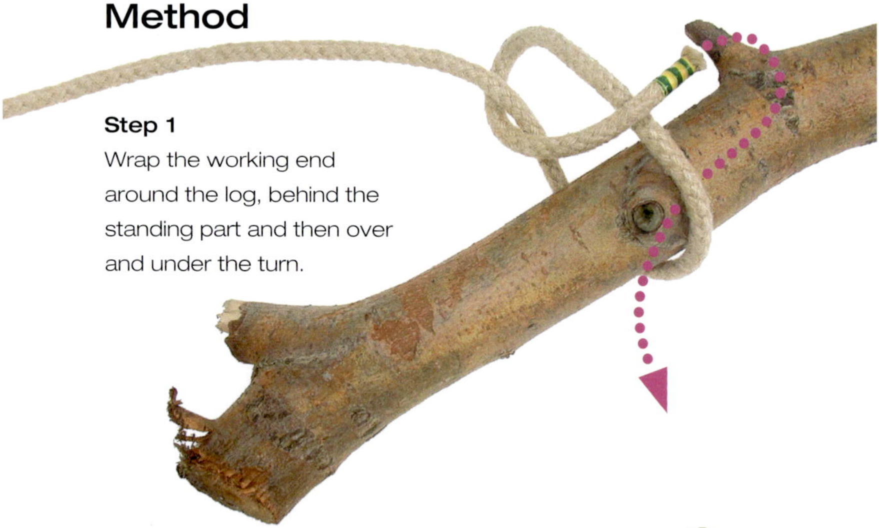

Step 1
Wrap the working end around the log, behind the standing part and then over and under the turn.

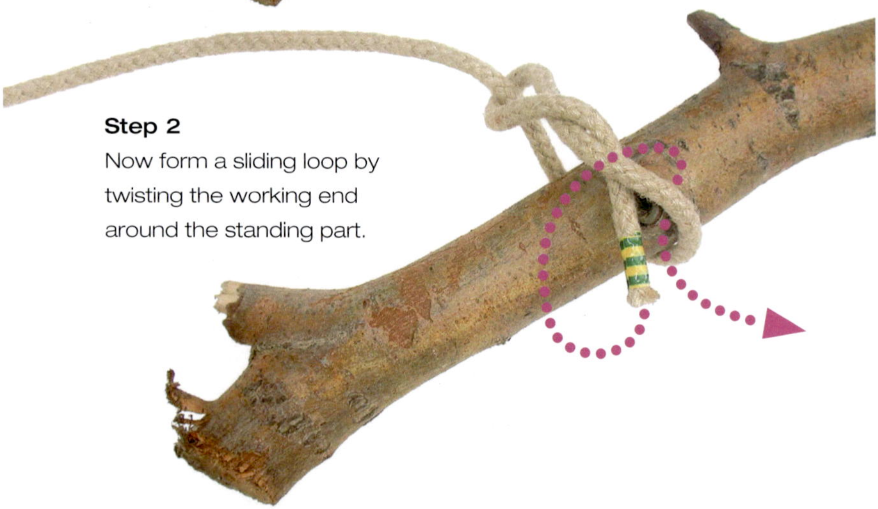

Step 2
Now form a sliding loop by twisting the working end around the standing part.

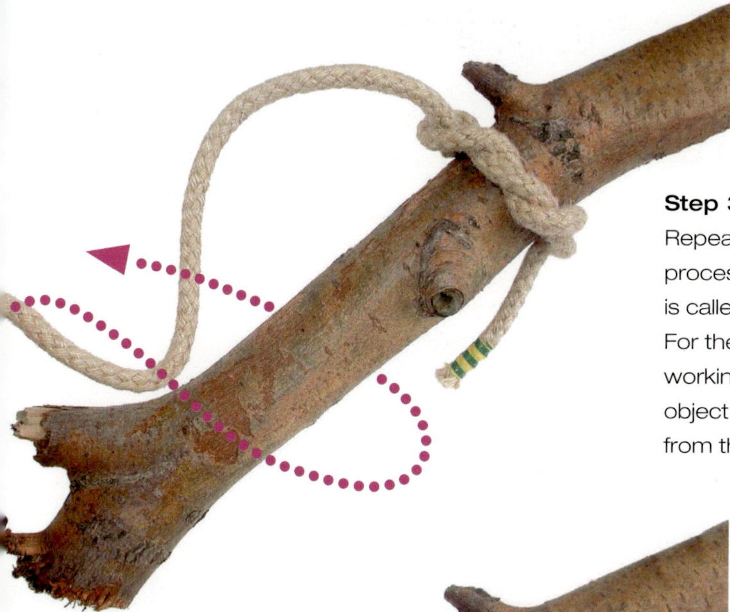

Step 3

Repeat the above process and tighten. This is called a timber hitch. For the Killick, pass the working end around the object some distance from the initial knot.

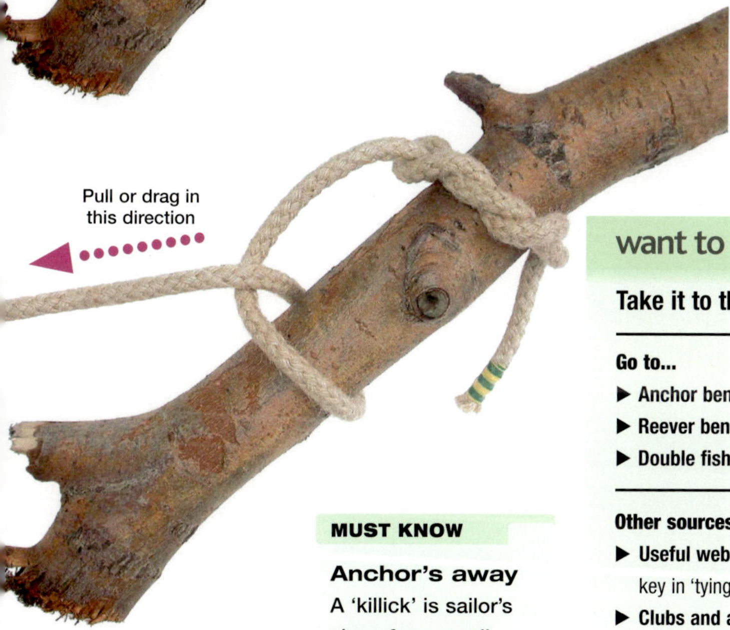

Step 4

By making this half hitch you will ensure a straight pull. On smooth objects, use two or more half-hitches.

MUST KNOW

Anchor's away

A 'killick' is sailor's slang for a small anchor, and this hitch once held a large stone or other heavy object to anchor a small boat to the seabed.

want to know more?

Take it to the next level...

Go to...

- **Anchor bend** – page 53
- **Reever bend** – page 118
- **Double fisherman's knot** – page 120

Other sources

- **Useful websites**
  key in 'tying knots' to any search engine
- **Clubs and associations**
  membership of the Braid Society
- **Decorative knots**
  join a macramé or craft evening class
- **Knotting books**
  visit your local library
- **Magazines**
  subscribe to *Knotting Matters*

life-support

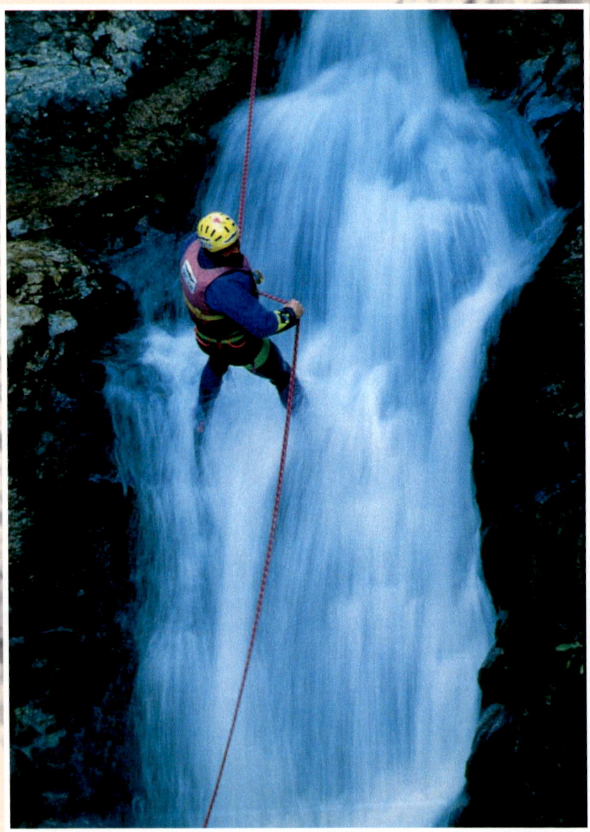

knots

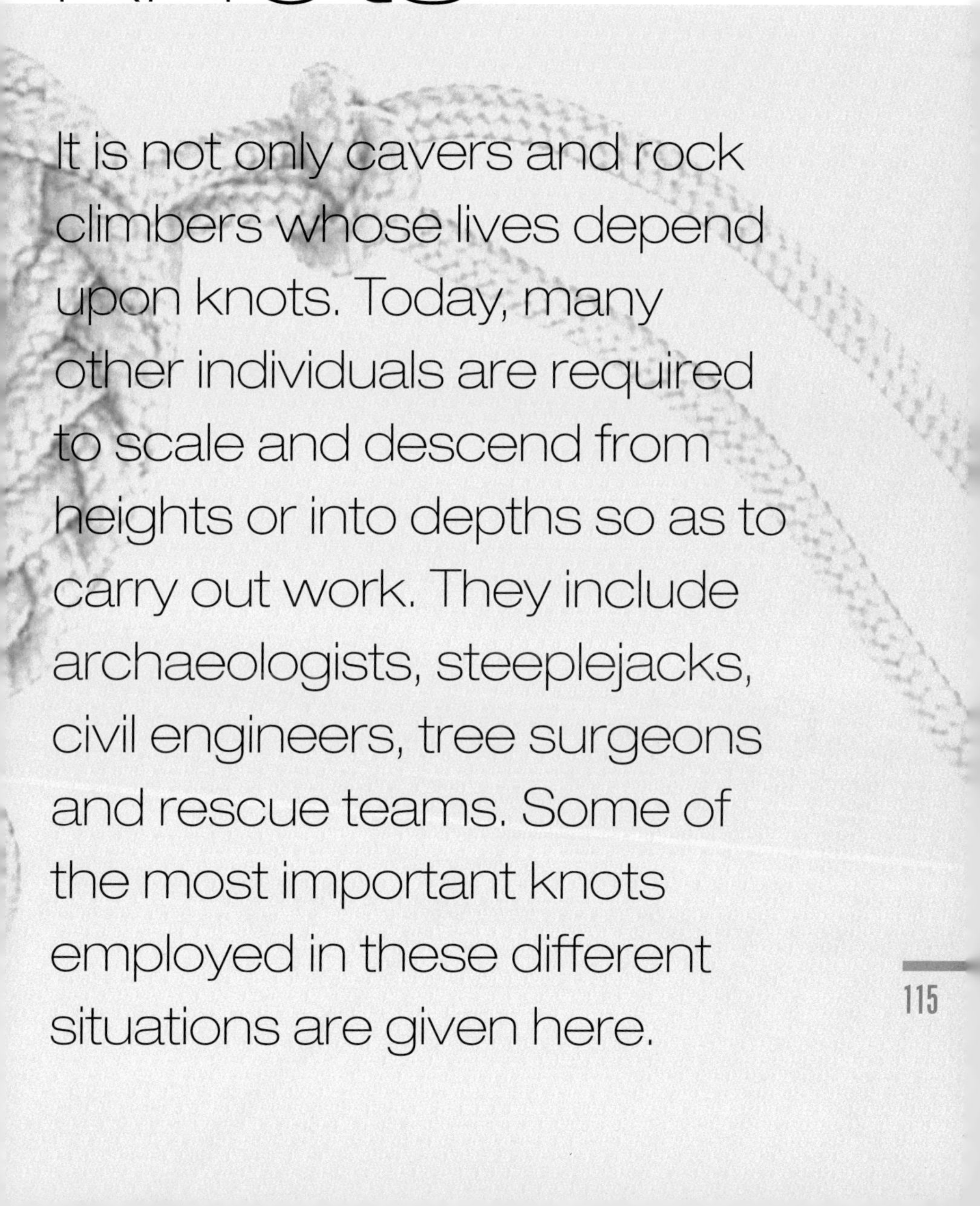

It is not only cavers and rock climbers whose lives depend upon knots. Today, many other individuals are required to scale and descend from heights or into depths so as to carry out work. They include archaeologists, steeplejacks, civil engineers, tree surgeons and rescue teams. Some of the most important knots employed in these different situations are given here.

Reinforced reef knot

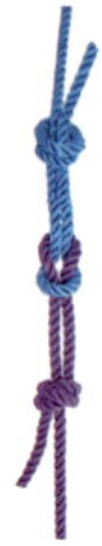

This knot is used to tie abseil or rappel ropes together. Because the combination resembles a double fisherman's knot (see page 120) that has consumed a reef knot, it is sometimes referred to as a reef-and-double-fisherman's or a square fisherman's knot.

The Roman historian and scientist Pliny the Elder (AD 23–79) wrote that wounds bound with a reef knot healed quicker and modern first-aid instructors still insist that slings and bandages are tied with it today, although they are probably unaware of the superstitious belief in the practice.

WATCH OUT!

Never employ a reef knot (known as a square knot in the USA) as a bend to join two working ropes unless it is backed up or locked off in this way.

Method

Step 1

'Left-over-right, then right-over-left' is the way most people remember this knot. You can, of course, go 'right-over-left, then left-over-right' if it is easier that way. Either way will prevent you tying an unreliable granny knot.

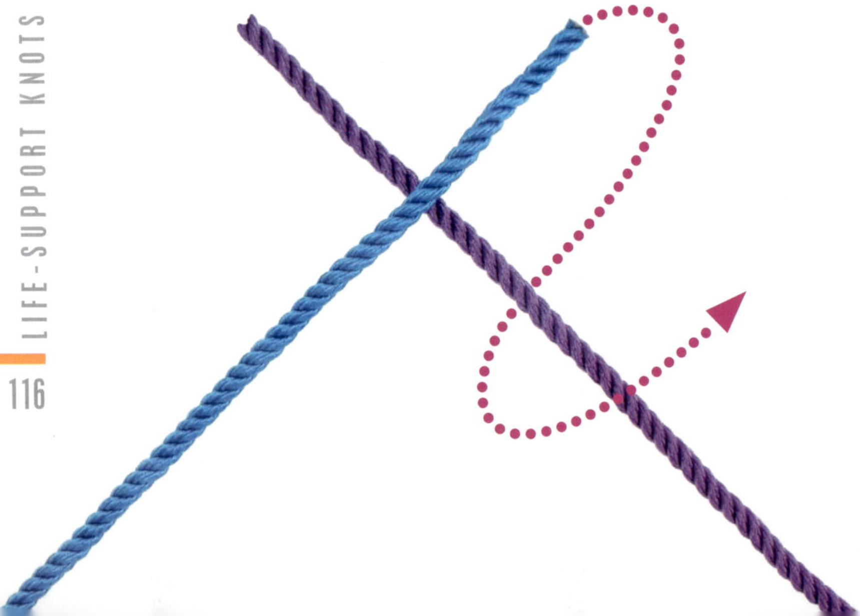

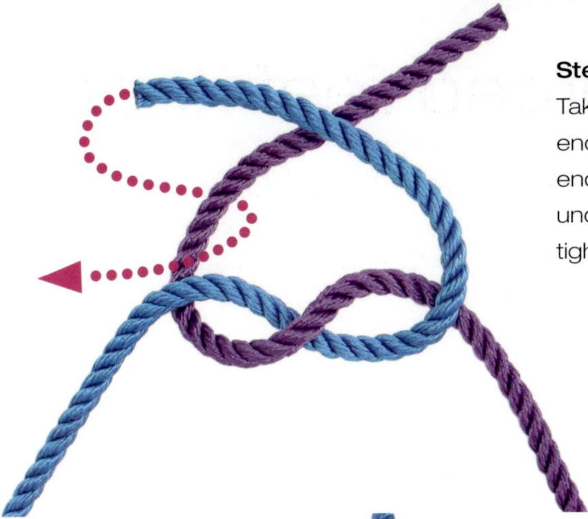

Step 2
Take the right-hand end over the left-hand end and tuck it underneath. Then tighten the reef knot.

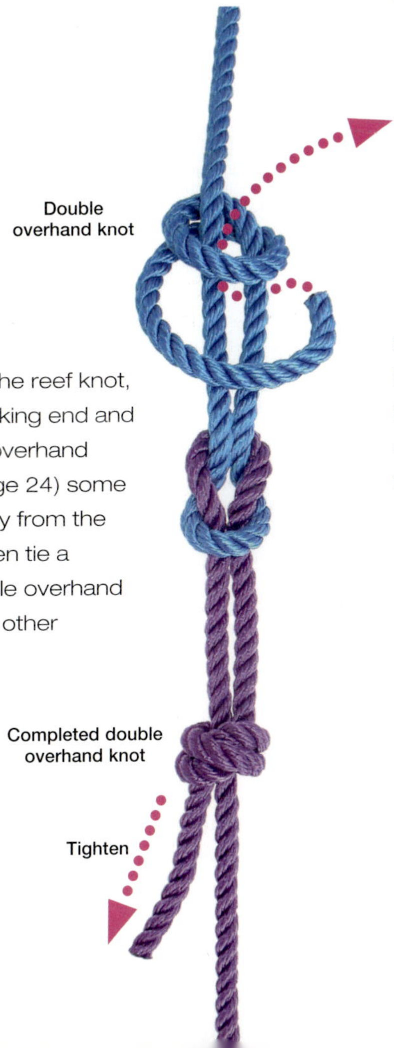

Step 3
To reinforce the reef knot, take one working end and tie a double overhand knot (see page 24) some distance away from the reef knot. Then tie a second double overhand knot with the other working end.

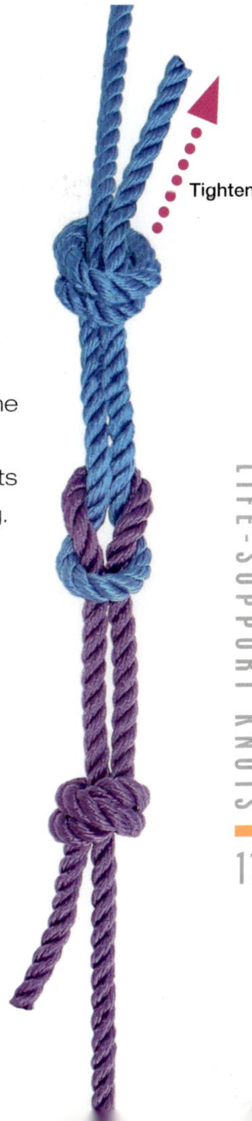

Step 4
Finally, work the two double overhand knots tight and snug.

Reever bend

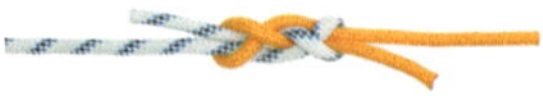

As well as joining natural fibre hawsers, the reever also works well with synthetic sheath-and-core (kernmantel) or braid-on-braid ropes and even holds firm in shock elastics.

This bend first appeared in *The Alpine Journal* (1928) when it was recommended for use in hemp or flax climbing ropes. Today, few climbers know of it but it is easier to untie than a double fisherman's (or grapevine) knot, and superior in every way to a reinforced reef knot.

Method

Step 1

Place two lines next to one another, with their ends pointing in opposite directions. Wrap one working end around the other line, over itself and back under the other line. Repeat the above process with the other working end.

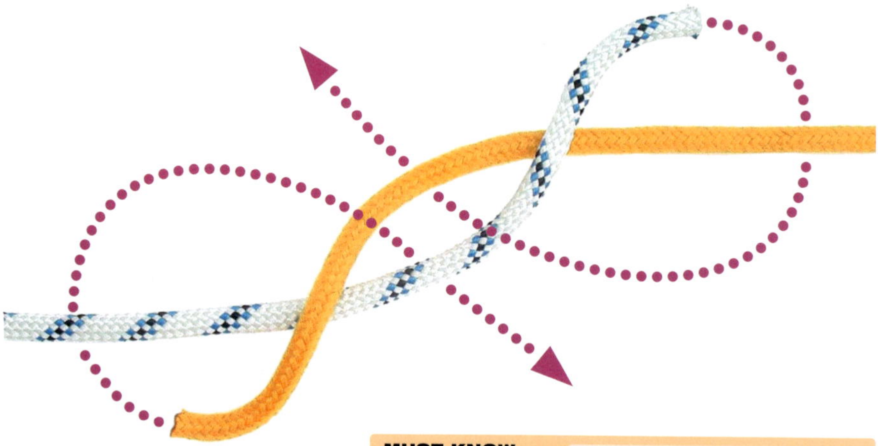

MUST KNOW

Well-supported

The basis of the reever bend is the harness bend (see pages 102–3), and the first two steps here follow the same method as for that knot.

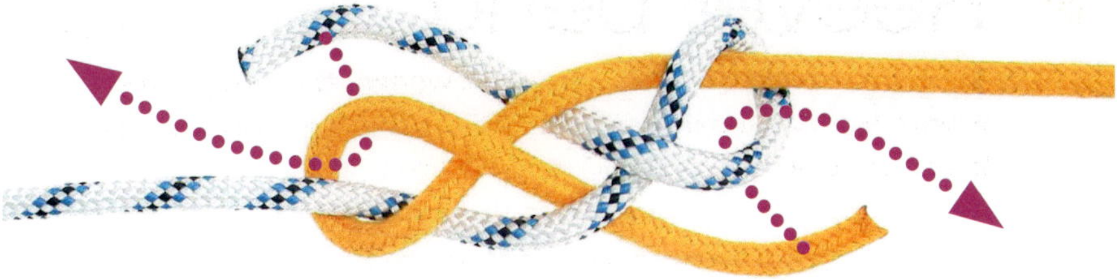

Step 2

Then simply tuck each working end through the loop that has formed at each end of the knot enclosing its own adjacent standing part.

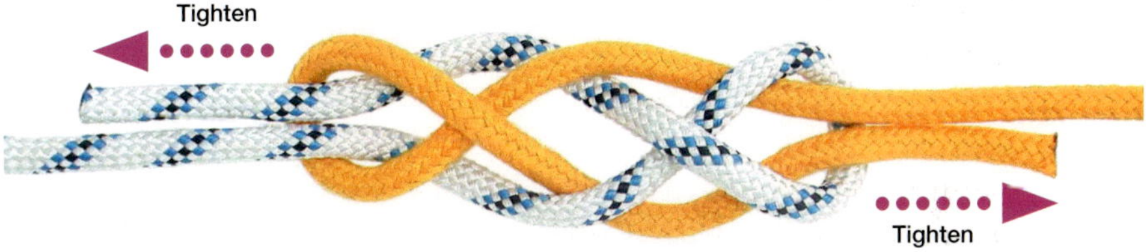

Step 3

Tighten the bend carefully, making sure that the turns lie neatly against each other.

Front view

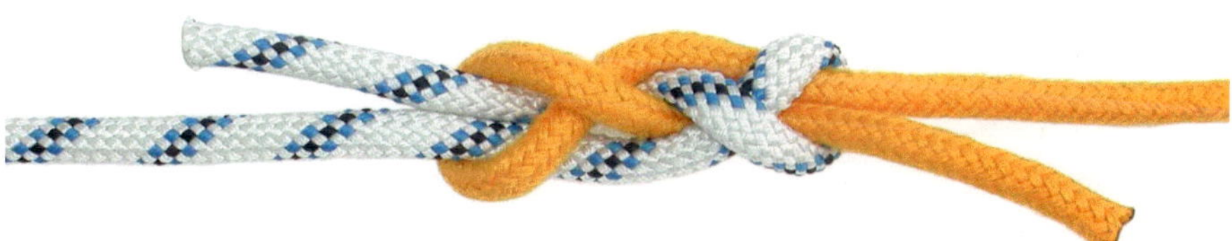

Back view

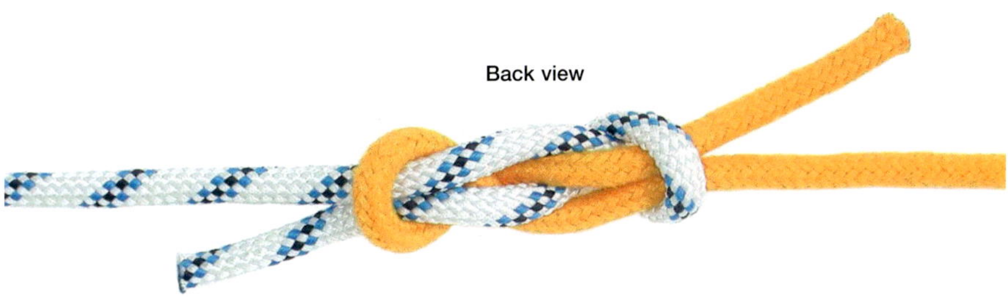

Double fisherman's knot

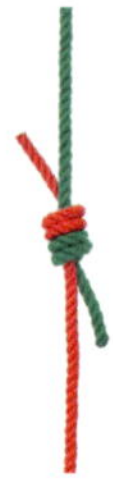

Tie this beefed-up version of the fisherman's knot to join two ropes together on long abseils or rappels.

Method

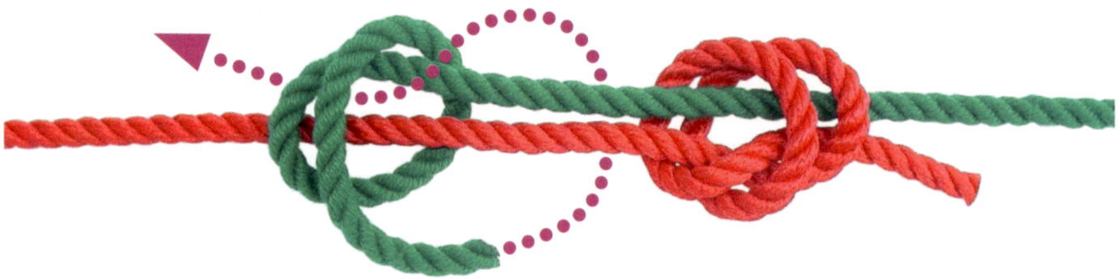

Step 1

Lay the two lines to be joined close together, parallel, with ends pointing in opposite directions. With the working end of the bottom red line, tie a double overhand knot around the standing part of the other line. Then, with the working end of the top green line, tie another double overhand knot of identical handedness (both either S-laid, or both Z-laid) around the lower standing part.

MUST KNOW

Other uses

A double fisherman's (or grapevine) knot has a secondary use for tying cords through nuts. It is also used to lock off the loose ends of other knots, such as the reef knot.

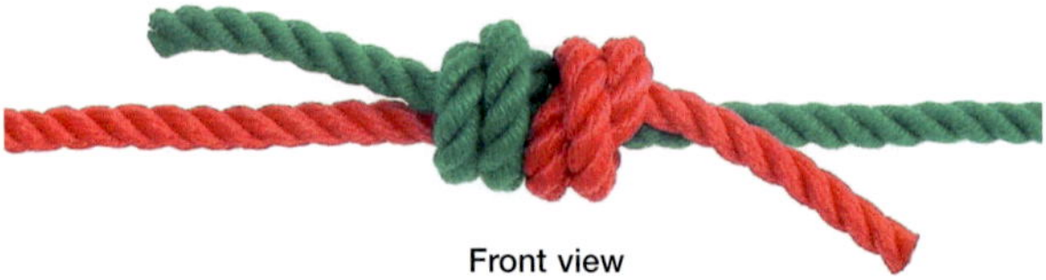

Front view

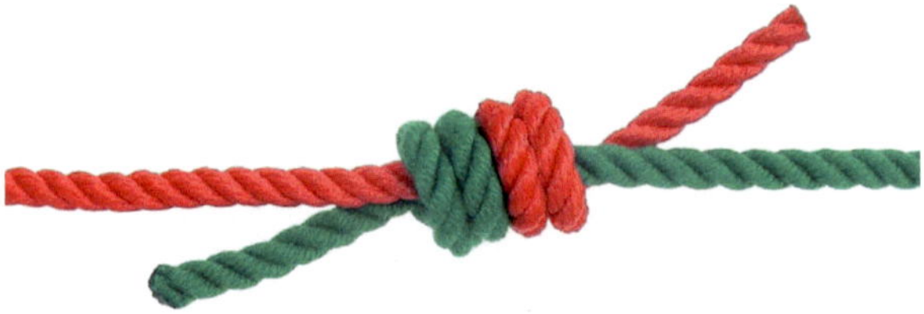

Back view

Step 2

Pull the two working ends to tighten the individual knots and then pull on the standing parts to bring them together. Make sure that the ends are left long enough to tape to their adjacent standing parts for extra security.

Triple fisherman's knot

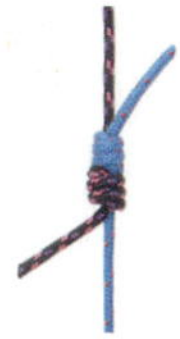

When the double fisherman's (or grapevine) knot may not cope, tie this even bulkier triple-wrapped version.

Method

Step 1

Lay the two ropes close together, parallel, with their ends pointing in opposite directions, and then tie a triple overhand knot with one end around the adjacent standing part.

WATCH OUT!

The double fisherman's knot is hard to undo once it has been loaded and this triple version is even more difficult to untie.

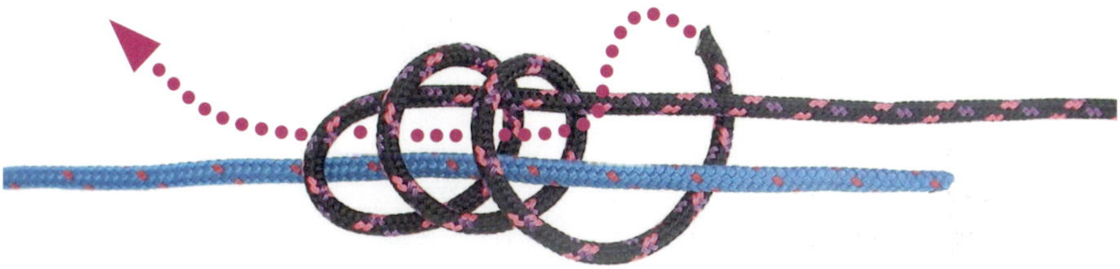

Step 2

Repeat the above process with the other end. Ensure that both knots are of the same handedness (either S-laid or Z-laid, see page 15).

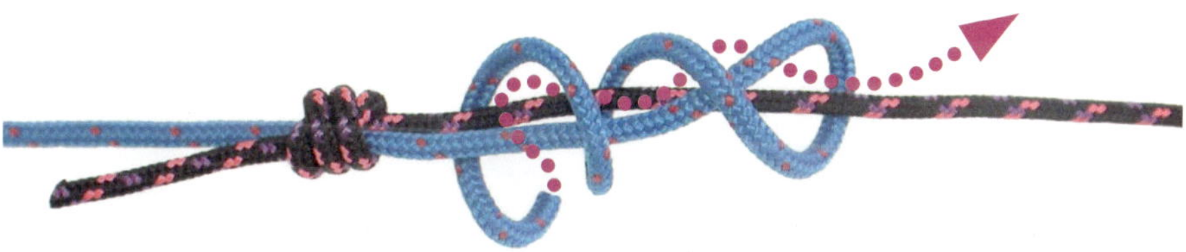

Step 3

Pull them tight and together as for the double fisherman's knot. The back view here clearly shows the three turns of each line placed neatly next to each other.

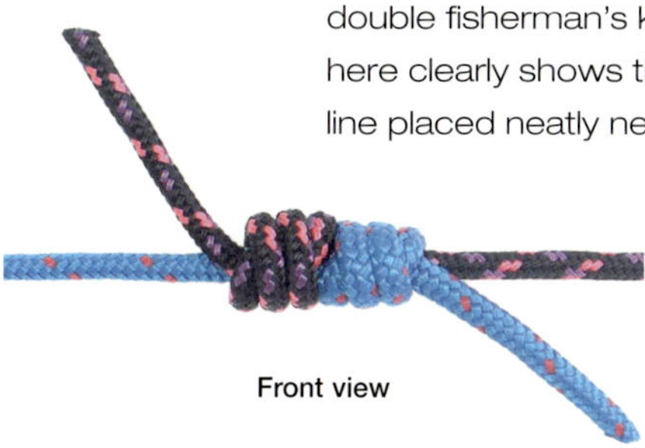

Front view

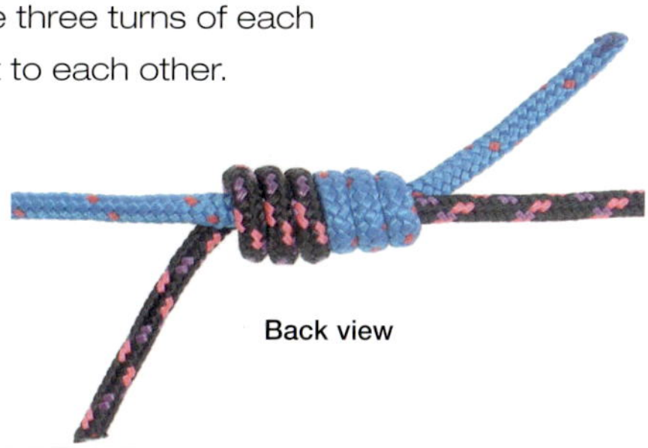

Back view

Alpine butterfly loop

This classic old knot enables the middle person in a team to clip onto the rope, a common practice when, for instance, crossing a glacier.

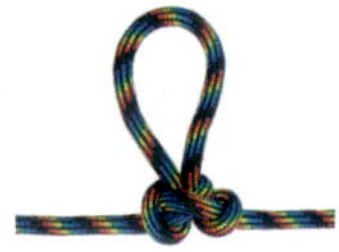

The alpine butterfly loop goes in and out of fashion, as each fresh generation of climbers first overlooks it then rediscovers it. This loop is tied in the bight of a rope.

Method

Step 1

Make a bight in the rope, twist a single loop and then add a second twist in the same direction.

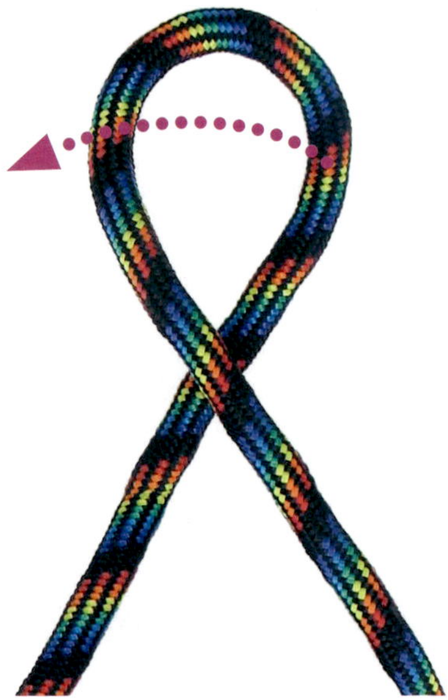

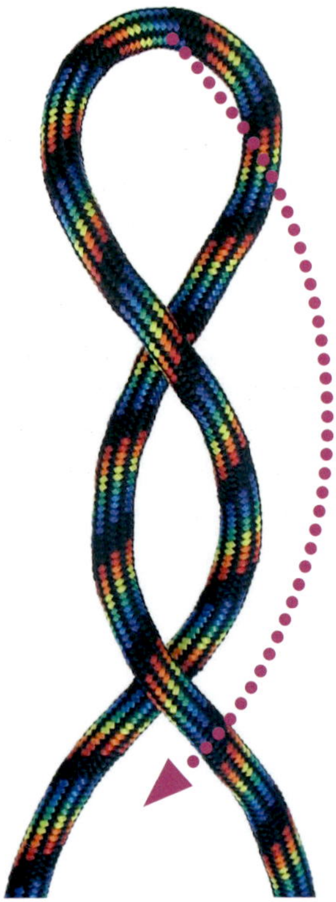

Step 2

Bring the upper loop forward and down over the lower loop to rest upon the two legs of the standing part of the rope.

WATCH OUT!

Beware, this knot will prevent the rope from passing freely through any protection, abseil or rappel device.

Step 3

Then tuck the initial loop up, forward from behind, through the second loop.

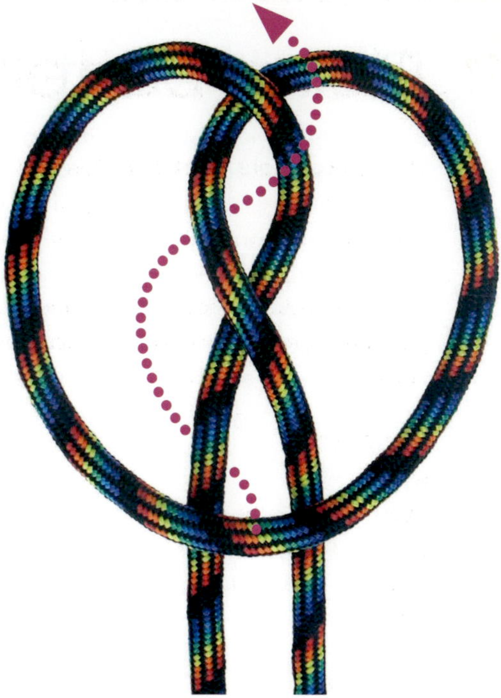

MUST KNOW

Build a bridge

This knot might also be used – temporarily – to bridge a damaged section of rope. There are several ways to tie it (in the bight) – whichever you use, always seek the advice and guidance of experienced climbers.

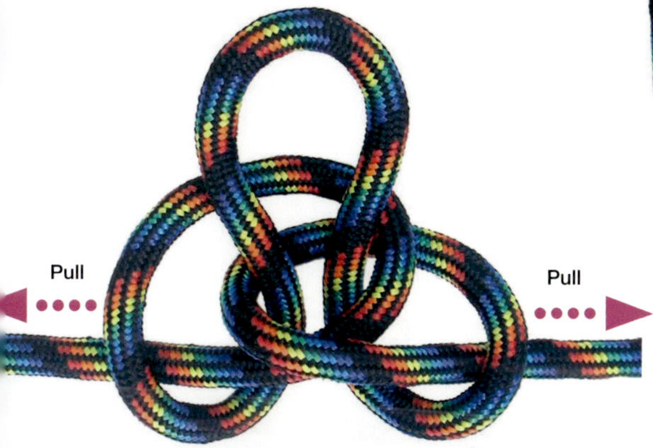

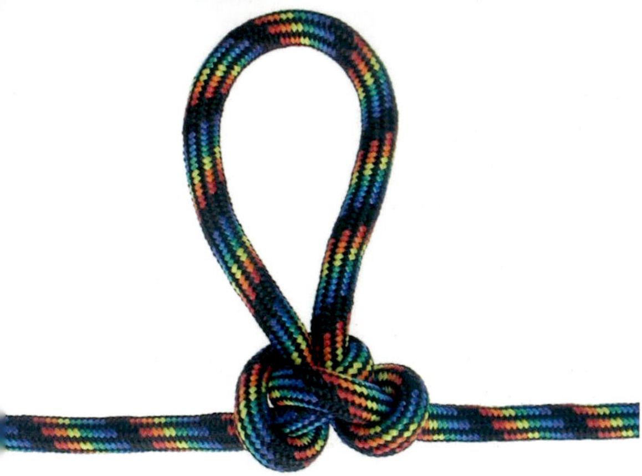

Step 4

Carefully pull the loop and then the standing parts to tighten the knot. You can distinguish this knot from other mid-rope loops by the way the two standing parts of the rope cross on one side where they enter the knot and the twin bights nestle like spoons on the reverse side.

Prusik knot

In climbing, the Prusik knot is invaluable for horizontal or diagonal crossings.

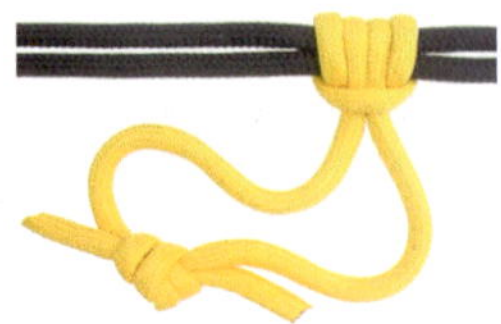

However, mechanical aiders and webbing étriers or stirrup ladders, when carried, are preferable and have superseded the Prusik knot for vertical ascents. It is also a useful abseil or rappel back-up, enabling a climber to fashion a prusiking loop and climb back up footage that has been lost in a slip or fall.

WATCH OUT!

Keep all prusiking slings short enough so that the Prusik knot itself remains within a hand's reach; and keep in mind that these slings are fraught with the potential for melt-down due to heat friction – the thinner ones more than thicker ones – if the knot does not grip instantly.

Method

Step 1

Make an endless sling in a length of 5–6 mm (¼ in) accessory cord by joining the two ends with a ring or double fisherman's knot (see pages 138 and 120).Then tie a ring hitch by placing the sling around the the single or doubled rope (or foundation) and tuck it through itself. Take a second wrap and re-tuck it, as indicated.

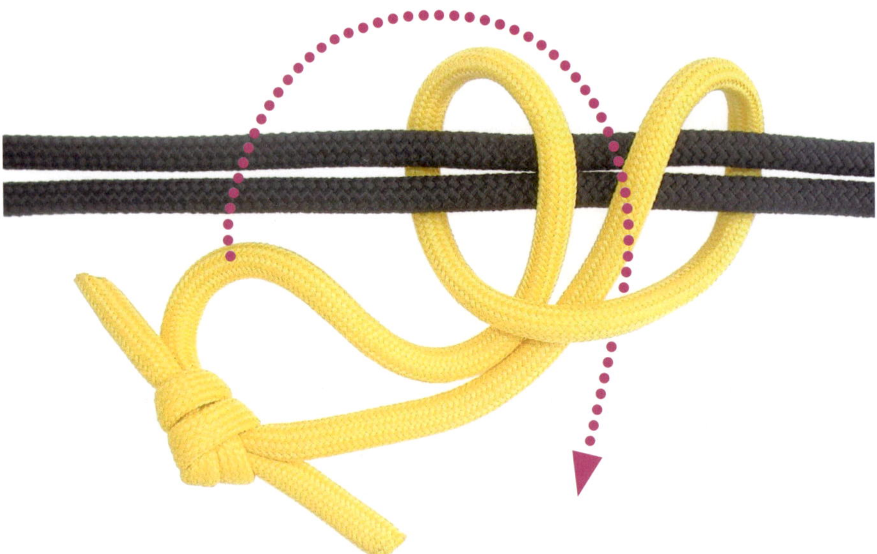

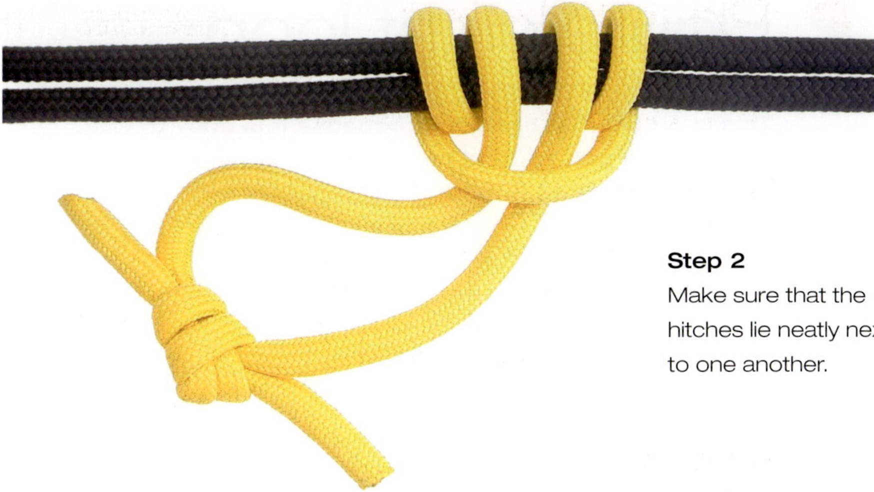

Step 2

Make sure that the hitches lie neatly next to one another.

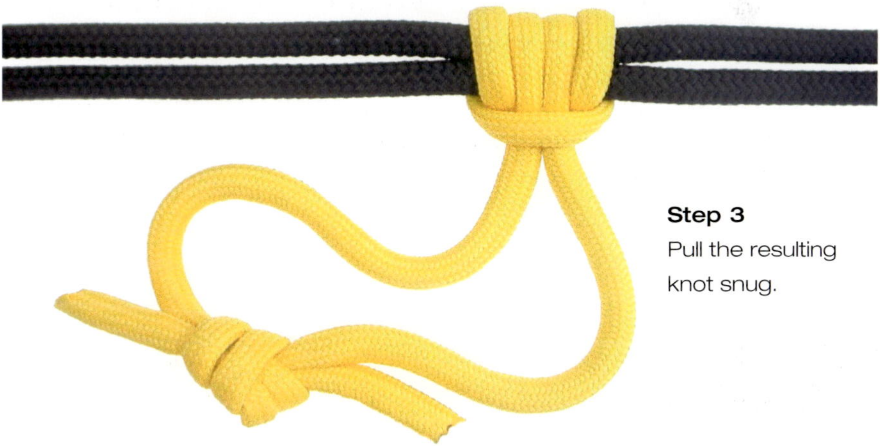

Step 3

Pull the resulting knot snug.

MUST KNOW

The good doctor

This slide-and-grip hitch was devised and made popular as a means of self-rescue by the musician Dr Karl Prusik in 1931, his Prusik knot (with an upper case 'P') having been devised in the first place to mend the strings of musical instruments. It led to a variety of other prusiking knots, loops and slings (with a generic lower case 'p').

Figure eight loop

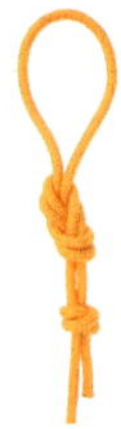

This is a favourite fixed loop because it is easy to learn, recall and tie (and for a leader to check) in extreme situations.

The figure eight loop can be tied in the bight or (with an end) onto a closed foundation. It is sometimes called the 'guide knot'.

Method

Step 1

Form a long bight in the end of the rope and then make it into an overhand loop. Next, add a 180 degree twist by taking the two right-hand parts of the loop beneath the two left-hand parts.

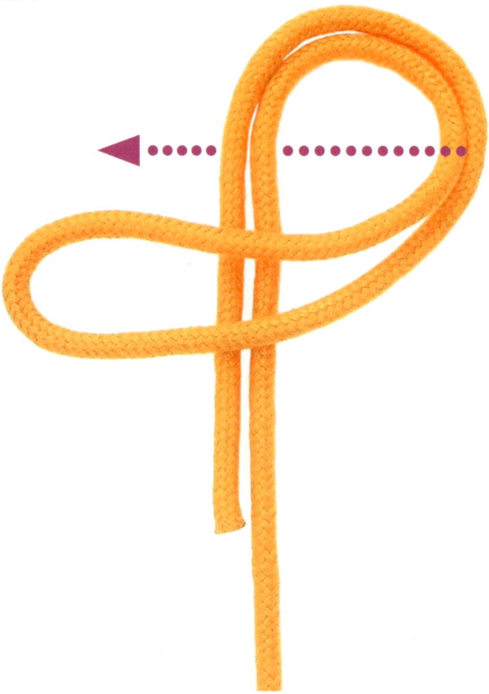

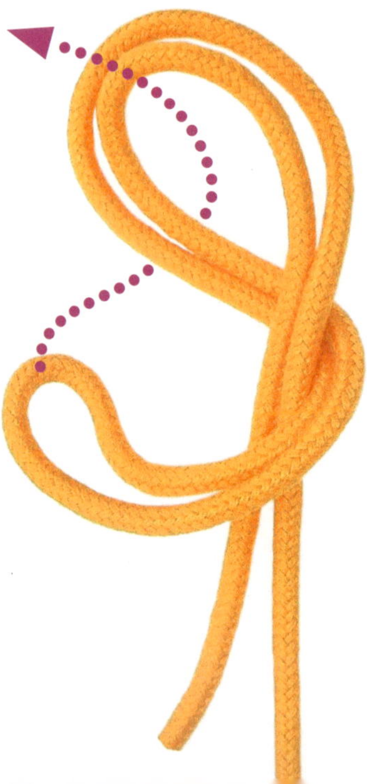

Step 2

Tuck the end of the bight up through the initial loop to complete the figure eight knot.

Step 3

Carefully arrange and tighten the knot. It is a good idea to make the doubled parts swap sides in order to streamline the sharp curves at each end of the knot (do not allow them simply to lie parallel).

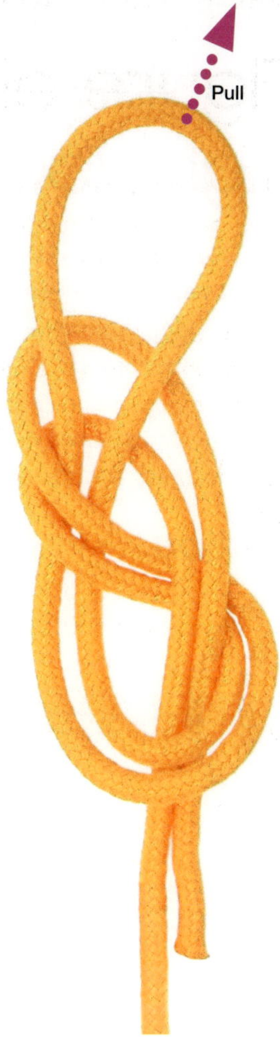

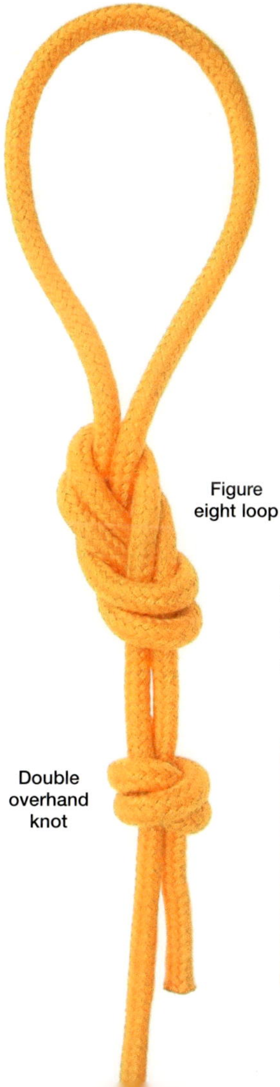

Step 4

Lock off the end or tail with a double overhand knot (see page 24).

MUST KNOW

A versatile loop

This tried-and-trusted loop can also at a pinch be used for the middle climber of a team (like the alpine butterfly on pages 122–3), as well as to bridge a damaged section of rope temporarily.

Double figure eight loop

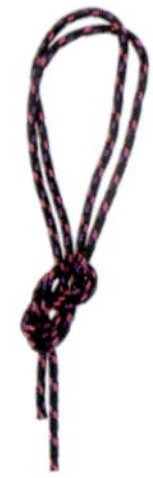

This chunky alternative to a bowline in the bight (see page 133) can be used to belay to twin anchorages.

The double figure eight loop will also serve (with suitable safeguards) as an emergency chair knot to lower an injured person, with one loop acting as a seat and the other as a chest sling.

Method

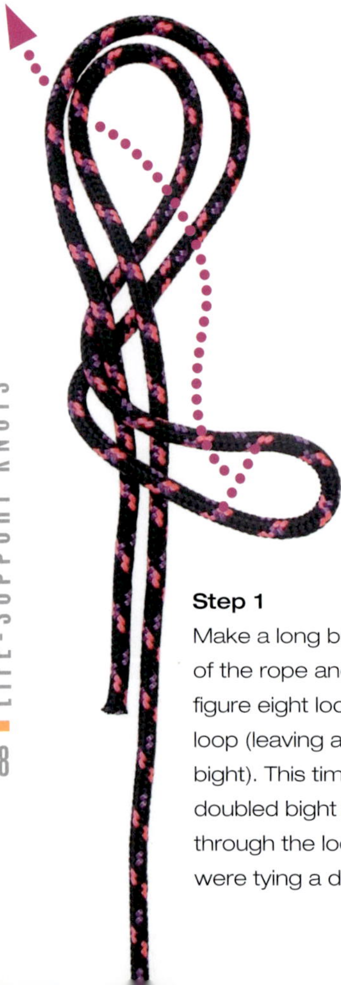

Step 1
Make a long bight in the end of the rope and begin to tie a figure eight loop by making a loop (leaving a long length of bight). This time bring the doubled bight legs part-way through the loop, as if you were tying a draw-loop.

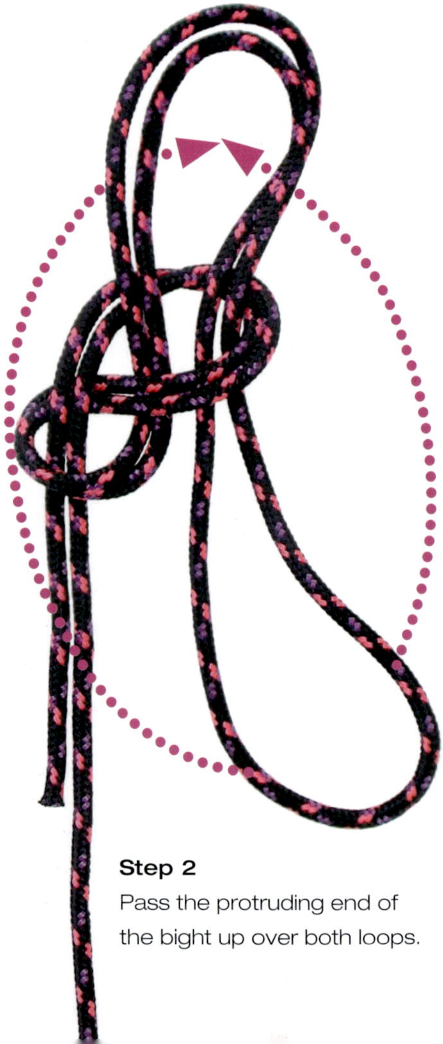

Step 2
Pass the protruding end of the bight up over both loops.

Step 3

Then bring the single loop down behind the knot to form a third part around the standing part and end.

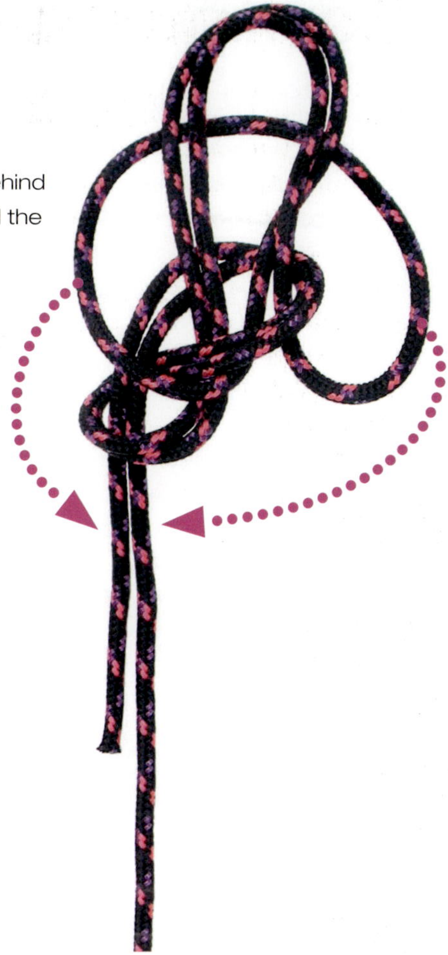

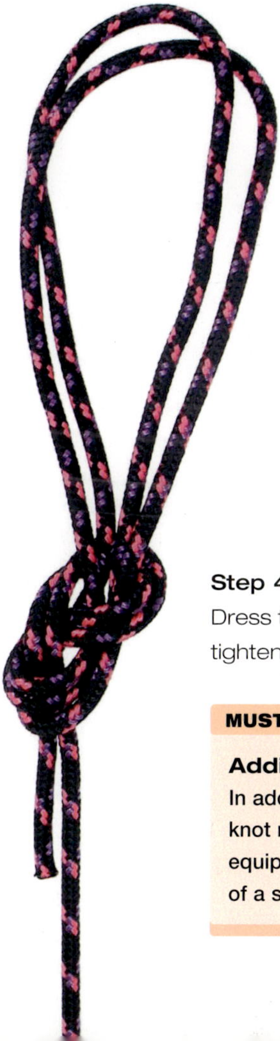

Step 4

Dress the knot neatly and tighten it carefully.

MUST KNOW

Additional applications

In addition to the uses already mentioned, this knot may be employed to lift or lower equipment, and also be made fast to both ends of a stretcher holding an ill or injured person.

Bowline on a coil

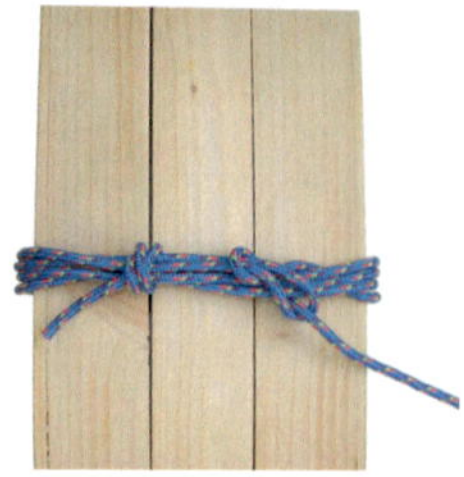

This unique knot is used to secure a climber (or other person in trouble) to a rope without a harness and should only be used in an emergency or as a last resort.

Initially learn to tie the knot around a piece of wood or a book.

Method

Step 1

First wrap the rope several times (at least four) snugly around the wood (or waist). Then pull a bight from the lowest turn up beneath the others and twist it into a loop.

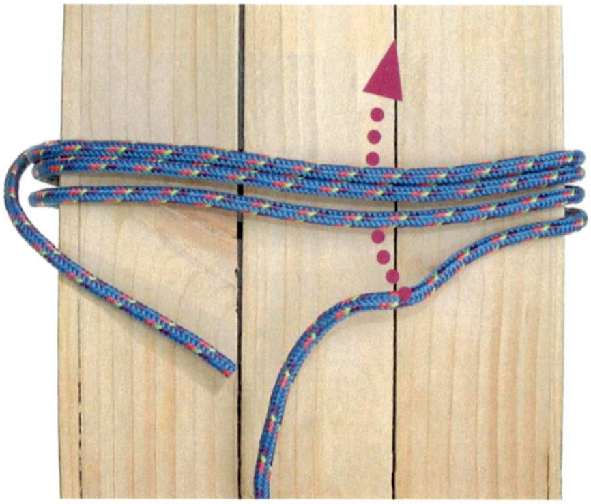

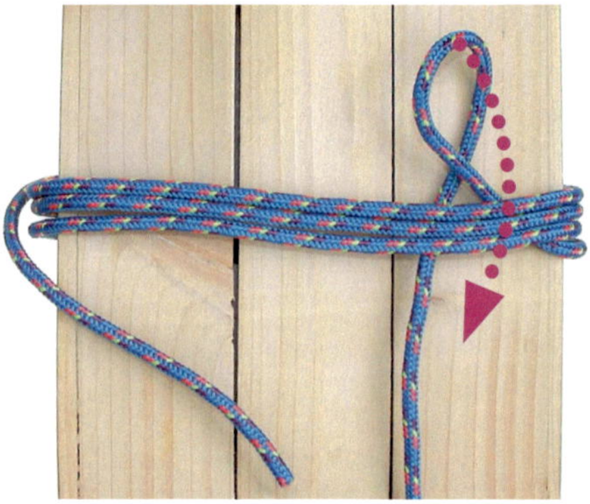

Step 2

Bend the loop downwards over the wraps and rest it on the standing end.

Step 3

Next tuck the working end over the loop, under the standing end and over the loop, so as to lock into the standing part of the rope.

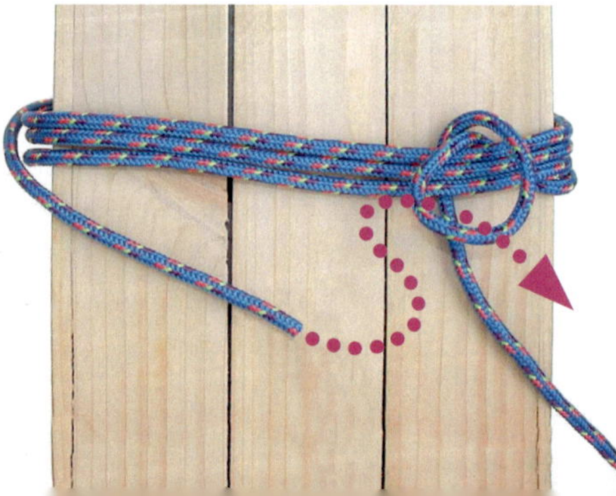

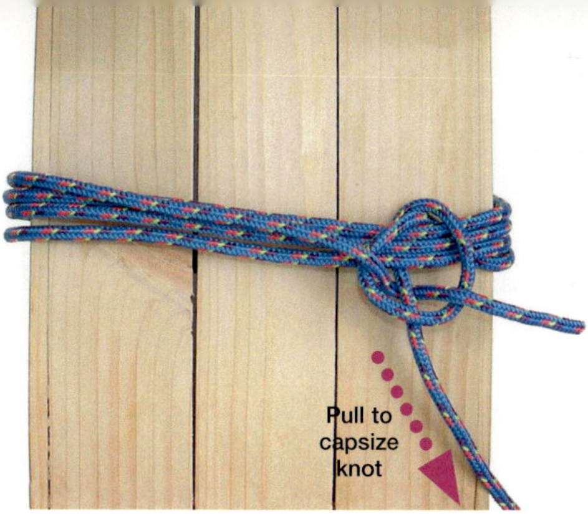

Step 4
Capsize the knot into the familiar bowline layout by means of a firm pull on the standing part.

Step 5
Finally, be sure to lock off the resulting knot with a double overhand knot (see page 24).

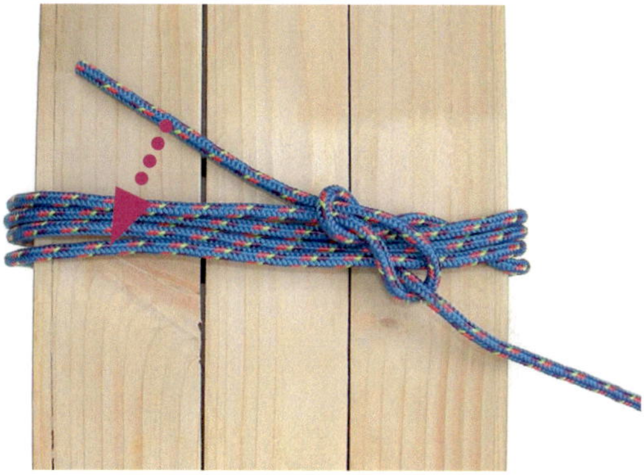

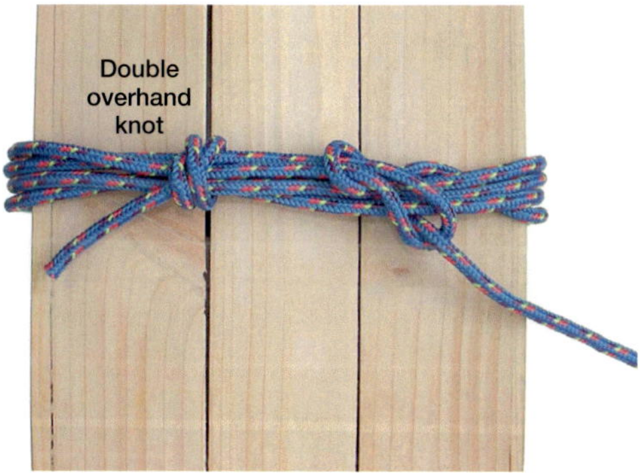

Step 6
Tighten the knot carefully, making sure the turns lie neatly next to each other.

WATCH OUT!

Only use in an emergency. Do not hang suspended by this knot for a long time as it could constrict and lead to severe internal injuries and damaged ribs as well as breathing difficulties. These risks may be reduced by slipping one turn of the rope down beneath one's buttocks to form a primitive seat.

Round turn bowline

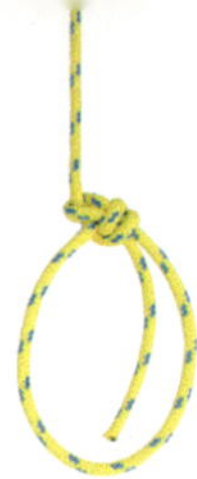

This particular bowline can be used as an effective alternative to the water bowline.

Despite its soubriquet 'King of knots', the basic bowline (see page 54) is neither very strong nor very secure. This variant is preferable, whether it is used for a crucial anchor or belay, or merely to hoist up or lower down a heavy rcksack full of useful gear.

Method

Step 1

First make a round turn (two overhand loops). Then tuck the working end up through it.

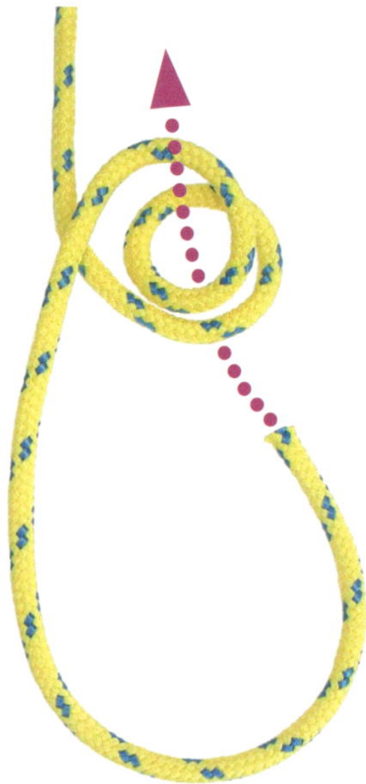

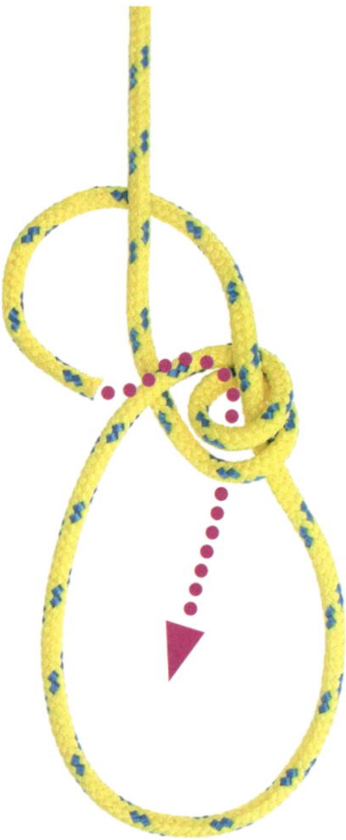

Step 2

Pass the working end behind the standing part of the rope and re-tuck it down through the turn.

MUST KNOW

Double puzzle
This fixed loop is also, misleadingly (since it has only one loop), called 'the double bowline'.

Step 3

Tighten the knot neatly, leaving a long end. This can be locked off with a double overhand knot (see page 24).

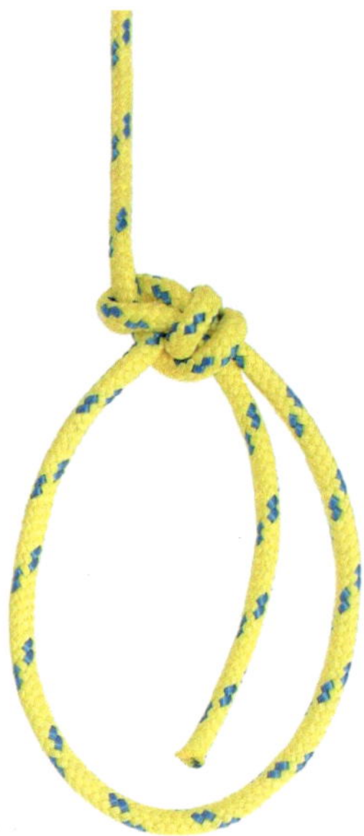

Bowline in the bight

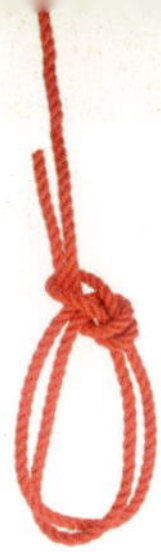

Use this twin loop knot between two anchorages or as an improvised chair knot with one loop for the seat and the other as a chest sling. It will also raise or lower a stretcher.

This double loop knot may be tied in the end of a rope or in the bight. When used instead of, say, an alpine butterfly knot, the middle climber should pass the double loop directly around the chest, as it is more comfortable than a single loop.

Method

Step 1

Make a long bight in a rope and with the doubled length form an overhand loop, before tucking the end of the bight up through the loop. Bend the bight down in front of the half-completed knot.

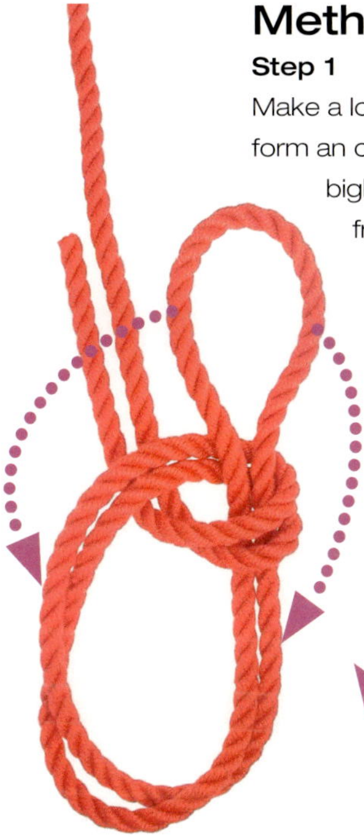

Step 2

Bring the twin loops forward up and through the bight eye. Then bring the bight eye up behind the standing parts of the rope.

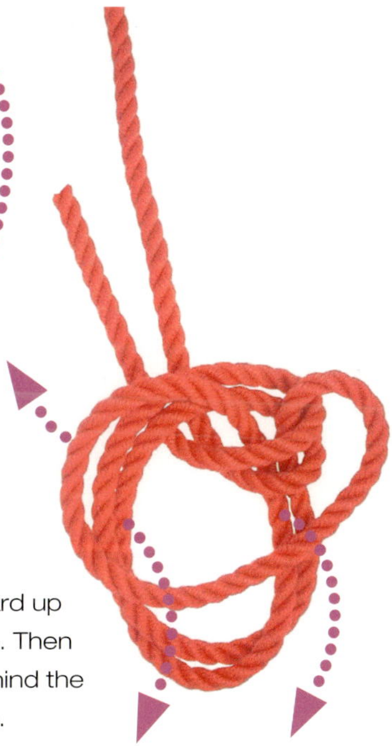

Step 3

Tighten the knot carefully. You can lock off the loose end with a double overhand knot.

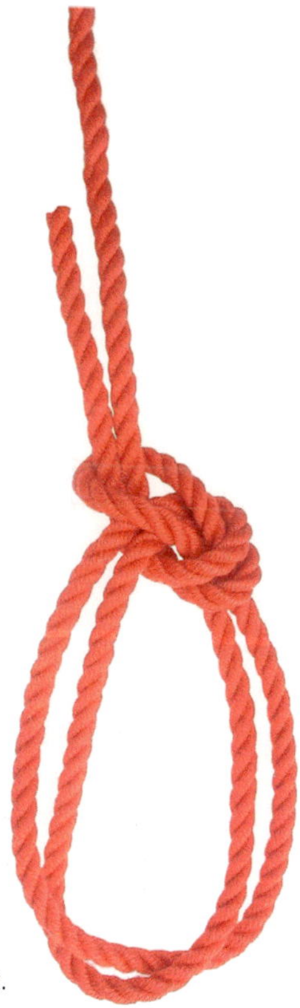

Triple bowline

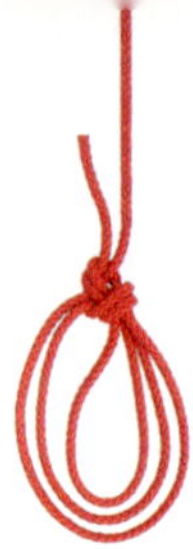

The main use of this knot, which can also be tied in the middle of a rope (or the bight), will be as a means of attachment to three anchor points.

Yet another variation of the bowline (see page 54), and like a bowline in the bight (see page 133), this knot may also be used as an emergency rescue chair knot, with two of the loops arranged as seat slings and the third as a chest sling.

There are other techniques for achieving three loops from a single knot, but this adaptation of the basic bowline is more easily taught and learned.

Method

Step 1

Make a long bight in the end of the rope and make an overhand loop with the doubled length. Pass the end of the bight through the loop.

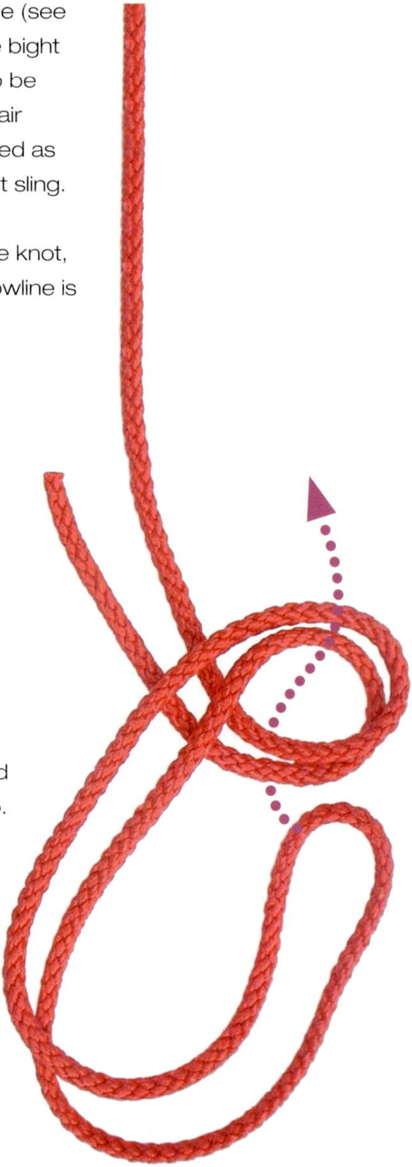

Step 2

Now bring the end of the bight behind the standing part and inert end then back down through the loop.

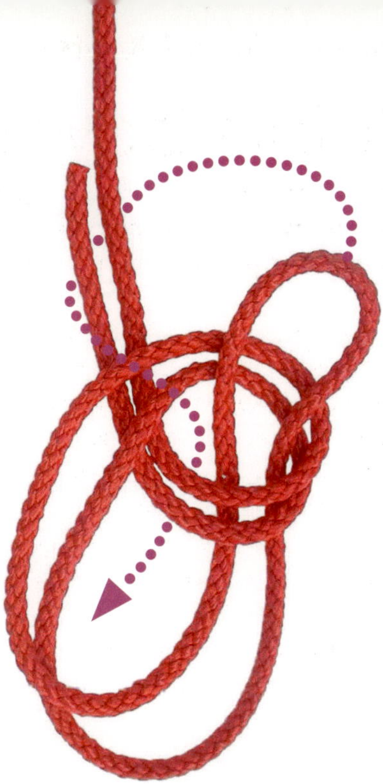

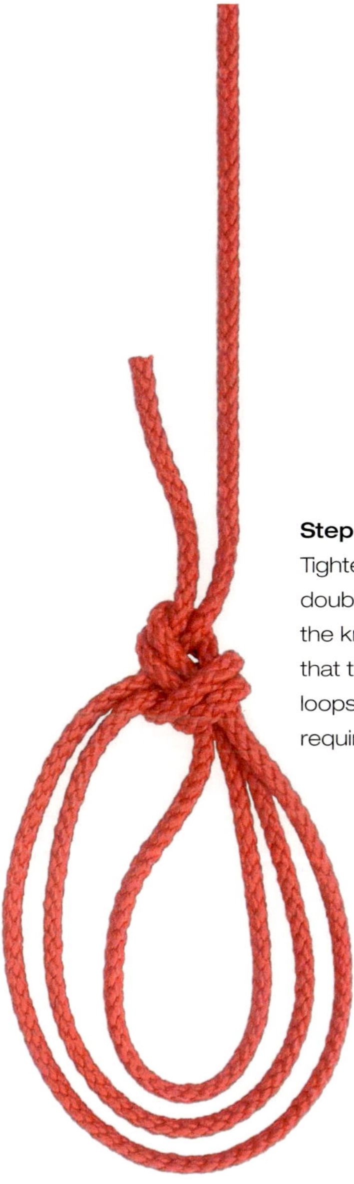

Step 3

Tighten all of the doubled parts of the knot itself, so that the three loops are of the required sizes.

want to know **more?**

Take it to the next level...

Go to...

- **Harness bend –** pages 102–3
- **Overhand shortening –** page 142
- **Cordage facts –** pages 166–83

Other sources

- **Scouting Association**
  www.scouts.org.uk
- **British Mountaineering Council**
  www.thebmc.co.uk
- **Video**
  Climbing Rock (see BMC website)
- **Magazines**
  Global Adventure, Trail
- **Film and book**
  Touching the Void

webbing

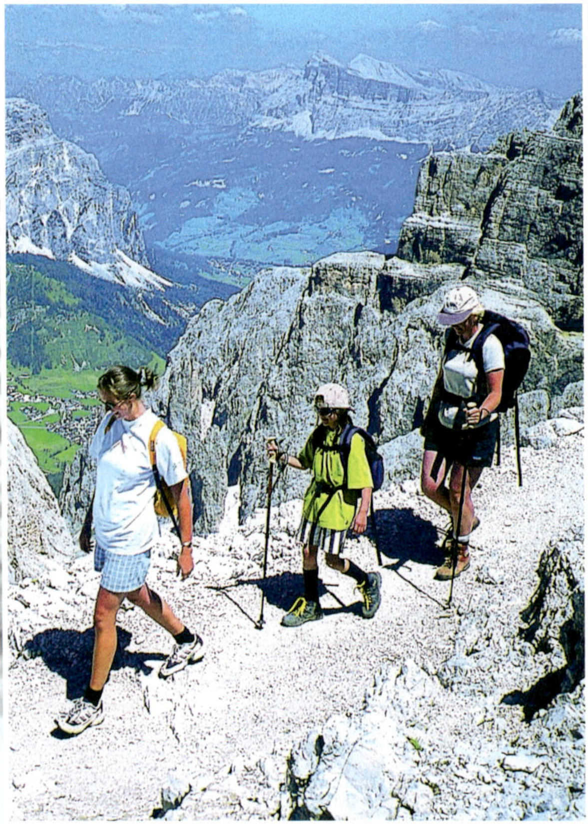

knots

Webbing is basically flat rope woven in synthetic materials. Mostly it was used for sailboat toe-straps or on land on construction sites as lifting slings. However, increasingly it is employed for a multitude of purposes ashore and afloat, commercial and domestic, including safety and barrier ropes, dog leashes, baggage straps and for lashing down awkward loads.

Ring or water knot

A ring or water knot is useful for joining two lengths of flat webbing.

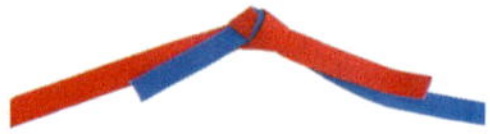

These conjoined overhand knots form the only bend recommended by climbers' technical and safety committees for slings and harnesses.

It is called the ring knot because of its circular shape. The knot works just as well in cordage but is known by the alternative name – water knot – because of its use for centuries by anglers in their horsehair and gut fishing lines.

MUST KNOW

Webbing facts

- Webbing is woven in nylon, polyester or polypropylene.
- Like other synthetic cordage it may be cut and heat-sealed.
- There are two main types of webbing: flat, such as car seat belts, and tubular, similar to a flattened hose.
- Flat webbing is only half as strong as tubular and is more liable to cuts and abrasions, but it is lighter, less bulky and fine for lashing loads to roof racks or onto road trailers.
- It can also be used for climbing étriers, 'aiders' or 'ascenders' (portable knotted ladders) and harnesses.

Method for flat webbing

Step 1

Tie a single overhand knot in the end of one length of the webbing. Then insert the end of the other length and follow the original knot around.

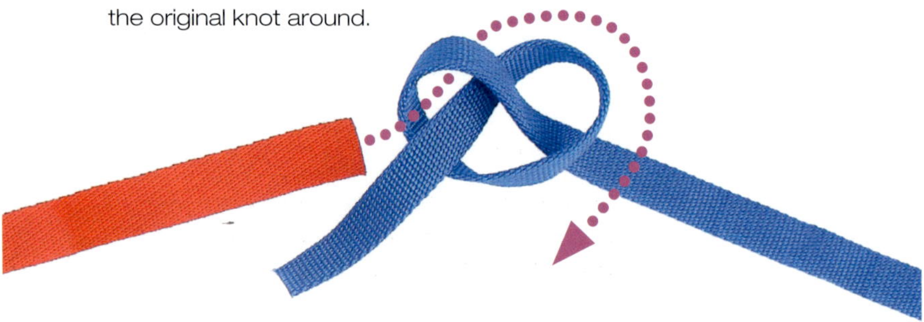

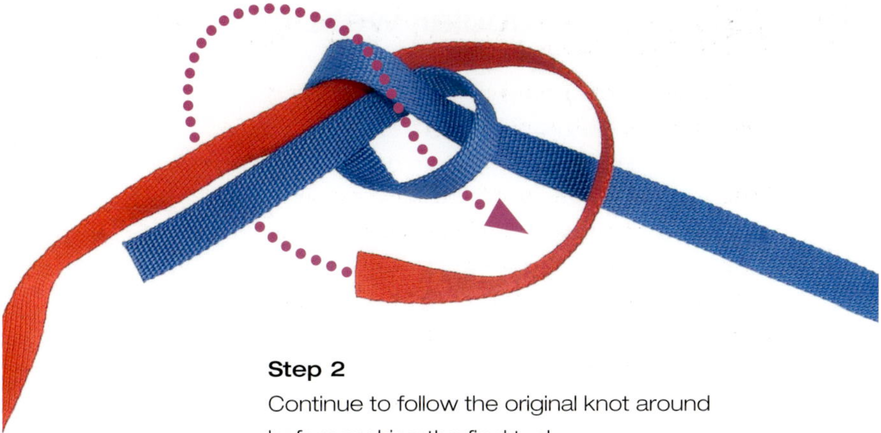

Step 2

Continue to follow the original knot around before making the final tuck.

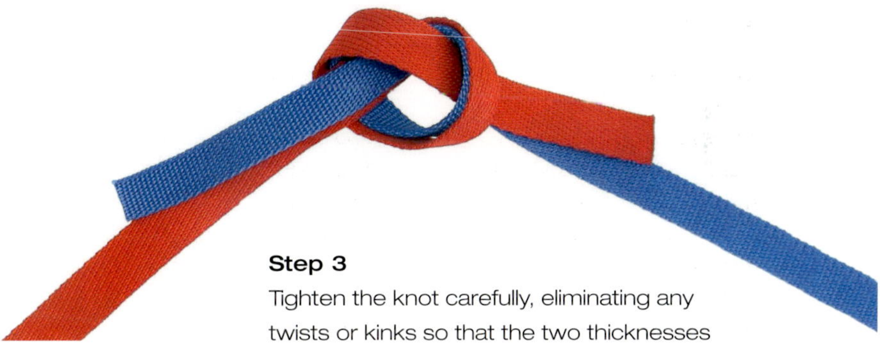

Step 3

Tighten the knot carefully, eliminating any twists or kinks so that the two thicknesses lie next to each other, neat and flat.

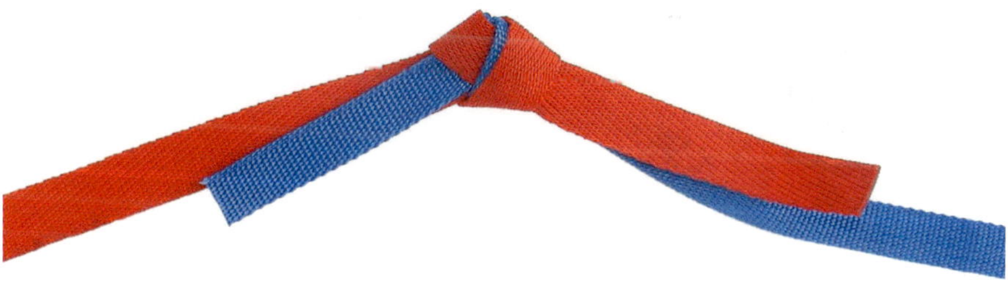

WATCH OUT!

It is recommended that you leave the working ends long enough to tape each one to its adjacent standing part as an extra precaution.

Method for tubular webbing

It is also possible to create an endless sling in tubular webbing using a ring or water knot.

With this technique, it is possible to contrive handy short slings to prevent open doors blowing shut, and to ease the load on suffering fingers when carrying full plastic shopping bags.

MUST KNOW

Quality not quantity

Tubular webbing comes in two forms. Avoid the sort that has been fabricated flat, then folded and stitched with a seam, and use only the best stuff that has been woven in the round.

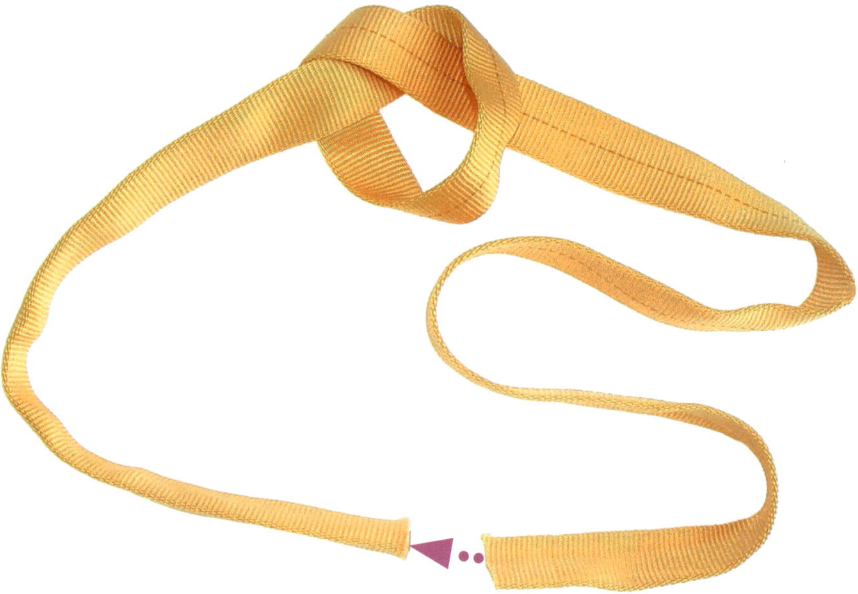

Step 1

Using a length of tubular webbing about 45 cm (1½ ft) longer than the required sling, tie a single overhand knot about 45 cm (1½ ft) from one end, then insert that end into the other end of the webbing so that the two overlap by as much as 30 cm (1 ft).

Step 2

Shift the loose knot until it is halfway along the double thickness of webbing.

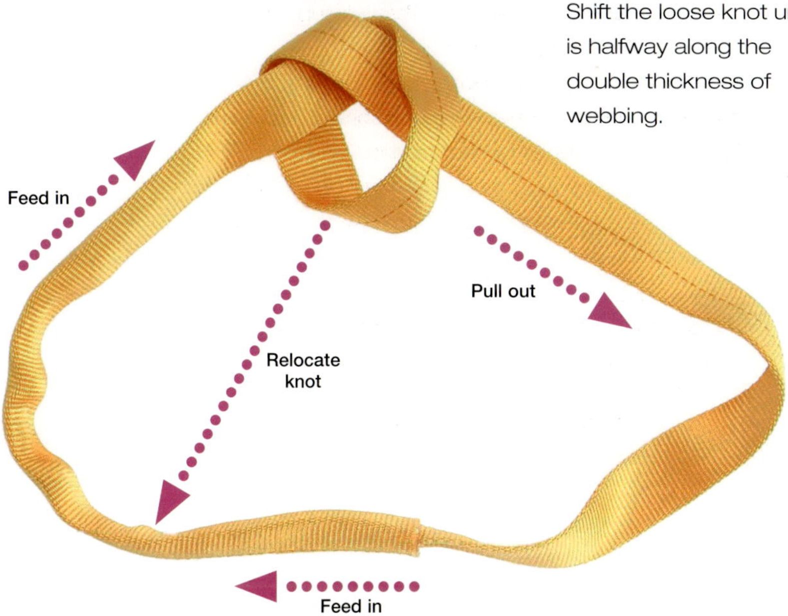

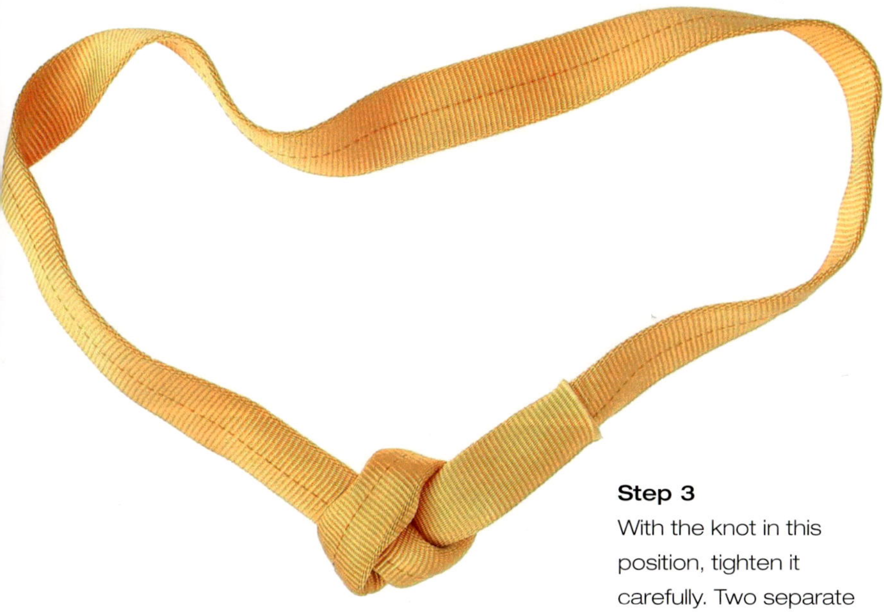

Step 3

With the knot in this position, tighten it carefully. Two separate lengths of tubular webbing may also be joined by this method.

Overhand shortening

The time-honoured sheepshank (see page 98) is far from ideal in webbing. Instead, use this similar technique in order to shorten a length of webbing.

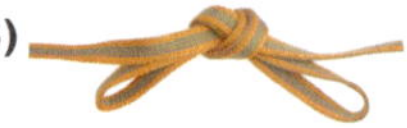

The twin fixed loops of this knot can also be used as points of attachment for snap-hooks, karabiners, shackles and such-like.

Method

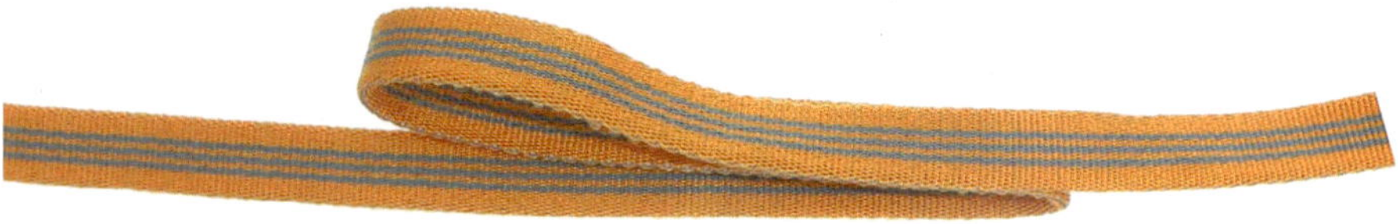

Step 1
First create a three-fold pleat in the middle of a length of webbing.

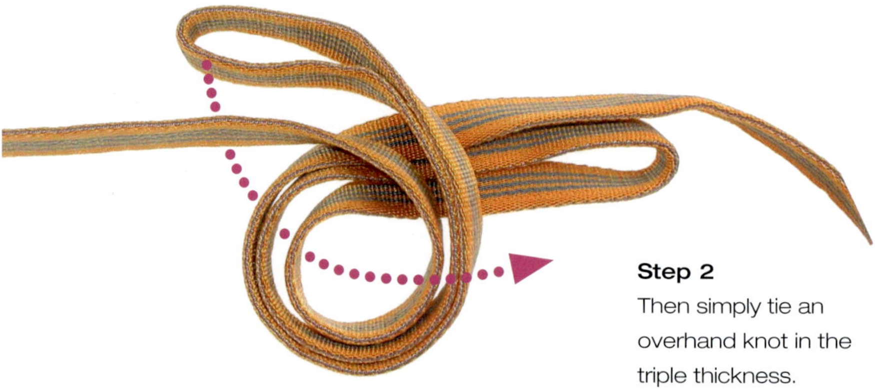

Step 2
Then simply tie an overhand knot in the triple thickness.

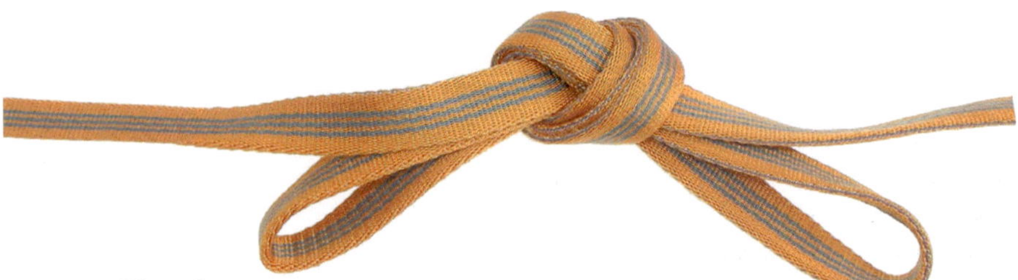

Step 3
Eliminate any unwanted twists and tighten it.

Frost knot

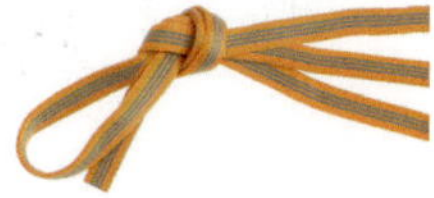

Use this loop knot to make endless slings that will be turned into the short stirrup ladders called étriers, 'aiders' or 'ascenders'.

This eponymous knot is named after Tom Frost who seems to have invented or discovered it in the 1960s.

Method

Step 1

Form a bight of sufficient length (for the desired size of sling) in one end of the webbing, and place the other end in the middle.

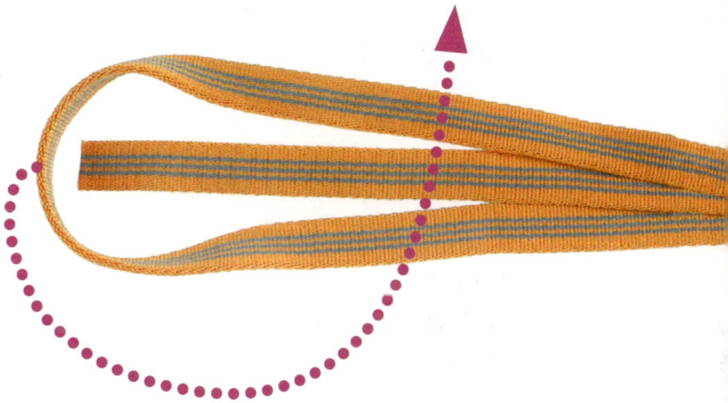

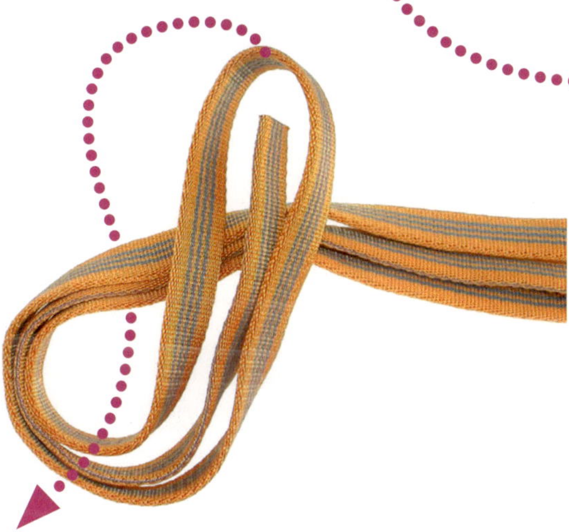

Step 2

Simply tie an overhand knot in the triple thickness – place the bight over and under the standing parts so as to form a loop.

Step 3

In 25 mm (1 in) wide webbing the triple overlapped section will be about 25–26 cm (10 in) long. Make sure that no unwanted twists intrude and then tighten the knot.

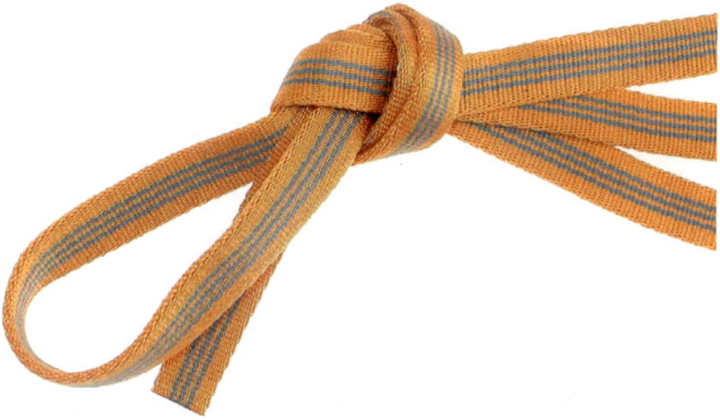

Overhand loop

This fixed loop has as many uses as any other fixed loop tied in rope or cord.

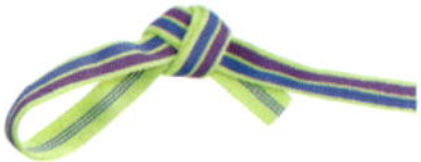

It is the webbing alternative to a bowline (see page 54) or the figure eight loop (see pages 126–7). Use it as an ad hoc handhold on a dog's lead, a climbing anchor or belay, the start of a luggage rack lashing, a mooring hitch and to start a parcel tie.

Webbing knots should also be applied to any cordage, such as paracord (see page 179), that has no core of heart-strands, and which consequently flattens when handled.

Method

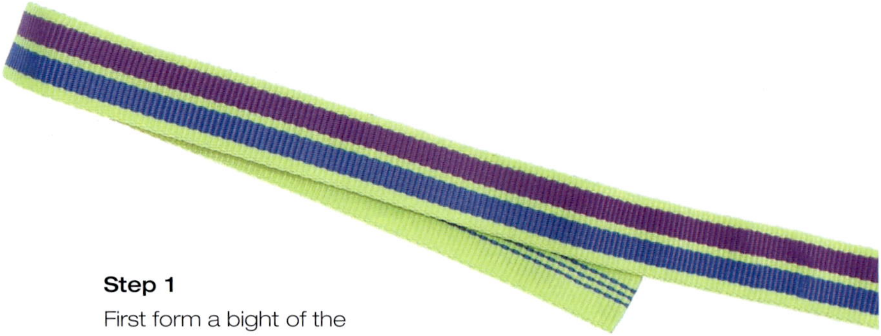

Step 1
First form a bight of the required length in one end of the webbing.

MUST KNOW

Buying webbing
Available from chandlers or outdoor activity stores by the metre, flat webbing is usually sold in 25 mm (1 in) and 50 mm (2 in) widths, while tubular webbing also comes in a width of 12.5 mm (½ in). Check the use for which it is sold – breaking strengths vary and may not always increase with the size of the webbing.

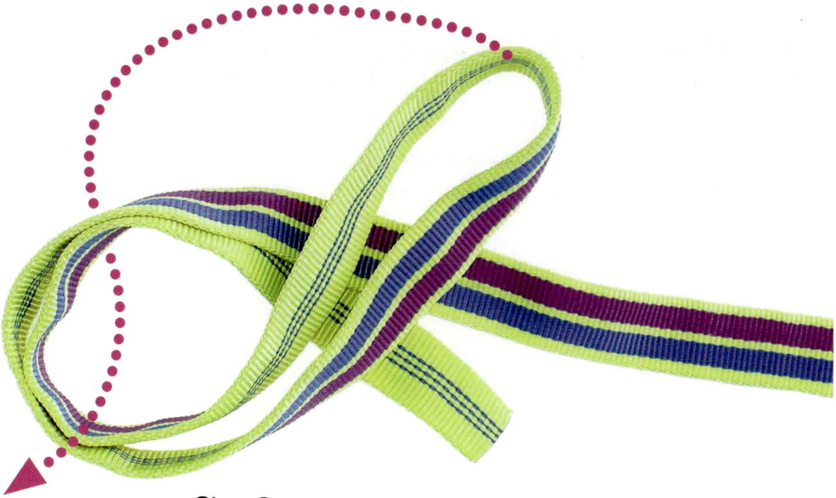

Step 2

Simply tie an overhand knot in the doubled part – place the bight over and under the standing part so as to form a loop.

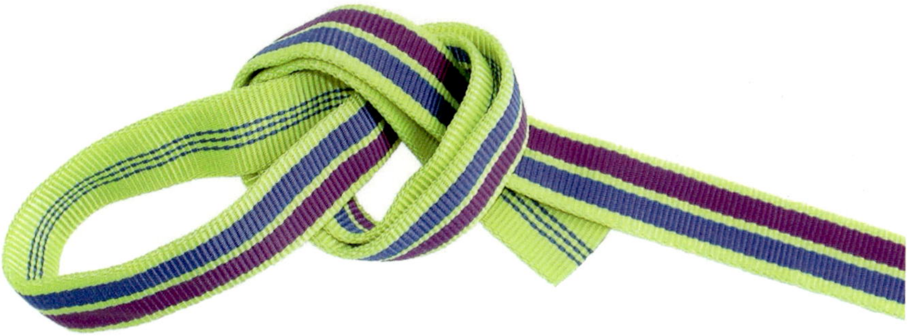

Step 3

Make sure that no unwanted twists intrude.

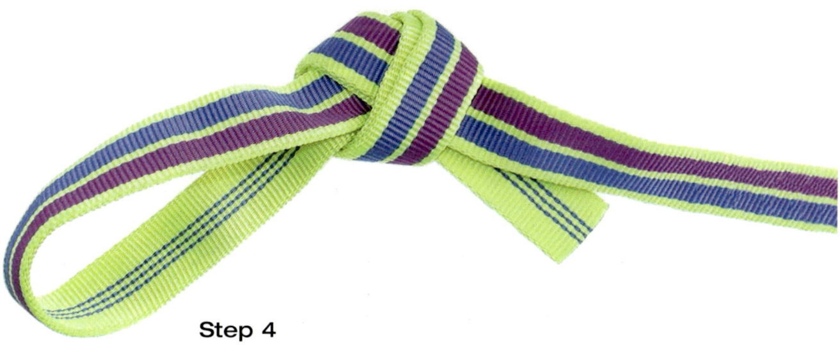

Step 4

Tighten the knot, pulling both the loop and the ends.

Sling hitch

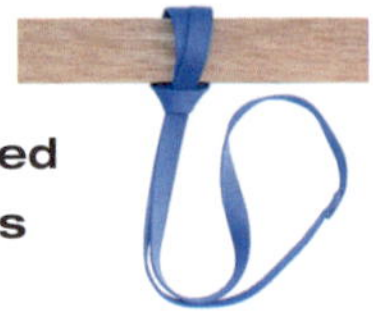

The hitch is akin to the rope ring hitch described on pages 108–9. Dockside workers and riggers may know this as a bale or hook hitch.

Drivers of forklift trucks or tractors, in warehouses and on farms, may find this webbing hitch handy, while gardeners can employ it to lug around weighty bags of peat or compost.

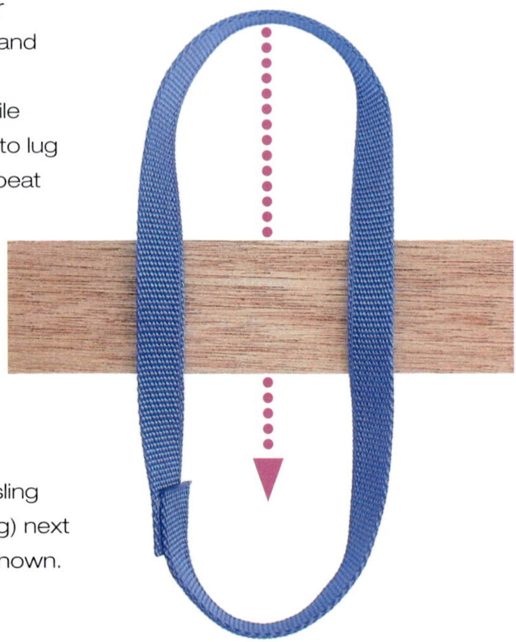

Method

Step 1

Firstly, place an endless sling (circular piece of webbing) next to the post or fixing, as shown.

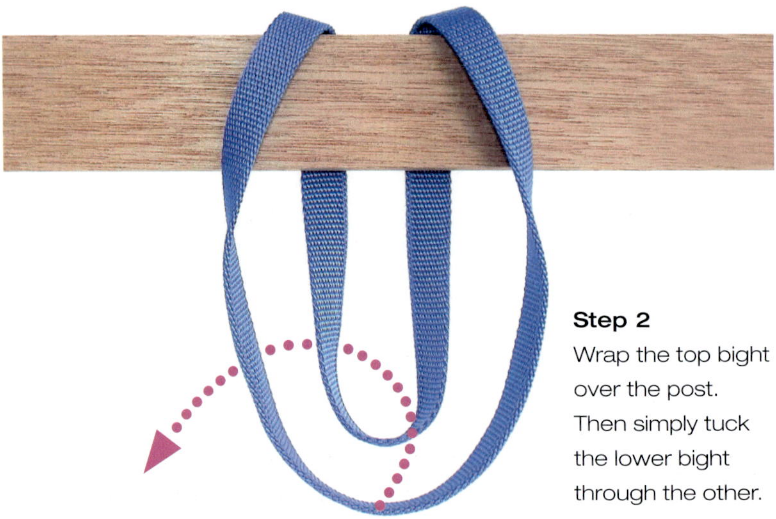

Step 2

Wrap the top bight over the post. Then simply tuck the lower bight through the other.

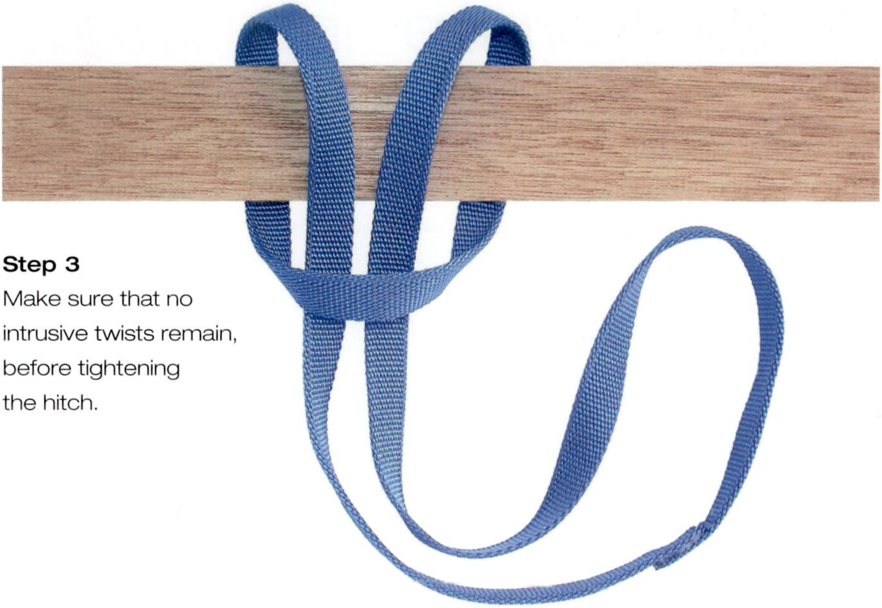

Step 3
Make sure that no intrusive twists remain, before tightening the hitch.

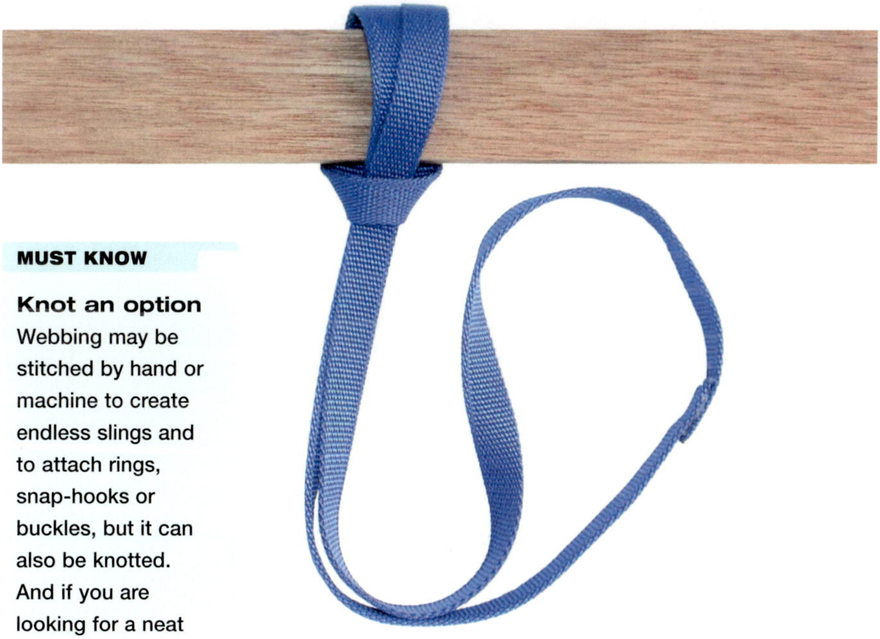

MUST KNOW

Knot an option
Webbing may be stitched by hand or machine to create endless slings and to attach rings, snap-hooks or buckles, but it can also be knotted. And if you are looking for a neat way to hang up webbing slings, use a sling hitch.

Step 4
While tightening the hitch, encourage one of the two legs to ride up over the other one.

Reinforced ring hitch

When a ring hitch can be slipped onto a hook, rail, spar or other point of attachment, you may choose to use this more secure variant, which is also tied in the bight.

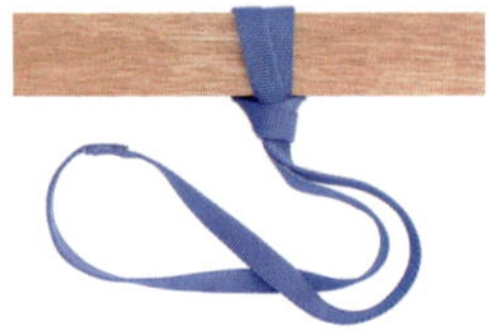

Method

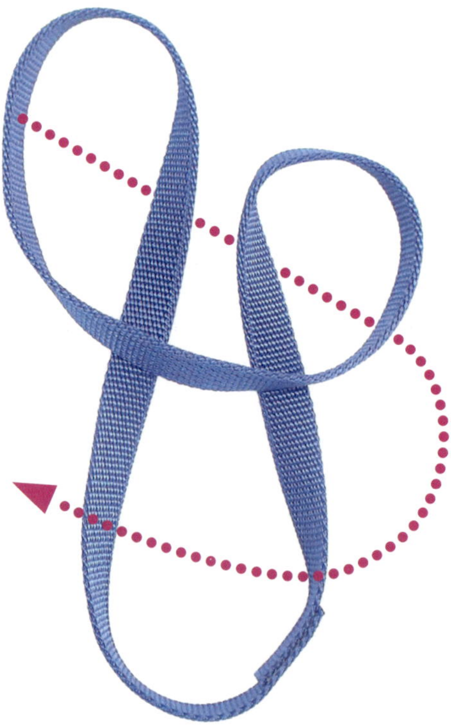

Step 1

Begin by forming a ring hitch (see pages 146–7) with an endless sling of webbing and without wrapping it around a post, but make one loop larger than the other. Wrap the larger loop behind and back across the front of the emerging knot to create an X-shape.

MUST KNOW

Crossed lines
Tying the hitch this way, with three extra crossing points, augments both its strength and security. It is possible to tie this hitch with an end, (see reinforced cow hitch on pages 150–1) so that the load is on a single standing part – like a robust form of the pedigree cow hitch on page 107.

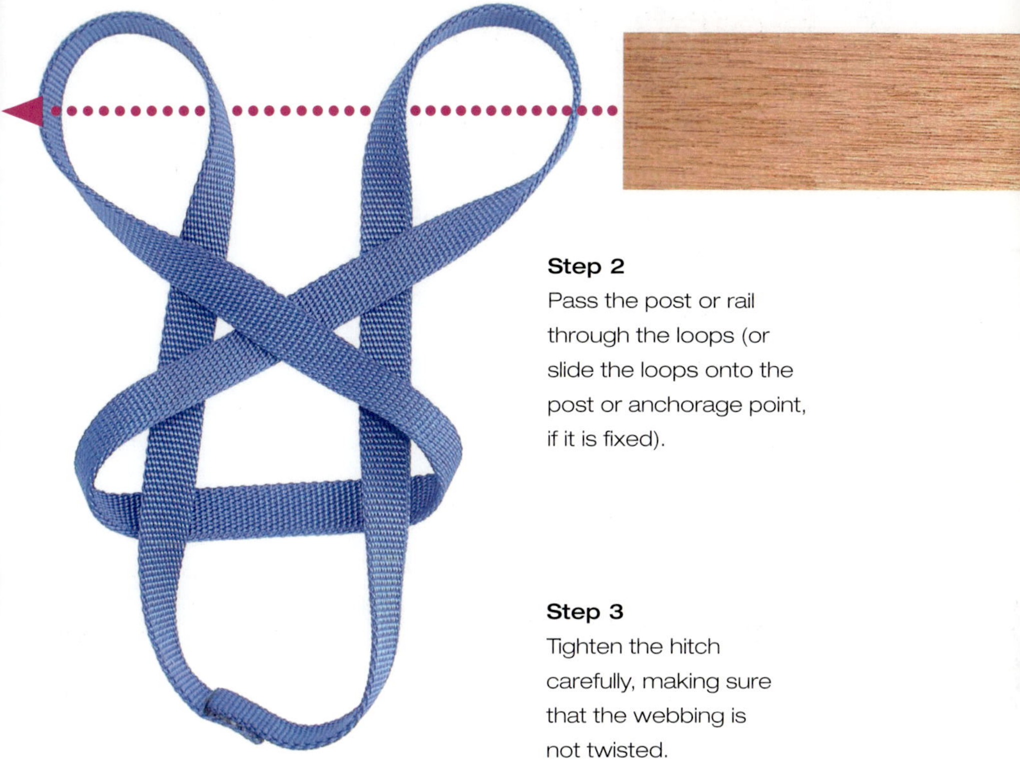

Step 2
Pass the post or rail through the loops (or slide the loops onto the post or anchorage point, if it is fixed).

Step 3
Tighten the hitch carefully, making sure that the webbing is not twisted.

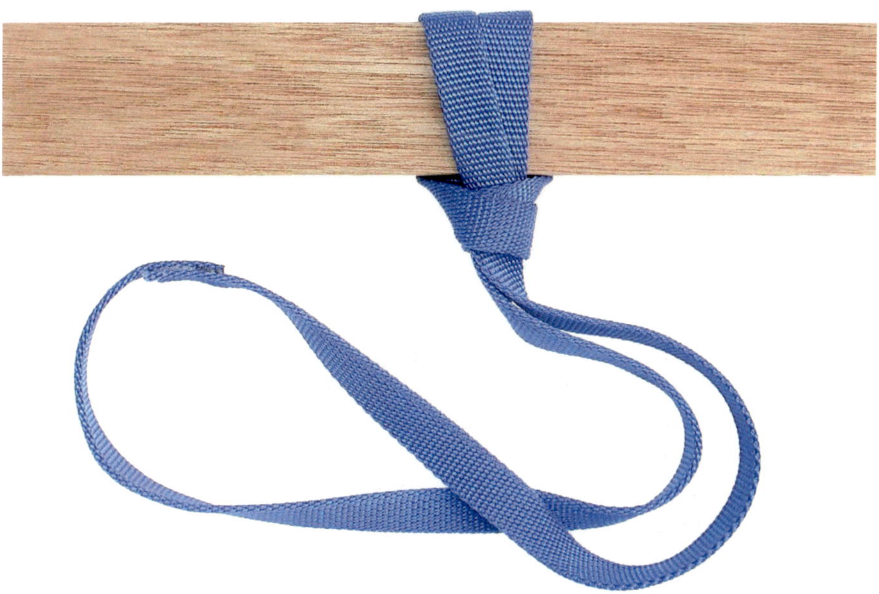

Reinforced cow hitch

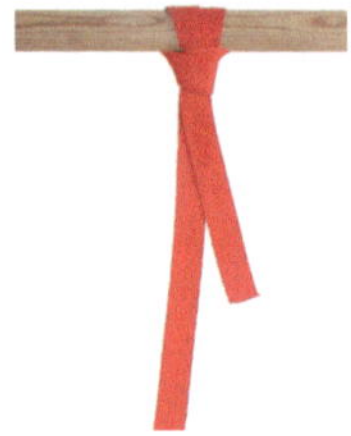

As neat as a necktie, try tethering a restless animal with this hitch.

When tying a cow hitch to a closed ring, rail or other point of attachment in webbing, you need to use an end. If tied with an endless sling it becomes a reinforced ring hitch described on pages 146–7.

Method

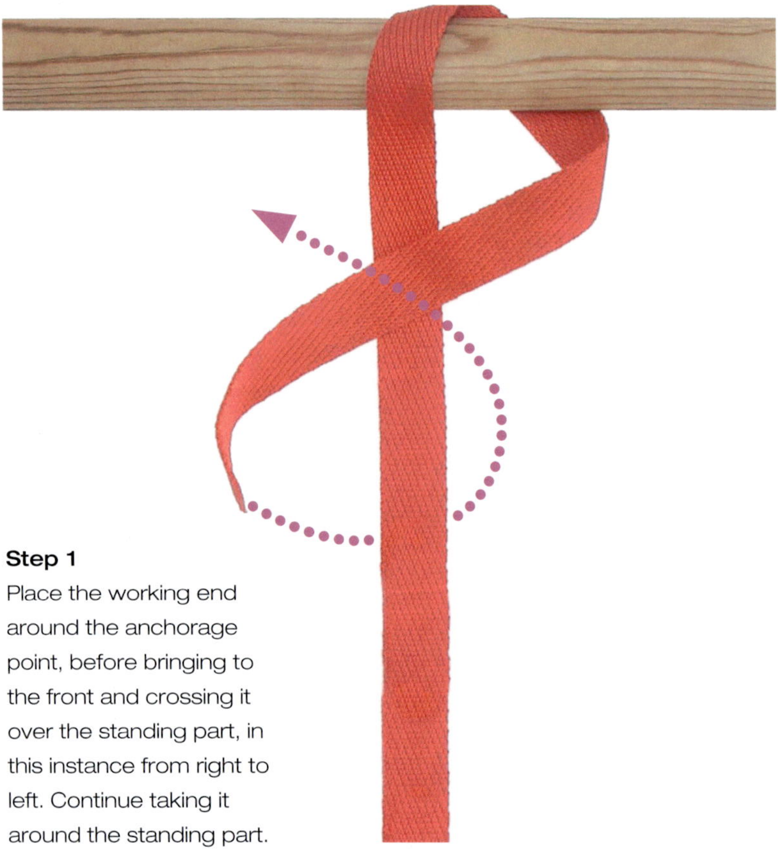

Step 1
Place the working end around the anchorage point, before bringing to the front and crossing it over the standing part, in this instance from right to left. Continue taking it around the standing part.

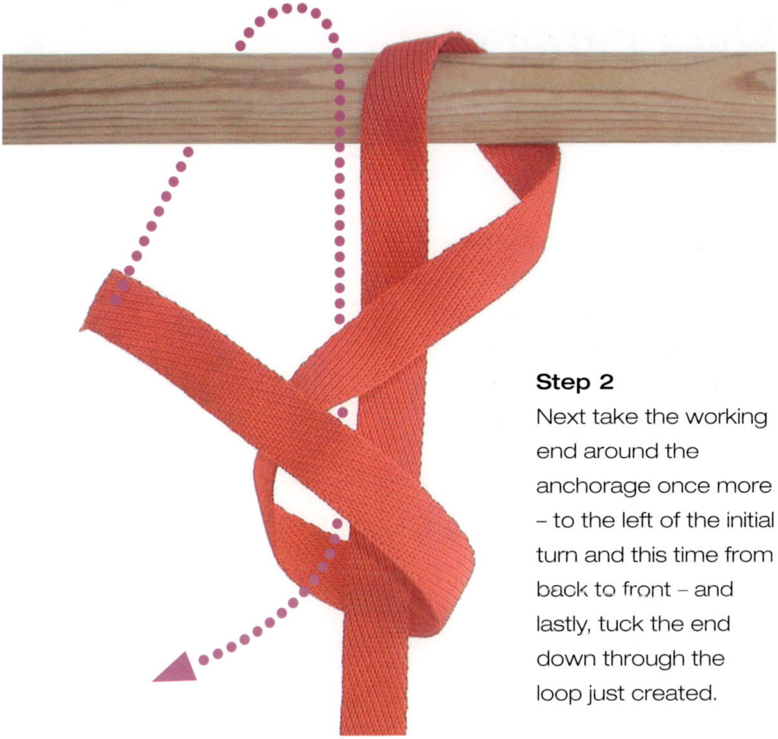

Step 2

Next take the working end around the anchorage once more – to the left of the initial turn and this time from back to front – and lastly, tuck the end down through the loop just created.

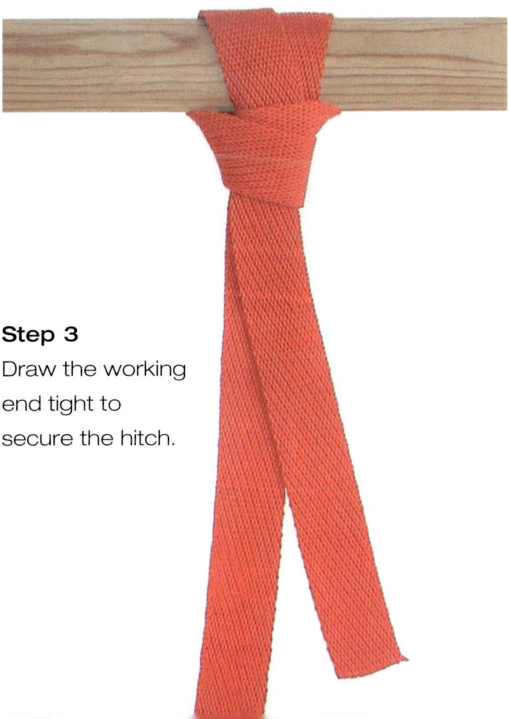

Step 3

Draw the working end tight to secure the hitch.

MUST KNOW

Taking the load

Superficially identical to the reinforced ring hitch, the dynamics of the reinforced cow hitch are different because only one leg is loaded. Ring hitches share their loads equally between both legs. (See also the pedigree cow hitch on page 107.) However, by tying this hitch with two legs of equal length, then stitching or knotting them together to reproduce an endless sling, the ring hitch can be replicated.

Pile hitch

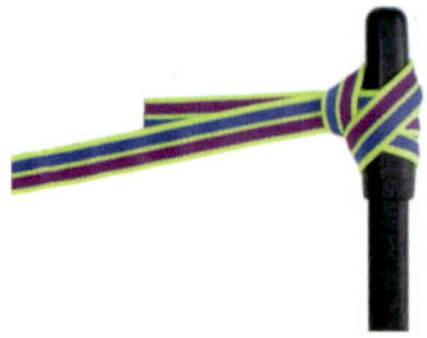

Moor a boat or tether a domestic animal with some webbing and this knot.

A pile hitch grips and holds better than a simple fixed loop because of the larger surface area in contact to generate friction, yet is cast off as quickly and easily.

MUST KNOW

Loose ends
For additional safety and security, you can stitch or tape the loose end to the standing part.

Method

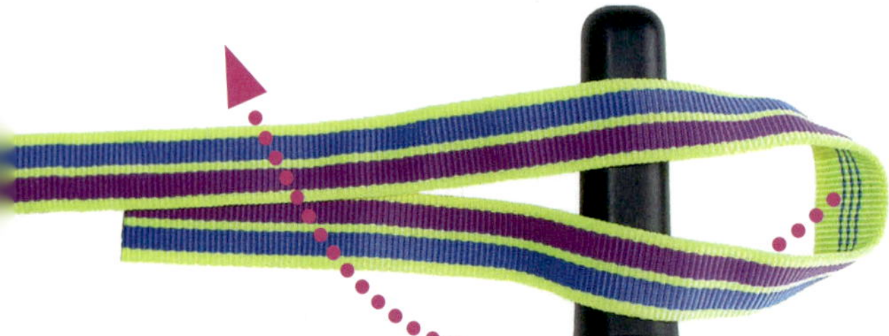

Step 1
Make a long loop in the end of a length of webbing, incorporating a 90 degree quarter of a turn. Wrap this loop around the post and pass it beneath the doubled standing part.

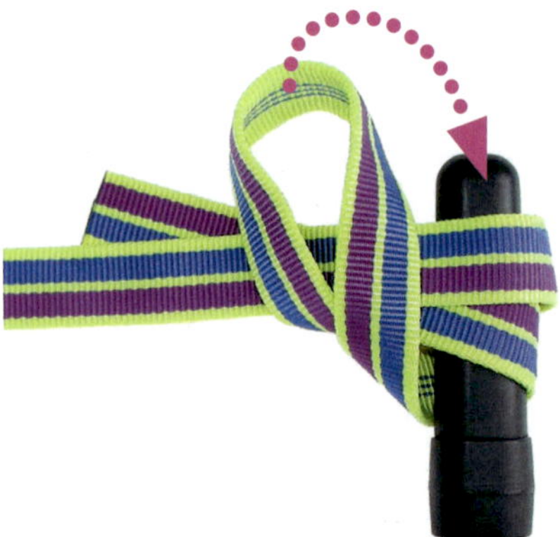

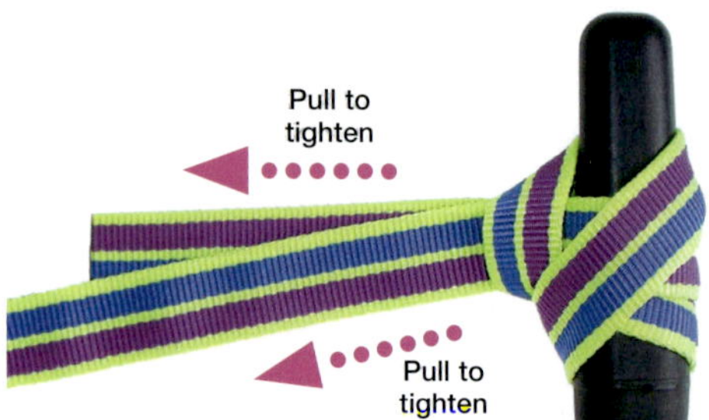

Step 2
Next, place the loop over the top of the post.

Step 3
Finally, making sure that there are no twists in the webbing, pull the hitch tight.

Ground line hitch

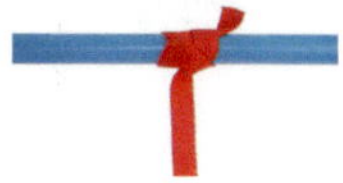

This hitch is similar to a clove hitch but is preferable to it when using webbing because it is noticeably more secure.

In cordage this versatile knot has been tied by millers around the necks of grain sacks and by solidiers on horseback – and, indeed, is still used by some western American horsemen and women – to tether their mounts to a picket line.

Method

Step 1

Take the working end around the post once, before crossing the standing part and making a second turn.

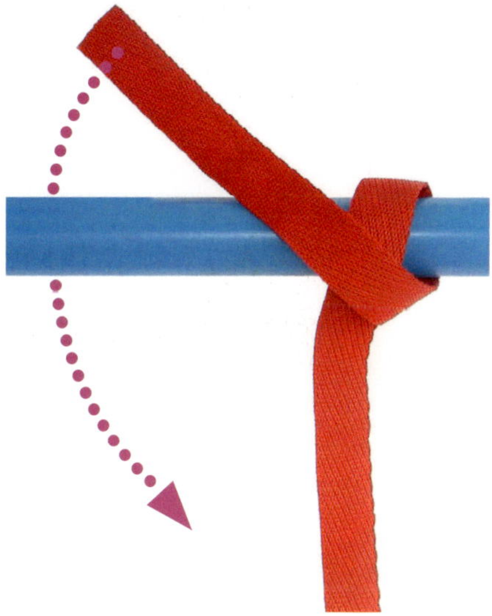

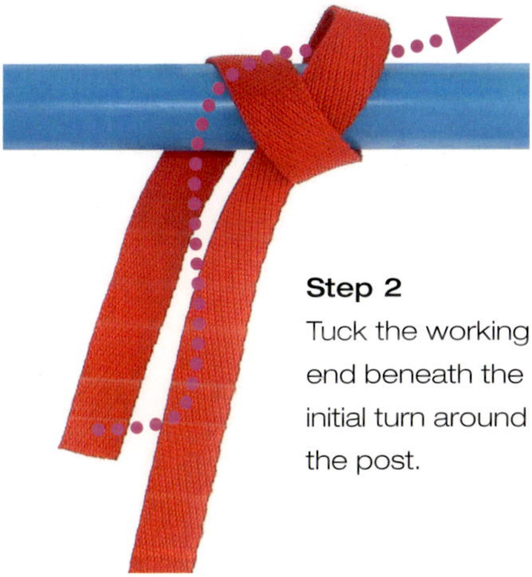

Step 2

Tuck the working end beneath the initial turn around the post.

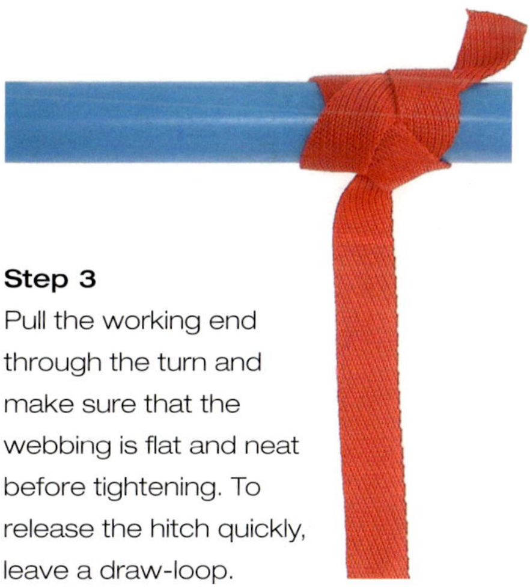

MUST KNOW

Land and sea

This strong but simple hitch was a favourite with professional cod fishermen who applied it (in cordage) to their nets. Tough when at sea, it works equally hard to earn its keep on land.

Step 3

Pull the working end through the turn and make sure that the webbing is flat and neat before tightening. To release the hitch quickly, leave a draw-loop.

Buntline hitch

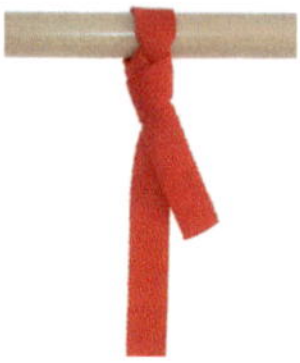

This knot jams when tightened, making it suitable for lines that are to be shaken or tugged intermittently.

Use it on flag halyards or down-hauls and out-hauls attached to dinghy sail eyelets.

Keep the working end shorter and load only the standing end of this compact yet gripping hitch.

MUST KNOW

Smart tie
Butchers once used this knot in string to prepare corned beef and salt pork, and anglers used it to attach lines of gut or horsehair to swivels. And it is, of course, the necktie knot still referred to by clued-up smart dressers as the 'four-in-hand'.

Method

Step 1

Place the working end around the foundation before bringing it to the front and crossing it over the standing part, in this instance from left to right. Continue taking it around the standing part and then lay it across itself.

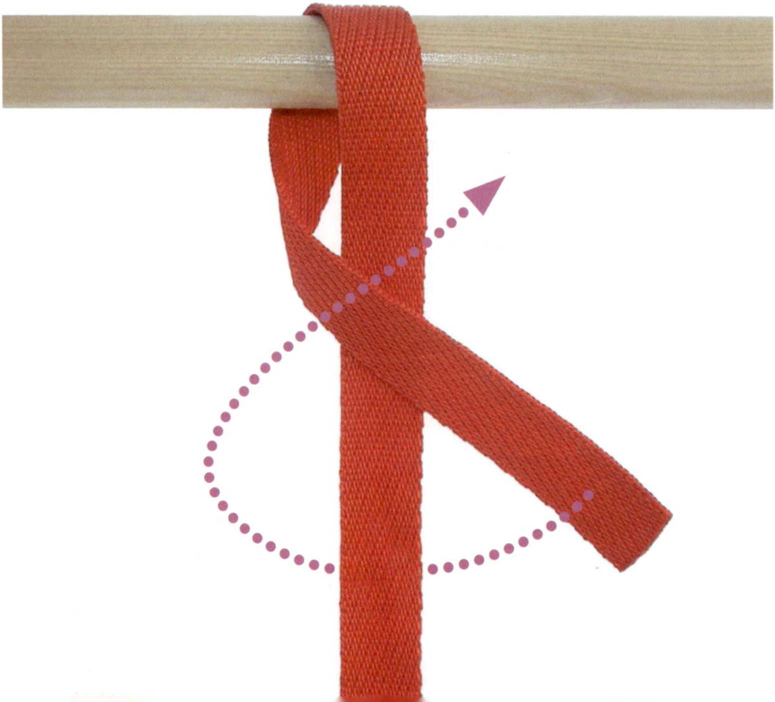

Step 2
Next, tuck the working end beneath the initial knot part – right to left – and back beneath itself from left to right.

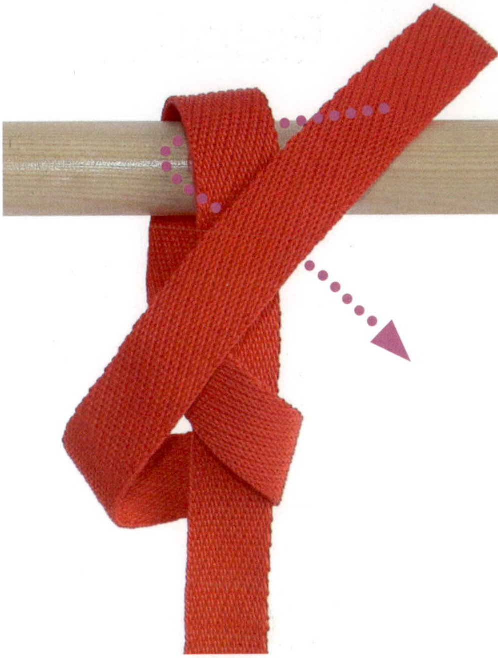

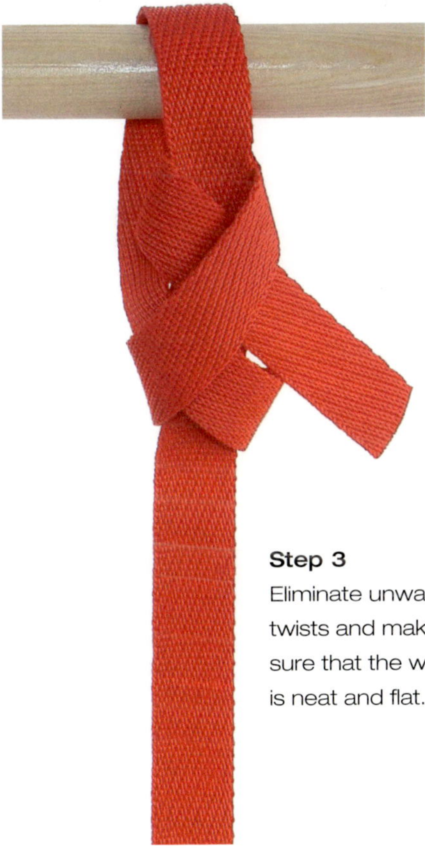

Step 3
Eliminate unwanted twists and make sure that the webing is neat and flat.

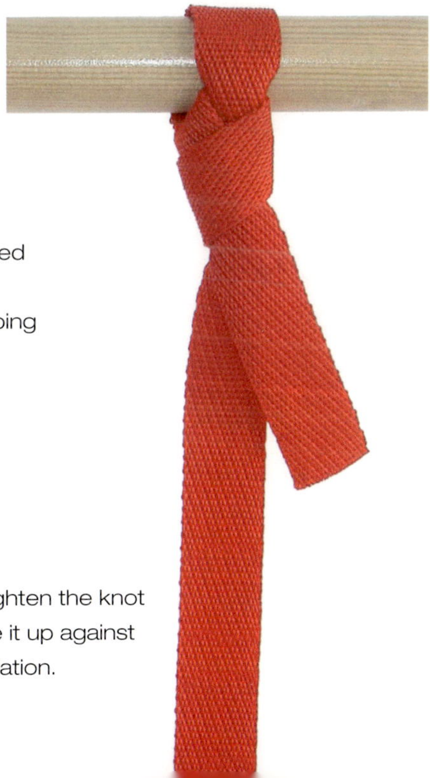

Step 4
Lastly, tighten the knot and slide it up against its foundation.

Ossel hitch

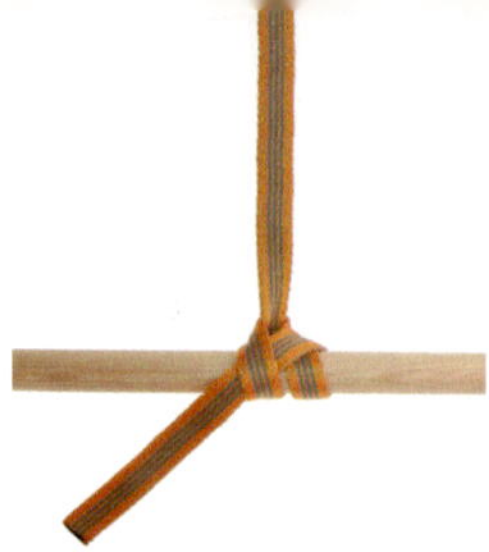

Traditionally employed by trawlermen, this is an extremely robust hitch.

You can use it as a secure alternative to the ground line hitch on page 153. The ossel hitch (with or without a draw-loop) requires only a little care to ensure that, as the working end is taken around behind the standing part, it resembles the collar of a jacket. Once done, it adheres to its foundation like superglue to skin.

MUST KNOW

Knotting options
Always use the quickest and simplest knot, bend or hitch to do any job, but when greater strength or security are essential consider a more elaborate version, which, in the case of the ossel hitch is the collared hitch (see pages 158–9)

Method

Step 1

Take the working end from back to front around the foundation, then behind the standing part of the webbing. Wrap it around the foundation once more before tucking it diagonally downward through the first turn.

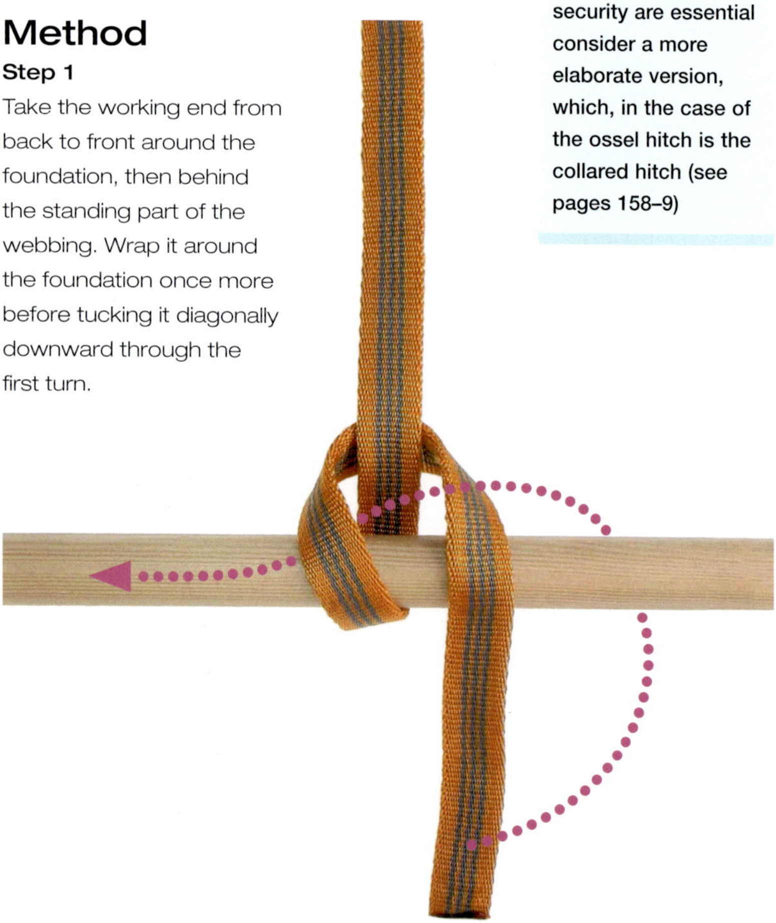

Step 2

Now make sure that all turns and tucks are neat and that there are no twists in the webbing.

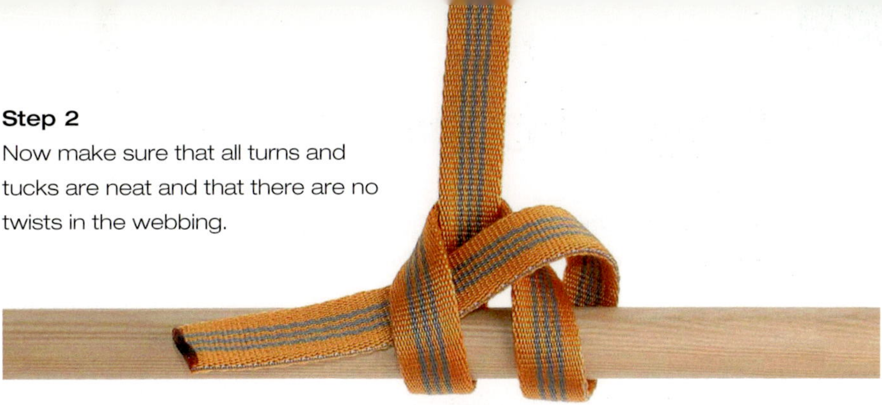

Step 3

Pull both ends tight to secure the hitch.

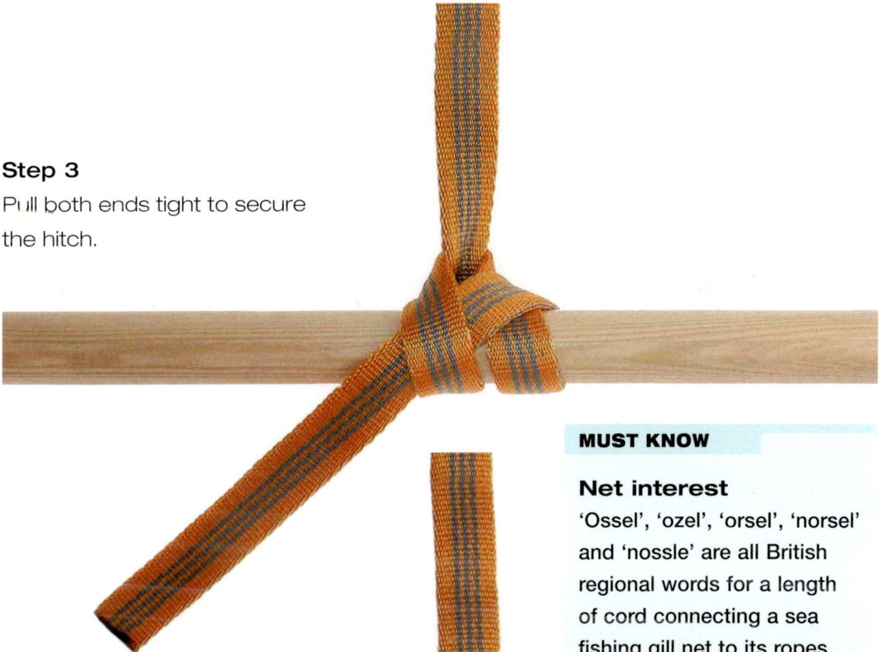

MUST KNOW

Net interest

'Ossel', 'ozel', 'orsel', 'norsel' and 'nossle' are all British regional words for a length of cord connecting a sea fishing gill net to its ropes.

Variation

Instead of tucking the working end through you can form a draw-loop, as shown here, for quick release.

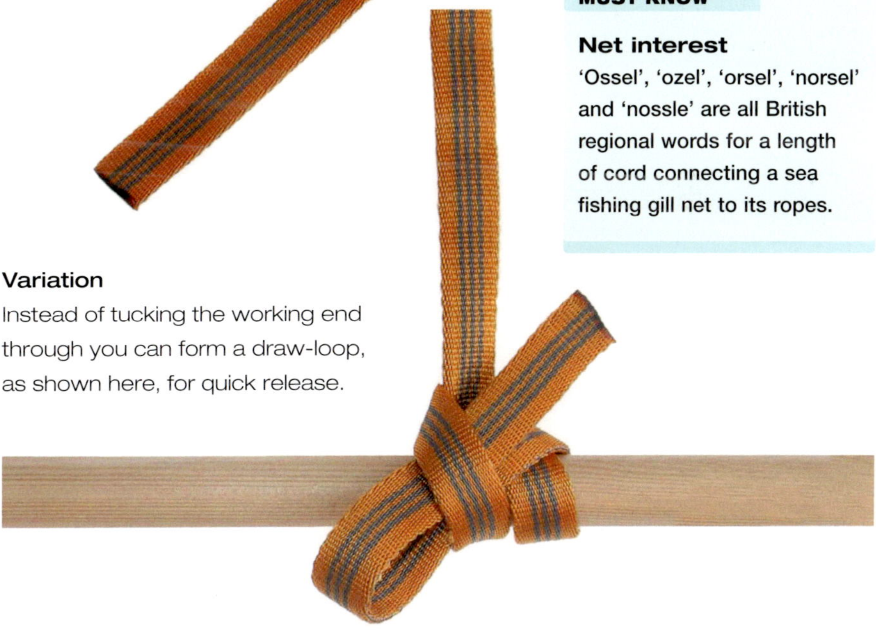

Collared hitch

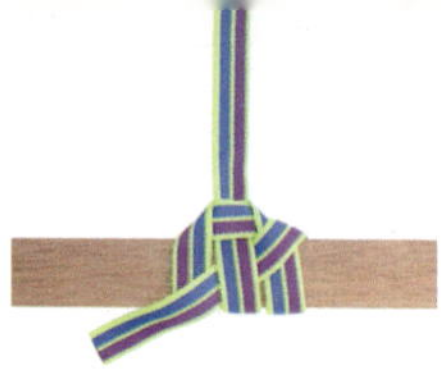

Employ a collared hitch on heavy vehicular loads and whenever pulls are liable to be from various directions.

It is stronger and more secure than the ossel hitch and a couple of these knots will even support a child's swing, but check the knot after each use.

Method

Step 1

Take the working end, from back to front, around the foundation, then behind the standing part of the webbing. Wrap it around the foundation once more but this time bring it in front of the standing part.

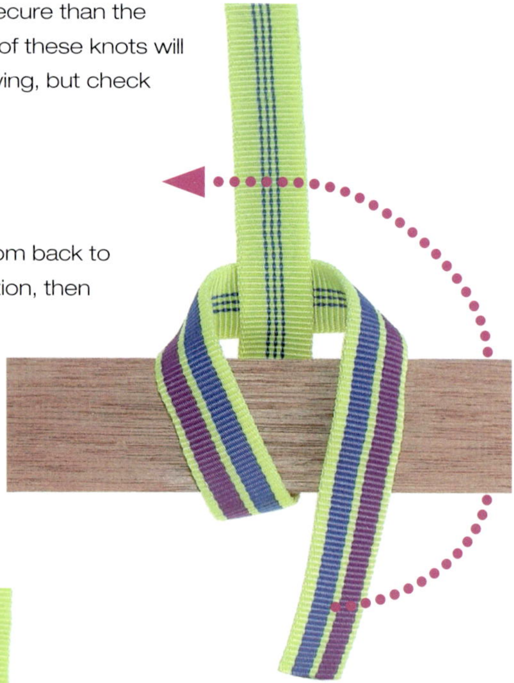

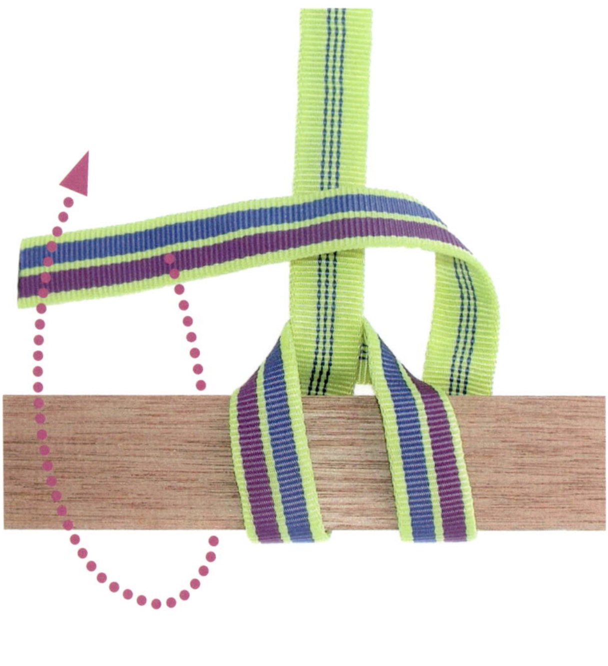

Step 2

Wrap the working end around the foundation a third time, making sure that the webbing lies to the left of the initial turn.

Step 3
Pass the working end behind the standing part and around the foundation, from front to back, a fourth time.

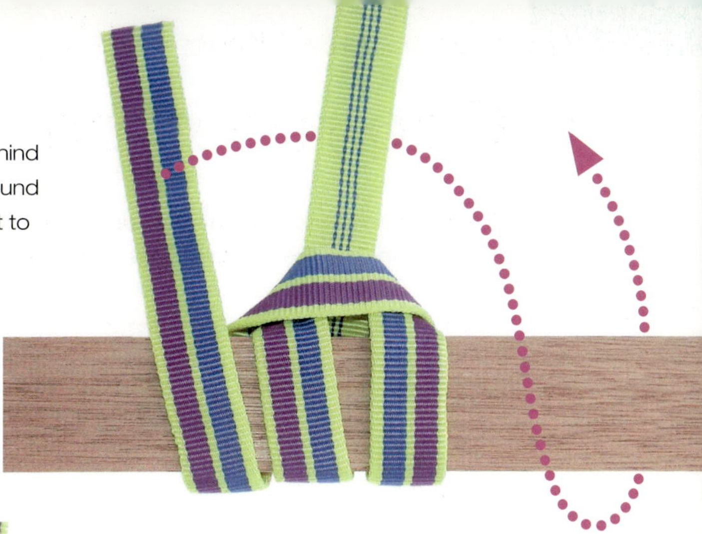

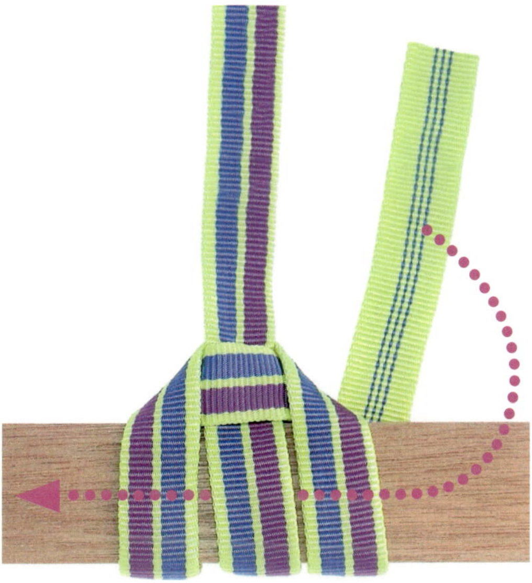

Step 4
Lastly, working from the back, tuck the working end beneath the central piece of webbing.

Back view

Step 5
Arrange each 'collar' neatly, so that between the two of them they enclose the standing part and tighten the entire knot.

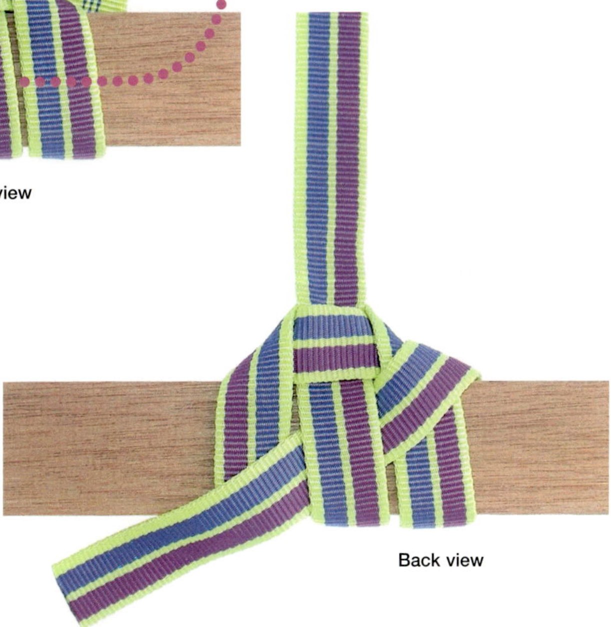

Back view

Boom hitch

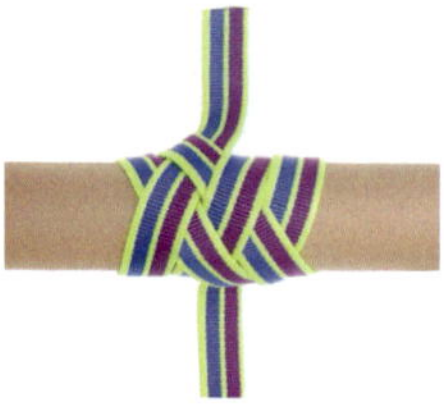

This is a very strong and secure, semi-permanent hitch for when the load comes from a more or less steady direction.

It is almost ornamental in appearance, like a particularly bulky clove hitch.

One dinghy sailor, whose mainsheet came adrift from its boom fixing, reattached it with a lanyard and this hitch. He not only made it back to the jetty without any more trouble, but he left the knot in situ and used it for the remainder of the sailing season.

MUST KNOW

No slacking

- Learn the mantra 'over, over, over, over and tuck' and you will remember how to tie this knot.
- Work this hitch tight a bit at a time so that there is no slackness remaining in any of the knot parts.

Method

Step 1

Take the working end, from back to front, around the foundation, then bring it to the front across itself and wrap it diagonally around the foundation a second time. Bring it to the front and this time across itself in the opposite diagonal direction and wrap it around the foundation a third time. Bring it back to the front and once again across the standing part and you're ready to make a fourth turn.

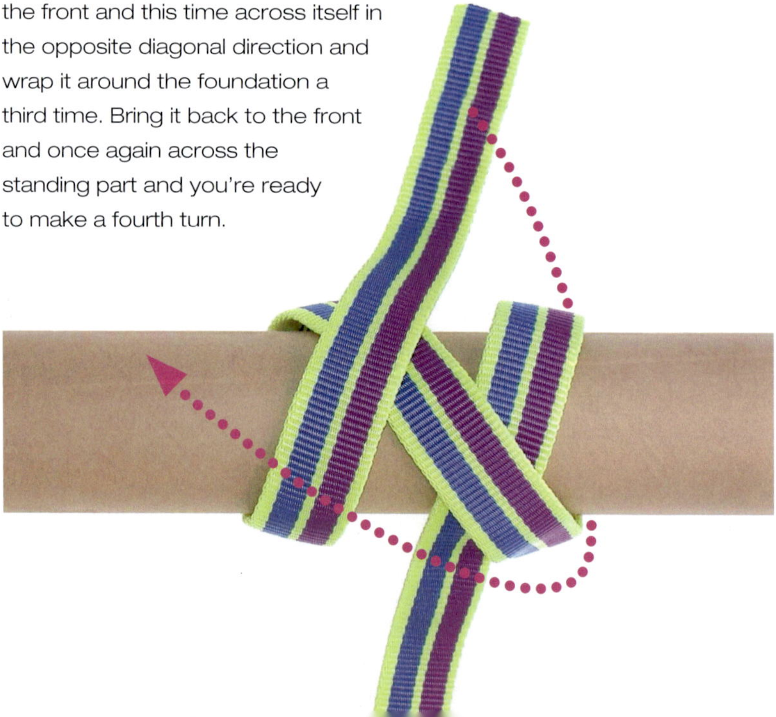

Step 2
Complete the fourth turn, bringing the working end across itself diagonally and then tuck it beneath the adjacent webbing.

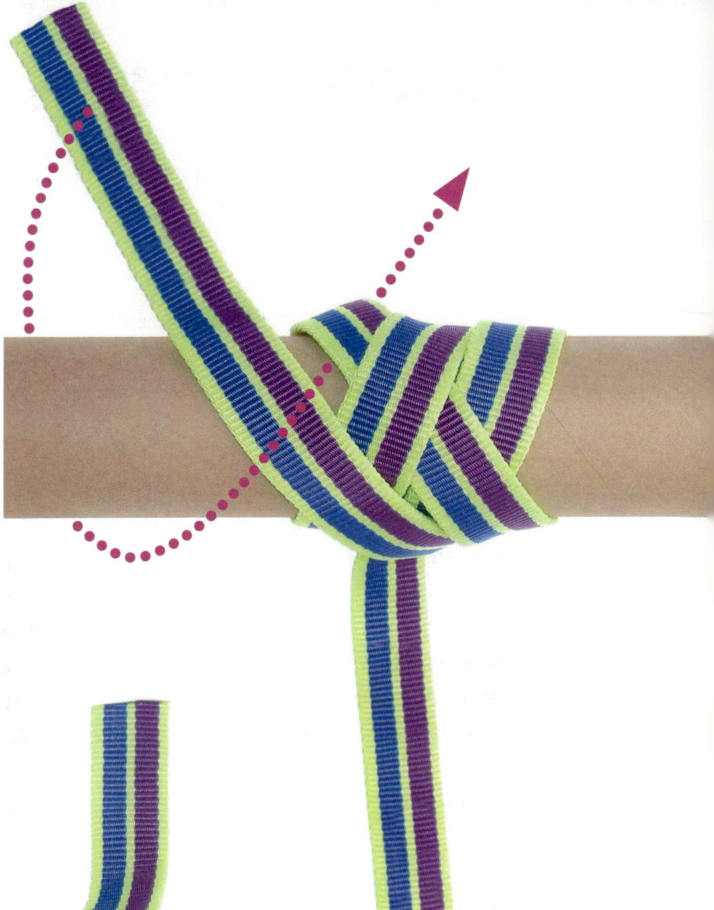

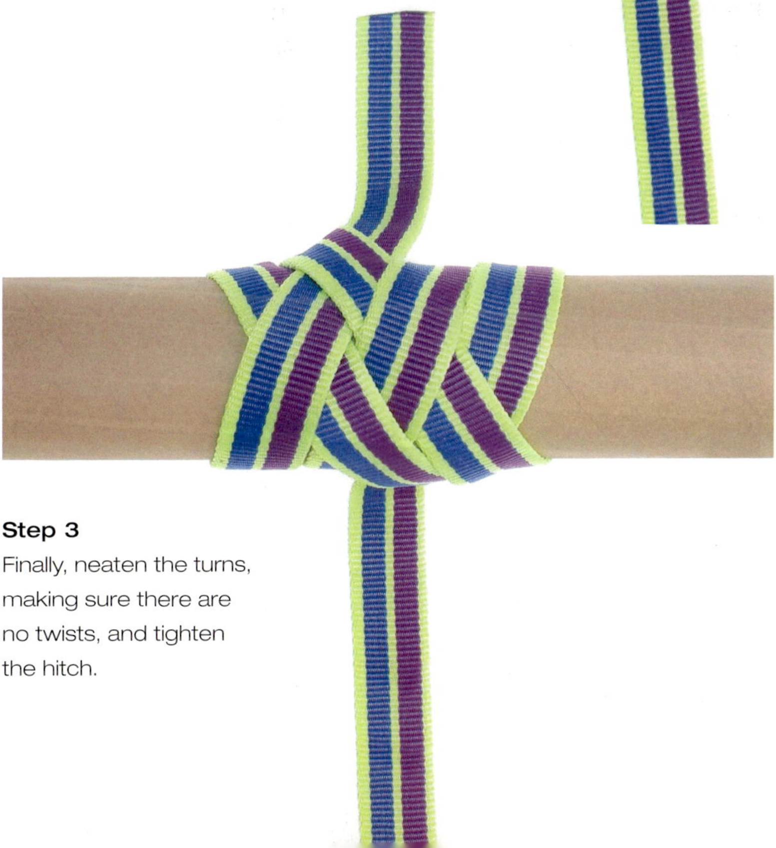

Step 3
Finally, neaten the turns, making sure there are no twists, and tighten the hitch.

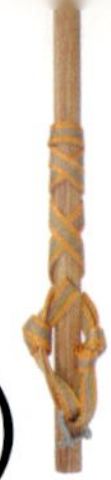

Slide-and-grip hitch (end-loaded, one-way)

This innovative hitch does not grip firmly until the load is low enough; it absorbs the energy of a shock loading by sliding.

It is as close to the imaginary 'sky hook' (an elevated fixing, third hand or other helpful support) as one can contrive.

Method

Step 1

Tie an overhand loop (see pages 144–5) in each end of a length of 25 mm (1 in) webbing. Position the middle of the webbing on the foundation and pass both ends in opposite spirals around the foundation, crossing one over the other where they meet.

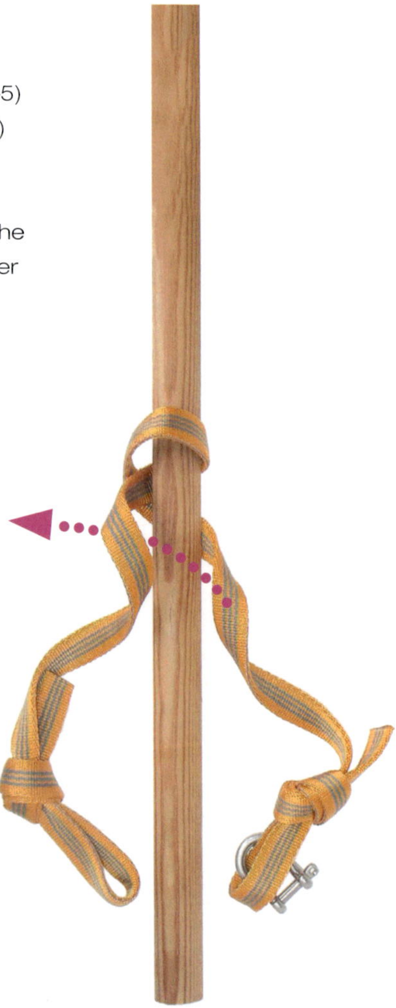

MUST KNOW

Load bearing

Loading this arrangement causes it to lengthen, decreasing its diameter, so that it grips and holds like the toy known as a Chinese finger trap. Release the load, take hold of the knot and push it from either end, when it will shorten, loosen its hold and shift readily enough.

Climbers are comfortable with the fact that, under a sudden load, this knot may slip to some extent before it holds, because that will absorb some energy until the load is low enough for the sling and rope (single or double) to withstand it.

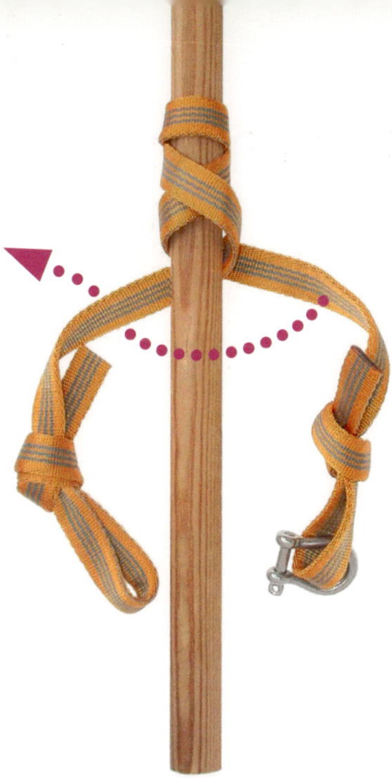

Step 2

Take both working lengths around to the back of the foundation, where the one that went over at the previous crossing point now goes under.

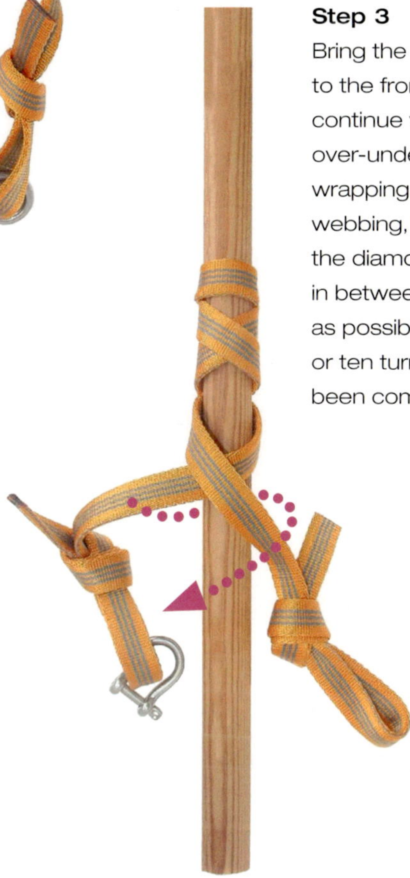

Step 3

Bring the ends around to the front again and continue with this over-under-over wrapping of the webbing, keeping the diamond spaces in between as small as possible, until eight or ten turns have been completed.

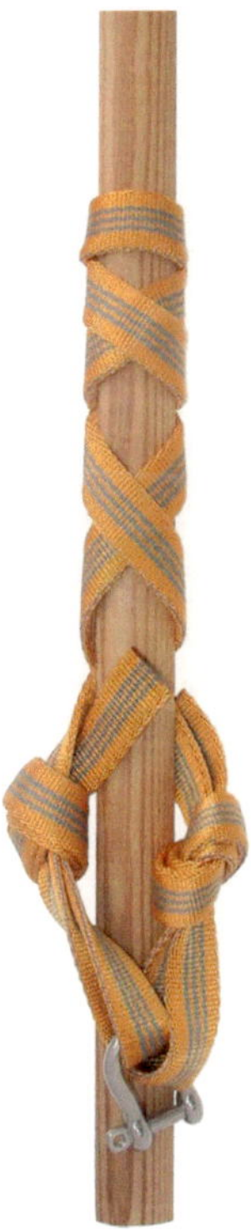

Step 4

Lastly, neaten any twists in the webbing. Attach the load to the two loops by means of a shackle or karabiner.

WATCH OUT!

This hitch glazes and loses friction with use, so be prepared to retire it before that occurs.

Slide-&-grip hitch (centre-loaded, two-way)

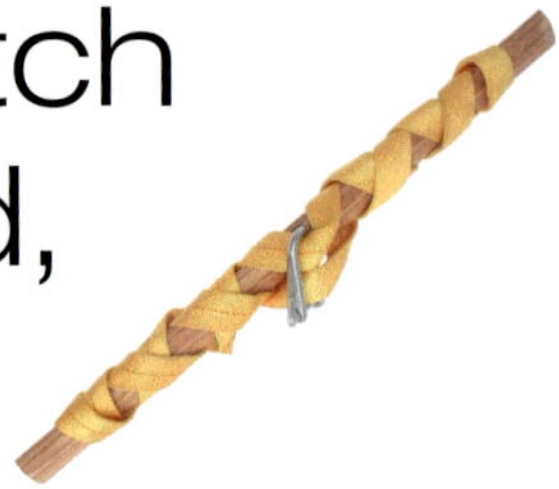

Anchor a block and tackle or an animal with a reputation for untying its tethers with this two-way hitch.

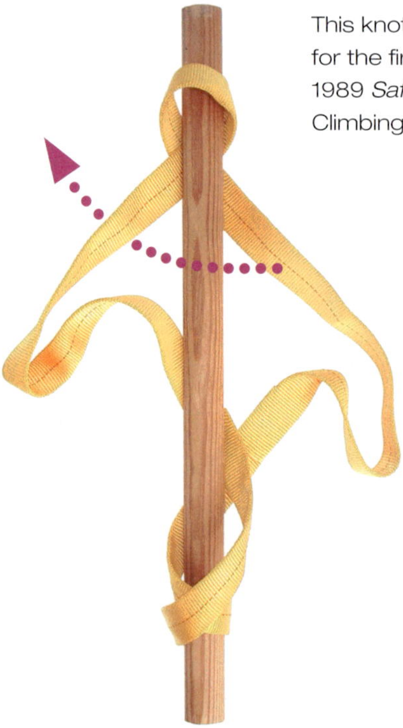

This knot seems to have appeared in print for the first time when it was featured in the 1989 *Safety Manual* of the Ontario Rock Climbing Association.

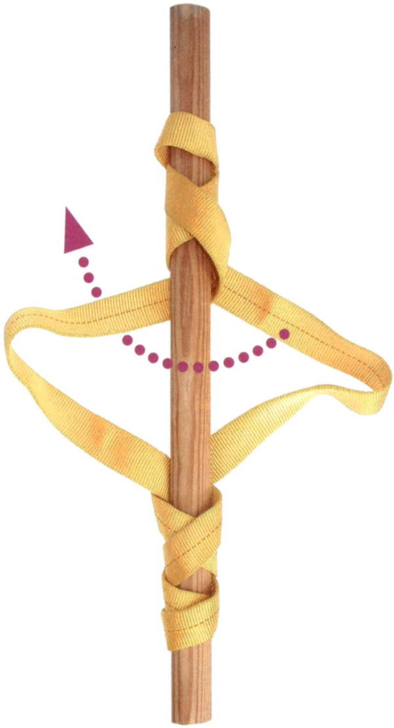

Method

Step 1

Wrap an endless sling of webbing around the foundation in two positions – top and bottom – leaving a gap in the middle. Cross the webbing over at the back (as if tying the end-loaded slide-and-grip hitch on pages 162–3).

Step 2

Repeat step 1, allowing a mirror-image wrap to develop at both ends of the foundation.

MUST KNOW

Hand-powered
The lengthen and grip, shorten and slacken off mechanism is the same as for the end-loaded version of this hitch on pages 162–3, but this powerful arrangement will withstand a severe pull in either direction yet may be shifted easily enough by hand.

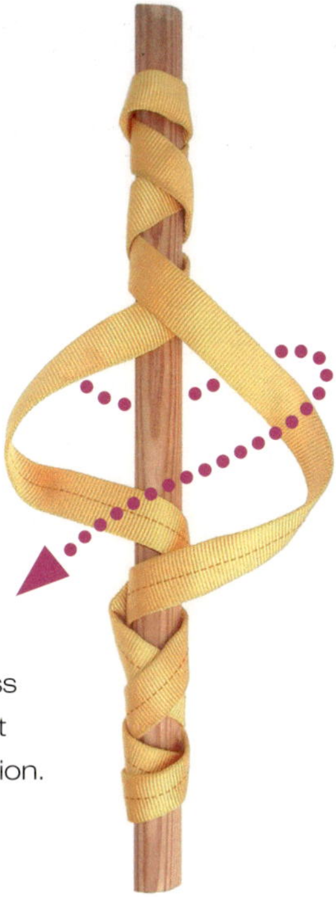

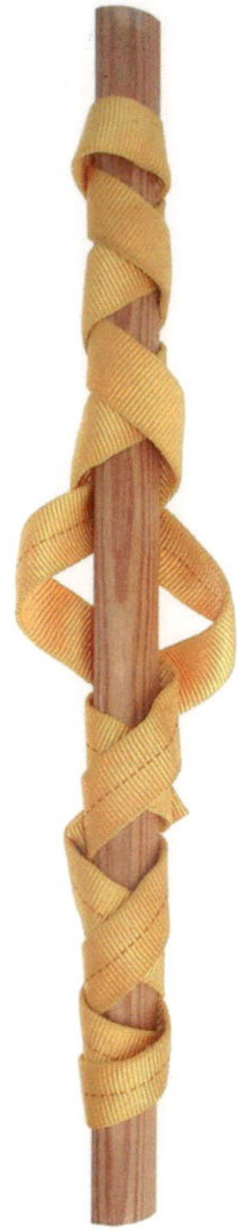

Back view

Step 3
Continue this process until you have almost covered the foundation.

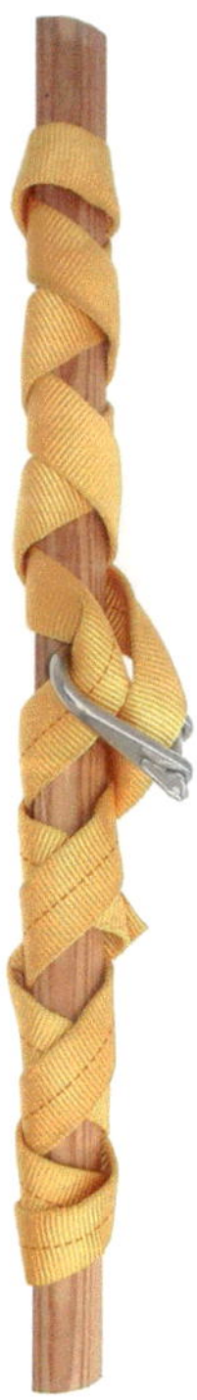

Back view

WATCH OUT!

Like the preceding one-way version of this hitch, it glazes and loses friction with use.

Step 4
Where the two bights meet in the middle, tighten the arrangement carefully, then secure them with a shackle or karabiner and attach the load.

want to know more?

Take it to the next level...

Go to...

- **Life-support knots –** pages 114–35
- **Cordage facts –** pages 166–83

Other sources

- **Webbing and cords**
  www.acesupplies.co.uk
- **Chandlers and outdoor activity stores**
  for supplies of all types of webbing
- **Clubs and organizations**
  membership of the IGKT
- **Video**
  www.thetievideo.com
- **Publications**
  Simplified Turk's-heads by Ron Edwards, (2003), ISBN 1-875872-70-1

cordage

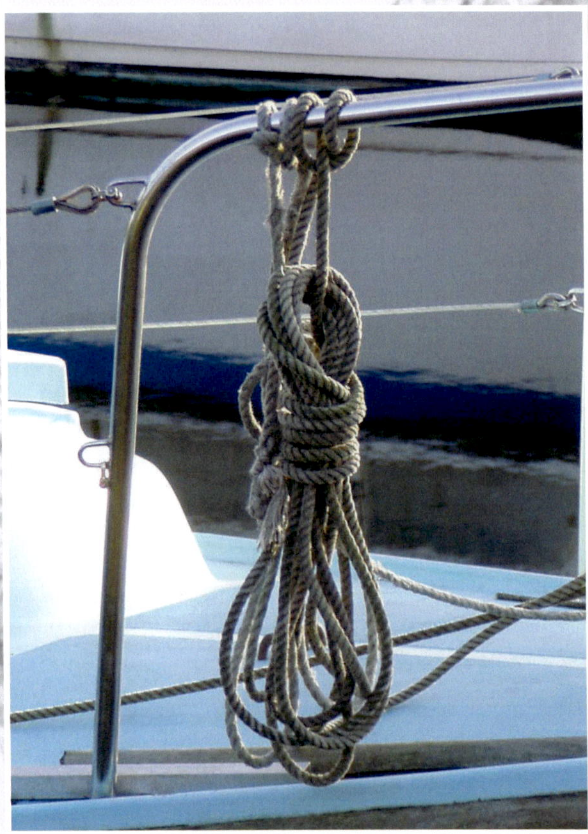

facts

While it is imperative to choose the most suitable knot for the job, it is equally important to use the appropriate cordage. Generally, boating knots are tied in marine ropes, fishing knots are intended for angling monofilaments and braids, and domestic quality cord is used around the home. Life-support knots employ climbing ropes. The latest material to need knots is webbing.

Cordage materials

The collective term for the rope, cord and twine of all kinds in which knots are tied is cordage, but it is also referred to casually as stuff (thick stuff, thin stuff, cheap stuff, expensive stuff) and it is either synthetic or natural.

Synthetic

The market is now dominated by artificial cordage materials, invented or discovered by chemists, the majority of which are one or other of the four P's, namely:

- polyamide (known as Nylon®)
- polyester (otherwise marketed as Terylene® and Dacron®)
- polypropylene
- polyethylene

All of these are generally strong, flexible and durable, although polypropylene reacts poorly to UV radiation which shortens its life considerably, and it is also susceptible to abrasion. They can be stored wet without the risk of mildew or rot.

Nylon loses up to 15 per cent of its strength when wet, but recovers once it has dried out. Polyester is slightly weaker than nylon, but it remains as strong wet or dry. Of greater practical application, however, is the fact that nylon stretches considerably under load, while polyester has little inherent stretch (and what it has is often removed by pre-stretching during the production process).

Polypropylene is weaker than either nylon or polyester, but it is cheaper and lighter, and it floats. To overcome its natural stiffness, and improve handling, polypropylene is constructed in several forms:

- monofilament – continuous synthetic fibre of uniform diameter and circular cross-section,

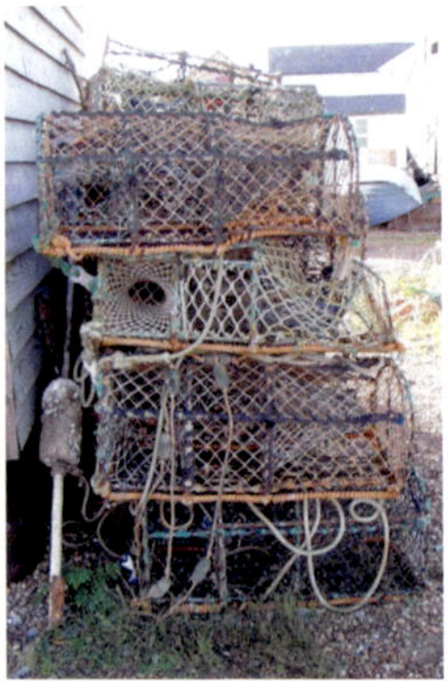

▲ Commercial fish traps and lobster pots are still handmade to age-old designs, but with synthetic twine and cord for the knotted netting.

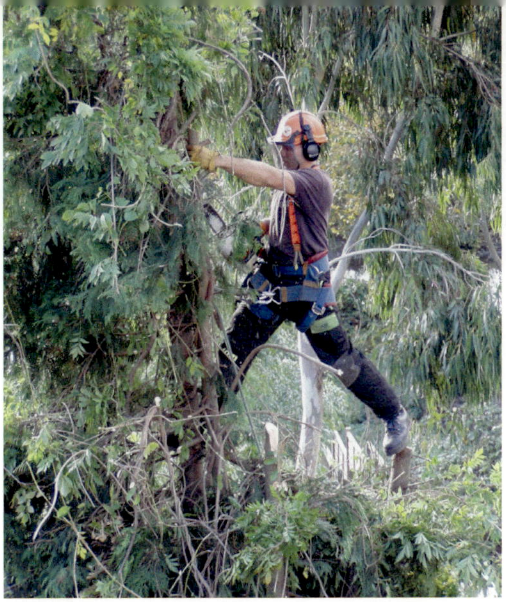

◄▼ Purpose-made harnesses – approved and tested in accordance with health and safety legislation, as well as best industrial practice – still require properly knotted ropes to put them to work.

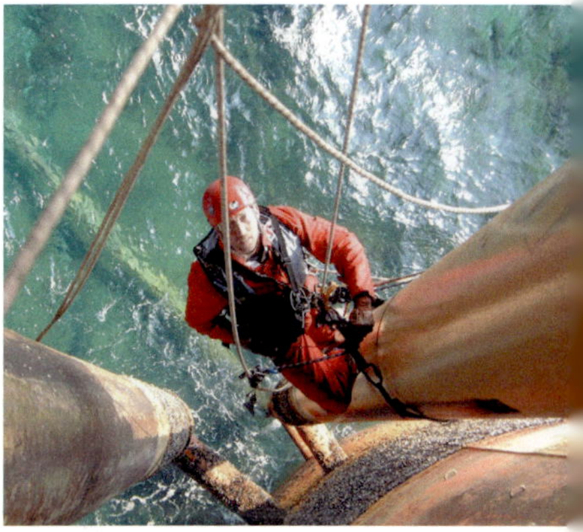

larger than 50 microns, which is the most resistant to chafing;
- multifilament – very fine continuous synthetic fibre of uniform diameter and circular cross-section, less than 50 microns, which is softer, more flexible and easier to knot;
- staplespun – in which long extruded fibres are chopped into shorter 'staple' lengths of about 15 cm (6 in) to produce a fuzzy surface texture resembling natural fibre rope;
- splitfilm – combed and spun into coarse, short-lived (but very cheap) stuff for one-off tasks.

Hi-tech newcomers

Fast becoming established are brands of cordage that are lighter yet stronger than wire rope, including:
- Kevlar/Twaron/Technora – aramid derivatives;
- Spectra/Dyneema – HMPE or high modulus, UV stable polyethylenes;
- Vectran – LCP or liquid crystal polymer, thermoplastic, multifilament yarn;
- Zylon – PBO or poly [P-phenylene-3, 6-benzo-bisoxazole] which is up to 20 per cent stronger than Vectran and HMPE (Spectra, Dyneema).

WATCH OUT!

Synthetic ropes can fail if subjected to heat-generated friction beyond their known melting points:
- **nylon = 210°C/410°F**
- **terylene = 260°C/500°F**
- **Dyneema/Spectra = 165°C/329°F**
- **Vectran = 500°/932°F**

but, be warned, they will glaze, fuse and weaken at lower temperatures.

All of these exotic 'super-fibres' are expensive but, because of their amazing strength-to-weight ratios and low stretch, appeal to extreme sportsmen and women whose sponsors can afford them. To overcome their known shortcomings, such as poor resistance to abrasion, low flex-fatigue, and vulnerability to UV radiation, these products are usually sheathed in polyester.

Natural fibre

Cordage made from materials of vegetable or animal origin is not employed as much by industrialized nations as it was 50 years ago, but it is still widely used elsewhere. So-called 'soft' cordage is made from fibrous plant stems (for example, flax, hemp and jute). 'Hard' cordage is made from leaves (such as sisal), as well as fibres attached to seeds (cotton) or even coconut husks (coir). Other natural fibre sources are date palms, tree bark, reeds and esparto grass, as well as material of animal origin (gut, hair, silk or wool).

One of the strongest and most durable natural fibres is **hemp** from the *Cannabis sativa* plant, although it is less than half as strong as synthetic cordage, but **manila** made from the leaves of *Musa textilis* (the wild banana plant)

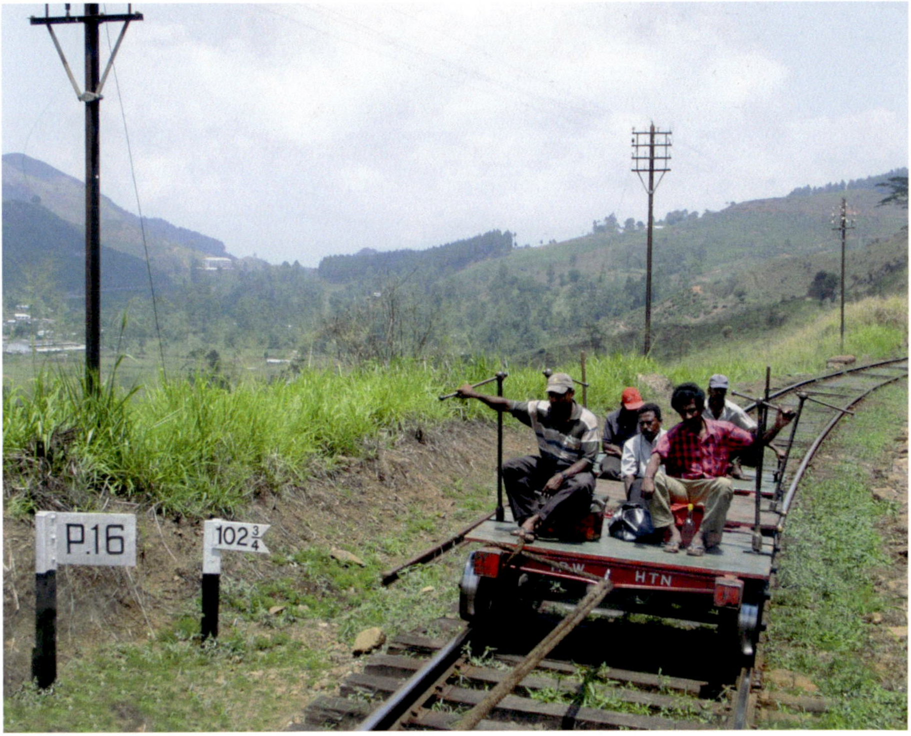

is more resistant than hemp to rot when wet. **Sisal**, derived from various aloe and agave plants, particularly *Agave rigidita* var. *sisalana*, is a cheap substitute for hemp and manila. The only vegetable rope that will float is **coir.** It is stretchy and resistant to immersion in salt water, so that – despite being a quarter the strength of manila – it is found as 'bass' fenders for small boats and 'grass rope' heaving lines. White **cotton** ropes, in contrast, are weak (because cotton fibres are short) but good looking. It is for these reasons that cotton ropes used to be prettily flaked down – not for serious use – aboard expensive yachts, and are still made into barrier ropes for crowd control in public meeting places. Cotton twines, treated to stop them rotting, were made into nets for the sea fishing industry.

▲ Tow-lines, such as this one attached to a railway bogie cart in Sri Lanka, should be stretchy (to absorb sudden jerks) and be secured without sharp bends (to safeguard the ropes' breaking strength).

Cordage construction

All cordage, natural or synthetic, may be floppy and flexible (soft-laid) or tightly twisted and stiff (hard-laid) as a deliberate feature of its manufacture.

Most natural fibre ropes and some synthetics consist of three Z-laid strands (spiralling right-handed or clockwise) and these are said to be hawser-laid. Four-strand rope is more flexible, but no stronger, and is called shroud-laid. Four or more strands create a hollow space along the centre of a rope, necessitating a thick yarn of some sort forming a heart (or core) to fill it. S-laid (left-handed or counter-clockwise) rope of three or four strands is less common.

Hawser-laid cordage

Natural fibre ropes that are hawser-laid are made by combing, lubricating and then spinning selected batches of natural fibres of limited (staple) length into Z-laid yarns, while synthetic

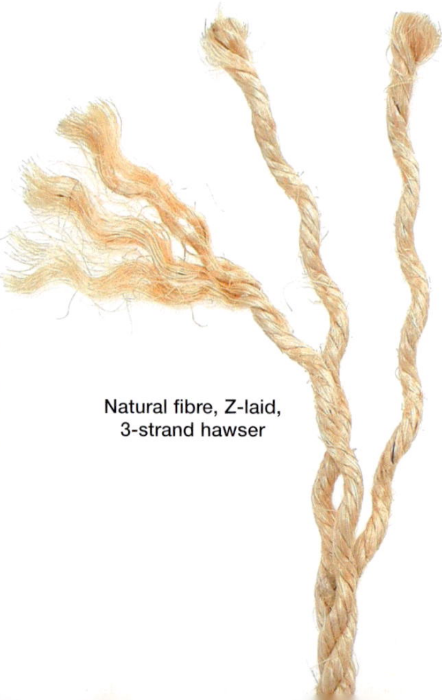

Natural fibre, Z-laid, 3-strand hawser

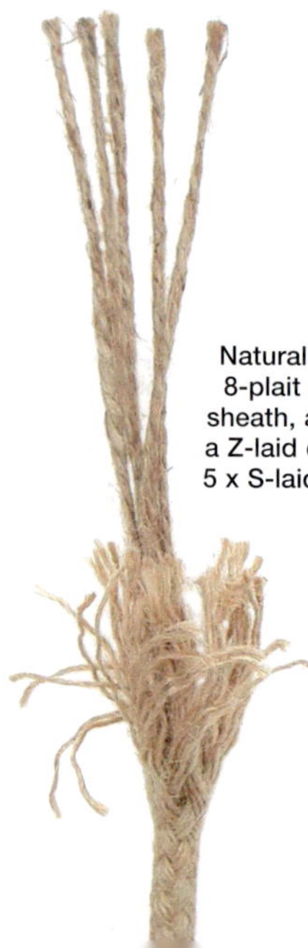

Natural fibre, 8-plait outer sheath, around a Z-laid core of 5 x S-laid yarns

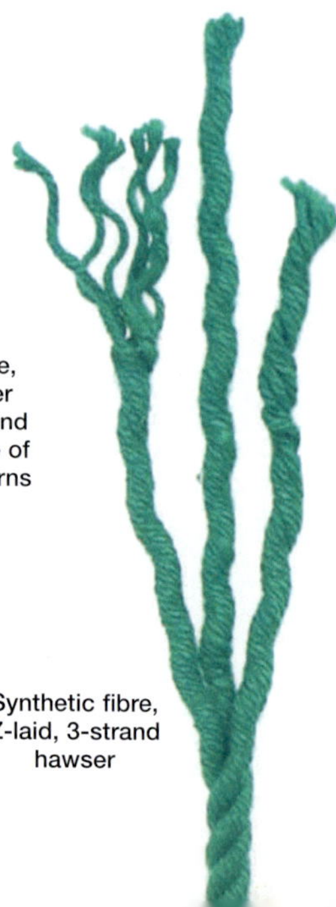

Synthetic fibre, Z-laid, 3-strand hawser

yarns are bunches of lengthy extruded monofilaments, multifilaments or splitfilm (and only occasionally staple-spun). A bundle of yarns is then spun to create S-laid strands; after which three of these strands are Z-laid to create the actual rope. This combination of twist and counter-twist gives a hawser-laid rope its geometry, cohesion, flexibility and strength. Tension determines whether or not any particular cordage is soft-laid or hard-laid. The number of fibres or filaments to a yarn, and yarns to each strand, dictates its diameter. A further subtlety, added by at least one manufacturer is the incorporation within each strand of a contrary S-laid yarn to combat kinks.

Synthetic construction

Most synthetic cordage is constructed from yarns of parallel monofilaments or multifilaments that are braided into 8-, 16- or 32-plait sheaths around a core. The core itself may be laid up into three strands, which makes it resistant to flex-fatigue; or it can be braided, making it easier to

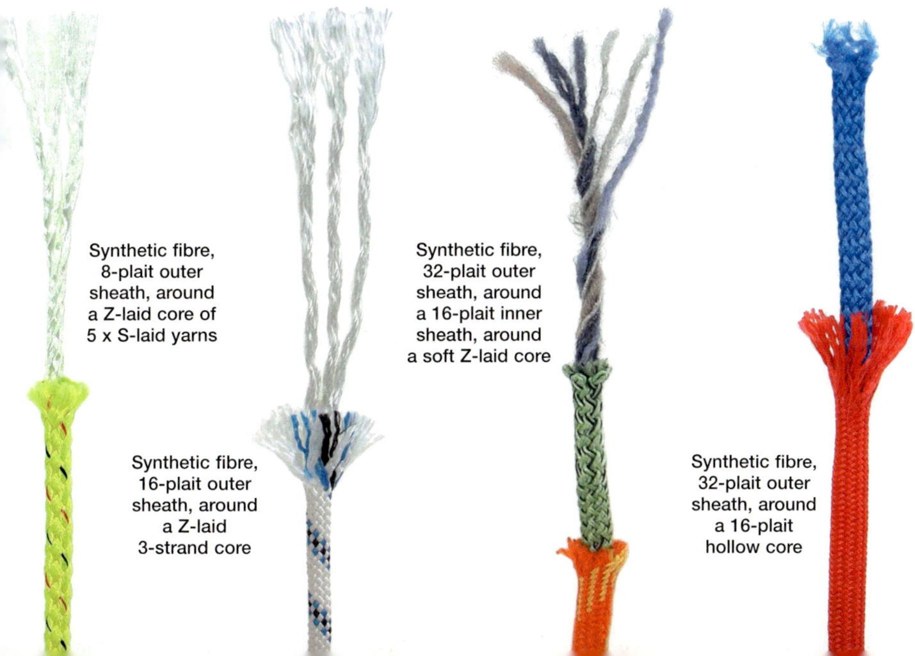

Synthetic fibre, 8-plait outer sheath, around a Z-laid core of 5 x S-laid yarns

Synthetic fibre, 16-plait outer sheath, around a Z-laid 3-strand core

Synthetic fibre, 32-plait outer sheath, around a 16-plait inner sheath, around a soft Z-laid core

Synthetic fibre, 32-plait outer sheath, around a 16-plait hollow core splice, or it could consist of parallel yarns which, despite being the strongest core construction, has poor flex-fatigue resistance and so tends to be used only in small diameter, eight-plait cordage. Depending upon their exact construction, therefore, synthetic ropes can be roughly identified as 'sheath-and-core' or 'braid-on-braid'.

Very little natural fibre cordage is braided, obvious exceptions being sash window cords, flag halyards, pulley cords for antique weight-driven clocks and washing lines.

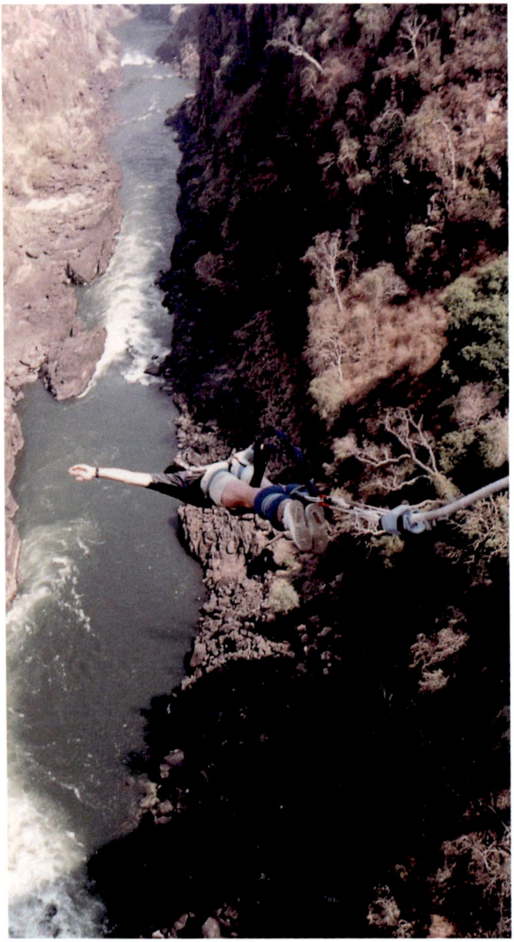

◀ Geronimo! In this extreme test of equipment strength and security, the falling daredevil's acceleration due to gravity is checked and absorbed by the elasticity of the bungee jump tether and harness. This spectacular dive took place at Victoria Falls in Zimbabwe.

Recent developments

The manufacture of synthetic tapered lines for running rigging aboard sail boats is one such development. A light but load-bearing core of high-strength, low-stretch Dyneema or Vectran is attached to spinnakers, then a smooth profile inner cover is added for taking turns around deck gear, and further along the standing part a thick outer sheath of soft matt polyester is applied for comfortable and effective handling (wet or dry).

One well-known space age product is shock (or bungee) cord, elastic yarn sheathed in tough polyester, short lengths of which are sold with hooks fitted at both ends for securing loads to car and motorbike luggage racks.

Synthetics are smooth and shiny because of their continuous filament construction which can make them less amenable to handling, knotting and splicing than natural fibre. It is to mimic some of the qualities of natural fibre ropes that continuous filaments may be staplespun to create a matt surface texture.

Thicker ropes are achieved in one of two ways: three Z-laid hawsers can be S-laid to create a cable or cable-laid rope of nine strands; or an eight-plait rope may be assembled in which two pairs of strands are S-laid and two pairs are Z-laid, resulting in a soft but solid rope with a square cross-section that is kink-resistant. Similarly, a 12-plait rope can be assembled in which two S-laid and two Z-laid strand triplets are plaited together.

These diverse rope types are marketed under a variety of trade names and, to guide buyers, the manufacturers and suppliers produce comprehensive brochures describing construction, use, breaking strengths and other performance test data. Specialist retailers will be pleased to explain what you need to know.

MUST KNOW

Telltale signs

Naval dockyards and large civil buyers and consumers of natural fibre cordage used to have a distinctive coloured yarn spun into their ropes to indicate ownership. This was the so-called rogue's yarn meant to deter larceny since thieves would find it hard either to use or to re-sell such ropes without revealing that they were in unlawful possession of them. Many synthetic ropes also included a telltale yarn or name tape to indicate the rope's manufacturer or materials.

Choosing cordage

Whether it is thick or thin, hard or soft-laid, cheap and crude or high-tech and costly, be choosy and select the best cordage for the work it must do.

Synthetic cordage is stronger than natural fibre. Sheath-and-core or braid-on-braid construction is stronger than laid line. A rope that is twice the diameter of a similar one will be four times as strong, but this extra strength costs more to buy, weighs more, and is subject to more friction in use.

In general, buy the thinnest cordage necessary. However, when the line is too thin to grasp comfortably, a thicker one (with needless extra strength) should be bought just to have something big enough to handle or to fit existing blocks, cleats, fairleads and other rigging tackle.

Cordage descriptions

A natural fibre rope or cord used to be referred to by its circumference in inches, so a '3-in hawser', for instance, was only about 1-in (25 mm) thick. After synthetics ousted natural fibre products, and the UK adopted metric measurements, cordage sizes changed to diameter in millimetres. That 3-in hawser became a 24 mm rope.

Anything less than 10 mm (⅜ in) is a cord, although very thin stuff is commonly called twine (if well-made) or string (if cruder). But this demarcation has become blurred now that many synthetic 'cords' are as strong as ropes, and some manufacturers have reverted to describing their products by circumference once more, so take care when consulting brochures from different suppliers to compare like with like.

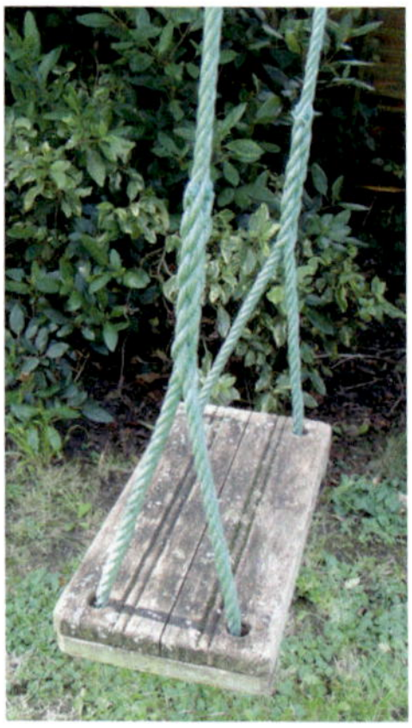

▲ Splices can be stronger than many knots and this garden swing relies upon a couple of load-bearing eye splices, the individual strands of which have all been tucked five or six times for optimum strength and security.

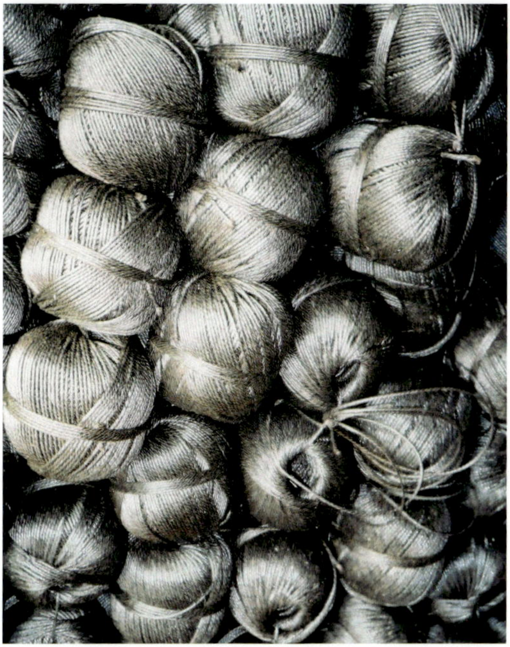

◀ These balls of oiled spunyarn were impregnated with a preservative during the process of manufacture.

MUST KNOW

Shocking news
A rope's advertised breaking strength may not be enough to cope with shock loading. Momentum = mass x velocity. In other words, a load that jerks or falls exerts a greater strain on a rope as it is brought to a standstill. Consequently, you may need rope with a breaking strength five to ten times greater than for a static load, if it is to be subjected to that sort of demanding usage.

Cordage uses

Use nylon, with its innate stretchiness, for dynamic climbing ropes (which may have to withstand the momentum of a falling climber), as well as for car tow lines and boat anchor warps. Nylon is also the preferred choice for most fishing lines.

Any rope with a specialized use is called a line (for instance mooring line, tow line, washing line). Afloat, shrouds and stays make up the standing (or static) rigging that braces masts. Halyards raise and lower sails while sheets trim them to the wind, and these constitute the running (or moving) rigging.

For any task demanding resilience with toughness, employ a braided polyester cover with a nylon core, which will stretch to absorb intermittent tugging while at the same time resisting abrasion. A three-strand polyester core within a polyester sheath, however, will act as

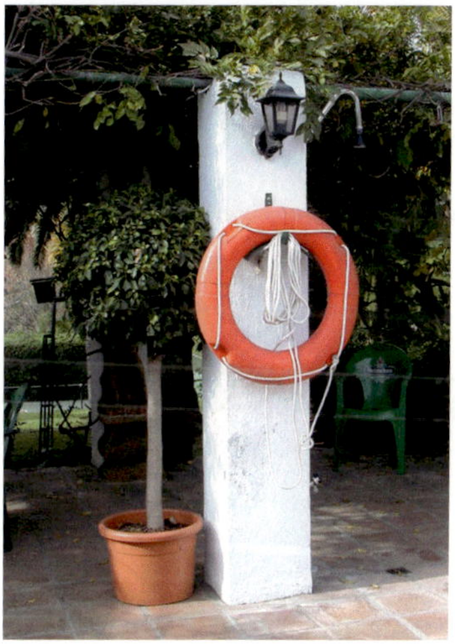

▲ The lines attached to lifebelts, such as this one, beside public swimming pools are likely to be made from polypropylene (because it floats).

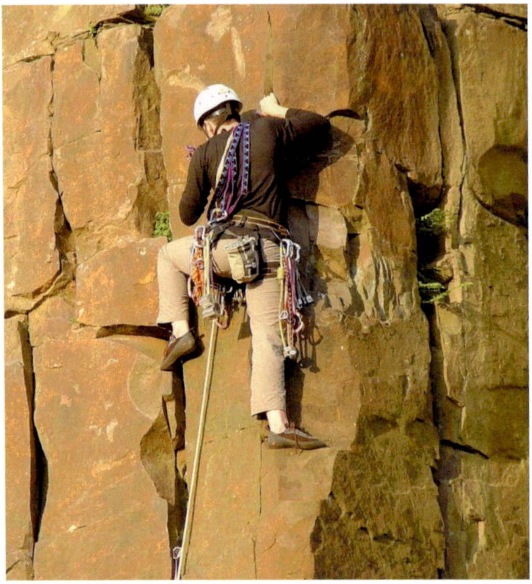

◀ Onwards and upwards – but peace of mind depends upon total confidence in the stitches and hitches that have gone into the manufacture and assembly of specialist equipment.

exceptionally strong, low-stretch halyards, shrouds and stays for radio, television, mobile phone and yacht masts, or any kind of flagpole.

An eight-plait, pre-stretched (4–8 mm) polyester cord is ideal for wind-surfing; and Dyneema or Vectran lines provide a combination of low water absorbance, light weight (without loss of strength) and reduced drag for the extreme sports of kite surfing, parascending and paragliding.

For owners of vintage boats, there is a long-lasting and UV resistant staplespun polypropylene rope that imitates old style hemp cordage without its shortcomings. Conversely, if you prefer clipper ship cordage and require the real thing, there is tarred hemp sold as balls of marline. This has a pungent smell – redolent of ancient rigging yards – that can clear blocked sinuses; and, because it is water-resistant, it is used to whip and weatherproof splices and heavy-duty static mooring lines. Be prepared to stain your hands and everything you handle, however, with this messy stuff.

MUST KNOW

A price to pay

Be aware that the general purpose and moderately priced synthetic and natural fibre cordage products sold in DIY or hardware stores will not have the same high performance specifications as the purpose-made (and often breathtakingly expensive) ropes acquired from camping and climbing shops or yacht chandlers.

But not all cordage applications are boating ones. If you need to hang a picture on a wall, or extend a bathroom light pull down to within reach of small children, a piece of cord and a couple of knots adeptly applied will do the trick.

Buying guide

Do not buy top-of-the-range rope to practise knots. Climbing rope is one of the most expensive types to buy.

Camping and outdoor pursuits shops sell 5 mm (⅜ in) inexpensive braided white nylon labelled 'Paracord' in 15 metre (49 ft) hanks, which is useful for all kinds of odd jobs; but, as it is hollow and has a tendency to flatten out, it is not ideal for learning and practising knots – unless you thread a smaller cord along its centre to act as a heart and keep it round.

Inexpensive olive green 5 mm (⅜ in) polypropylene is sold in similar lengths in army surplus stores. This is a hard-laid round cord that is suitable for knotting, although rather drab.

Keep a lookout in rope, cord and twine outlets for end-of-range cordage and bags of mixed off-cuts at bargain prices. If you think you might have a use for it, buy it there and then, for it will have gone when you have second thoughts and return for it later.

Colourful cordage

Natural fibre cordage is generally hairy and either blonde or brunette in colour; but synthetic ropes may be white, black, or any shade from discreet burgundy to outrageous fluorescent pink. You could choose mint green and peat brown in the garden, Mediterranean blue by the swimming pool, silver or gold for a dressing-gown cord, and psychedelic webbing straps around your travel bags (for easy recognition on the airport luggage carousel).

MUST KNOW

Varieties of cordage

Although cordage for yachting may have the glossiest brochures, ropes are also made and sold for banisters in houses; bell-ropes in church belfries; crowd control barriers for historic houses, museums and art galleries or scenes of crime; queue control ropes for banks, building societies, cinemas and post offices. There are knotted rope dog leashes, horse leads, halters and lunge lines and pet harnesses, knotted ropes to replace trellis-work for climbing plants and knotted netting to protect fruit and vegetables from predation by animals and birds.

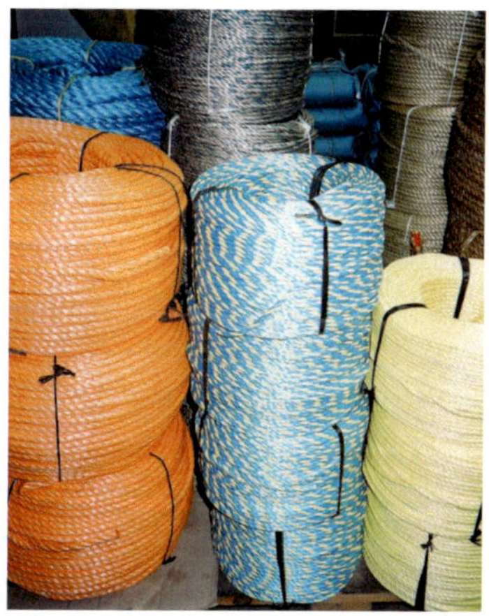

▲ Coils of rope of various kinds are secured with 'stops' of spunyarn (the dark strings) knotted to keep them intact during transit to retailers.

Care of cordage

Look after cordage, use it carefully and it will last longer. Failure to do so will lead to premature depreciation of an expensive asset and may impair the user's safety.

Maintainance

- Avoid needless rough treatment of ropes. Ensure predictable wear and tear is spread over different sections of a rope by regularly shifting its location or turning it end-for-end.
- Minimize overall abrasion by using the correct size of blocks, fairleads, cleats or other items of hardware, and avoid localized wear by inserting thimbles, fitting protective sheaths or taking other anti-chafe measures.
- Keep ropes away from oil and grease, dirt and grit.
- Prevent ropes from contact with strong chemicals and fumes.
- Avoid subjecting ropes to extremes of heat, including direct sunlight, heat friction and flying sparks, as well as to extreme cold with the likelihood of freezing and ice crystals.
- Wash, rinse and shampoo ropes whenever practicable if they have been immersed in sea water (to flush out abrasive salt crystals) or become impregnated with dirt and grit.
- Dry natural fibre ropes thoroughly before storage, otherwise they are liable to rot.
- Inspect all ropes and downgrade them to less vital work if they show signs of 'creep' (elongation of the core resulting in a wrinkled sheath), glazing and fusion due to heat friction, or the fuzziness that is an indication of cut and fraying fibres.
- Prise apart hawser-laid and cable-laid ropes to see if there is deterioration of internal strands, yarns and fibres.

MUST KNOW

Prime mover
A rope that is stiff and awkward to handle is probably in its prime. Perversely, once it becomes soft, pliable and pleasant to work with, it is likely to be past its best. Use it then for learning and practising knotting.

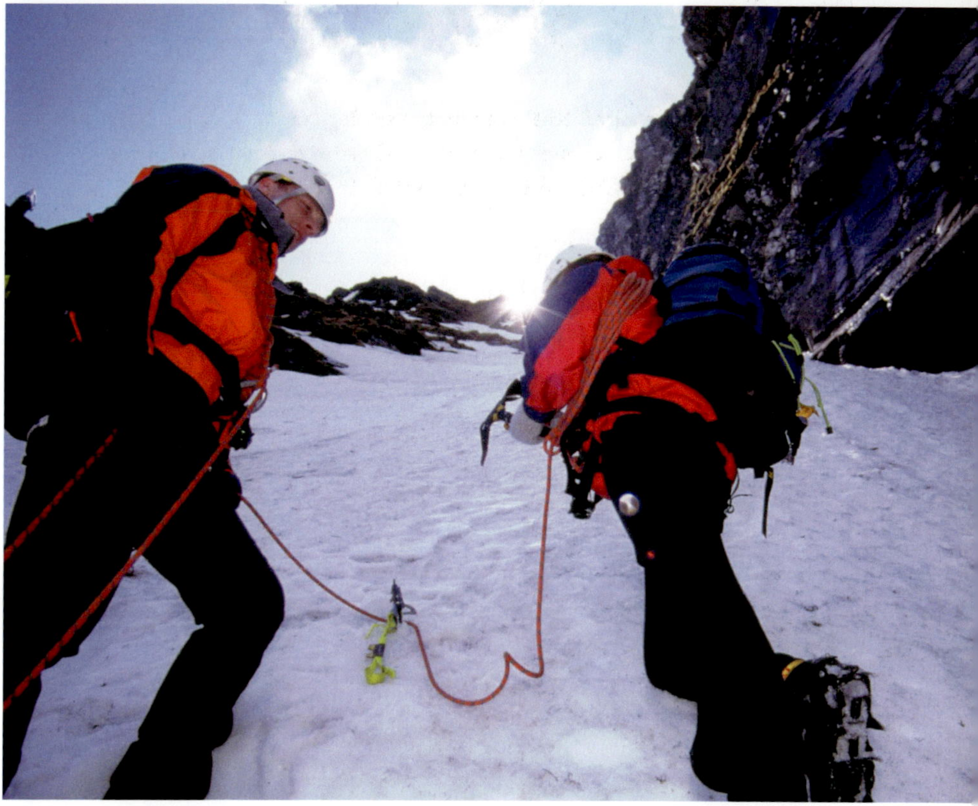

Other considerations

Assess the unseen internal condition of sheath-and-core or braid-on-braid ropes by studying their recent history of use. Dynamic climbing ropes should each have a log book, in which periods and kind of use are recorded, as well as any shock loading or other abuse to which they have been subjected. Ropes used only occasionally and carefully at lengthy intervals may remain safe for months or even years. However, the working life of those in continual heavy use may be measured in mere weeks and, after sustaining a heavy fall, friction-generated heat damage or other severe stress, a rope should be instantly discarded (or downgraded to a less risky use).

▲ Climbing ropes, cords and accessories must be fit for the purpose and wholly dependable, while knots and rope techniques (although practice-perfect) should always be checked by a companion.

Storage

Ropes should be tidily coiled when not in use. Braided cordage may be coiled either clockwise or counter-clockwise. When coiling clockwise, impart an extra half a clockwise twist with each completed circle of coil; and, going counter-clockwise, add half a counter-clockwise twist. This tames the rope's innate tendency to resist you and results in a far neater and more compliant coil.

When a coiled rope is run out, all of those accumulated half-twists remain, and they should be removed one by one as the rope uncoils. Z-laid hawsers must only be coiled clockwise (or right-handed); otherwise, when run out, they will acquire a series of cruel and ugly kinks that can distort and damage them. For the same reason, S-laid hawsers must be coiled counter-clockwise (left-handed).

▼ These bulky 8-plait ropes have been loosely coiled ready for use when mooring or berthing.

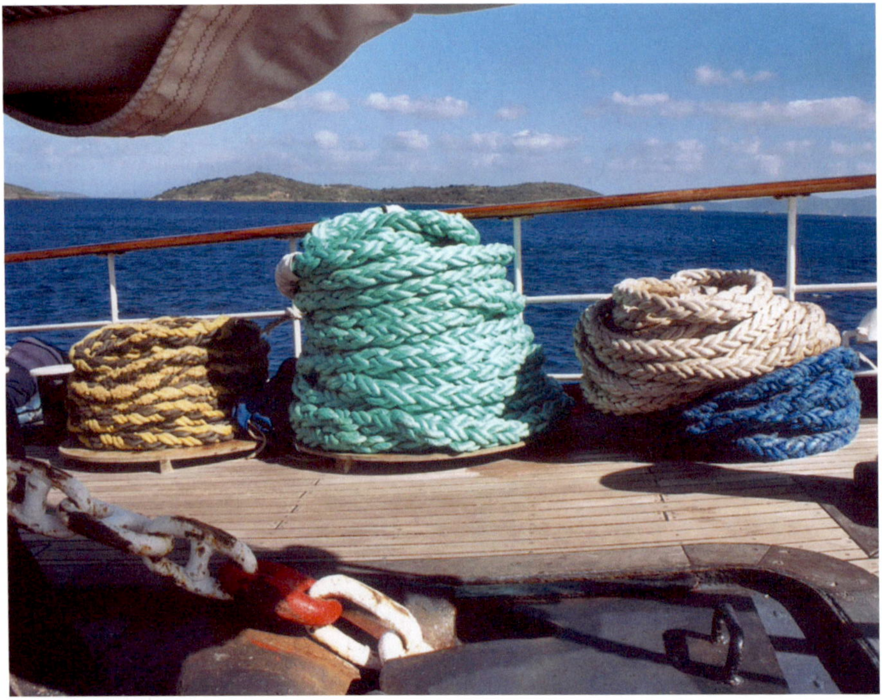

Coiling methods

There are numerous methods of coiling rope depending upon whether it is to be kept handy for immediate use, thrown as a heaving line, carried (hands-free) like a back-pack, dumped in a car boot (or trunk) and a sail-boat's rope locker, or put away in storage. Stored coils should be hung in a well-ventilated area where they cannot be trodden on, and a basic method of tying off a coil so as to create a loop from which to suspend it is shown here.

Basic coil tie

Step 1

Neatly coil the rope, and then make a fairly long bight in the working end. Wrap the bight around the coil.

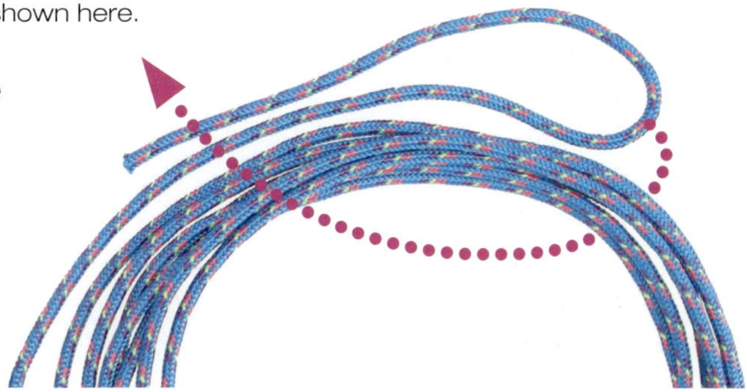

Step 2

Bring the bight across itself and then take it around the coil once more and tuck it beneath its own initial wrapping turn.

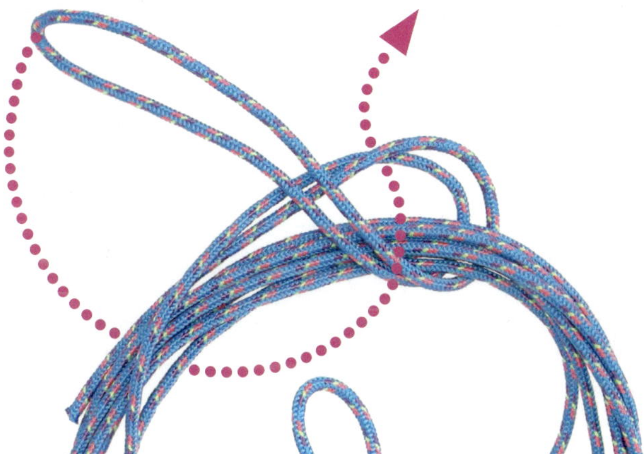

Step 3

Lastly, tighten the resulting knot and the coil is ready to hang.

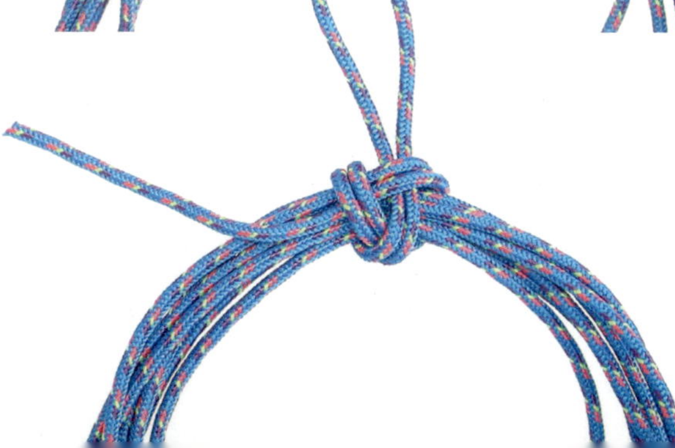

Glossary

Abseil To descend from an anchored static climbing rope that is usually retrievable.

Back up Securing or 'locking off' the working end of a completed knot by tying or taping it to the adjacent standing part.

Anchorage A secure belay; taking a rope around a fixed object.

Barrel knot See **Blood knot**

Belay Boating – making fast to cleat, post, ring, rail or spar; Climbing – securing a climber in case of a fall.

Bend A knot that binds or joins the ends of two ropes together, so that they may be untied again later.

Bight U-shaped partial loop in a line.

Blood knot A core-and-wrap knot or bend made with numerous wrapping turns.

Braid-on-braid A type of rope or cord construction consisting of an outer covering around an inner core or heart.

Breaking strength Manufacturer's calculation of the load a rope will hold before it breaks, taking no account of wear and tear, shock loading or knots that may drastically reduce this estimate.

Cable Three hawser-laid ropes (customarily Z-laid) laid up together left-handed (S-laid); but cable also refers to any large rope.

Capsize Spilling or deformation of a knot due to careless tightening, misuse or overloading. It may also be induced deliberately as a means of untying.

Cord Small stuff under 10 mm (½ in) diameter.

Core The yarns filling the space within four (or more) strand ropes, and within the outer covering of synthetic cordage.

Cordage The collective name for all kinds of rope and cord.

Draw-loop A bight of line left in a completed knot, making it easier to untie later.

Efficiency See **Strength**

Elbow Two crossing points created by an extra twist in a loop.

Eye A knotted, seized or spliced loop in a line.

Handedness The direction of twist by the strands in a hawser-laid rope or some part of a knot, either S-laid (counter-clockwise) or Z-laid (clockwise).

Hard eye An eye that is reinforced and protected from abrasion by the insertion of a thimble.

Hard-laid Stiff cordage.

Hawser A rope of three strands, either S-laid or Z-laid.

Heart See **Core**

Hitch A knot attaching a line to an object or an inert rope.

Karabiner Multi-purpose aluminium or steel snap-link, commonly oval or D-shaped, locking or non-locking, used by climbers.

Kernmantel The core-and-covering construction of all climbing ropes.

Kink A damaging deformation caused by an over-tight loop.

Knot Loosely speaking, any

complication in a line, but in particular those tied deliberately which are not bends or hitches.

Lanyard A short length of line with many applications, such as lashing, securing or suspending implements and accessories.

Lay The direction in which a rope twists (S-laid or Z-laid), as well an indication of its construction (soft-laid, hard-laid).

Left-handed Cordage S-laid.

Line A generic word for cordage with a specific use (fishing line, throwing line, washing line).

Locking off See **Back up**

Loop A bight with a crossing or one that is knotted or spliced.

Middle, To Verb: to double a length of line and locate its centre.

Monofilament Continuous synthetic fibre of uniform diameter and circular cross-section, larger than 50 microns (0.002 inch).

Multifilament Very fine continuous synthetic fibre of uniform diameter and circular cross-section, less than 50 microns (0.002 in).

Natural fibre Processed plant products used to make cordage.

Noose An adjustable or sliding loop.

Rappel See **Abseil**

Right-handed Cordage Z-laid.

Safe working load The estimated load a rope will withstand, taking into account predictable factors such as shock-loading and the weakening effect of knots. It may be as little as one tenth of the quoted breaking strength.

Security The ability of knots – distinct from strength – to withstand shaking, tugging or a steady load without slipping, deforming or capsizing and spilling.

Shackle The boating equivalent of a climber's karabiner, a D-shaped or U-shaped stainless steel link that is closed and secured with a threaded pin or similar patent locking device.

Sheath-and-core A type of cordage construction consisting of an outer braided covering around a number of heart-strands or yarns.

S-laid The counter-clockwise twist of strands or yarns.

Soft-laid Flexible cordage.

Spilling See **Capsize**

Standing end The inactive end of a rope or other cord.

Standing part The length of line (rope or cord) between standing and working ends.

Strength The relative efficiency of a knot expressed as a percentage of the breaking strength of the cordage in which it is tied.

Stuff An informal word for any type of cordage.

Synthetics Cordage made from artificial monofilaments or multi-filaments, staple fibres or split film.

Tag end Angling – the short end of a completed knot, as well as the active end in the tying process.

Thimble A metal or plastic lining, with a round profile or one like a hot-air balloon, concave in cross-section, to protect small knotted or spliced eyes from abrasion.

Working end The end of a rope or cord used in the tying process.

Z-laid The clockwise twist of strands or yarns.

Need to know more?

To tie a knot, you must attempt to tie that knot. Merely reading about it will not teach you how. At all times carry a length of cord with you and fiddle with it frequently, for a knot that cannot be recalled when required was never really learned in the first place. A good memory for knots is not a gift, it's a reward. Practise every new knot again and again, until you can tie it reliably, preferably without looking.

The Surrey six

If everyone had to learn the same six knots (and only six), what ought they to be? It is debatable. But the Surrey branch of the IGKT (the International Guild of Knot Tyers) came up with the following consensus (all of these knots are featured in this book):

- the bowline
- the constrictor knot
- the figure eight knot
- the rolling hitch
- the round turn and two half-hitches
- the sheet bend

Record breakers

The Guinness Book of Records credits the fastest time for tying six Boy Scout knots to Clinton R. Bailey Snr, of Pacific City, Oregon, USA. The knots are:

- the bowline
- clove hitch
- reef knot
- round turn and two half-hitches
- sheepshank
- sheet bend.

His time, achieved on 13 April 1977 when he was a 50-year-old disabled ex-naval veteran, remains an astonishing 8.1 seconds. This six-knot challenge has become a perennial crowd-puller at IGKT events but, despite many determined attempts, nobody else has recorded a time lower than 12 seconds (with most aspiring record-breakers clocking around 16 seconds). All of these knots feature in this book.

Places of interest

- Visit the ropewalk within the Historic Dockyard, Church Lane, Chatham, Kent ME4 4TG (tel: 01634 823800/fax: 01634-823801), a UK registered

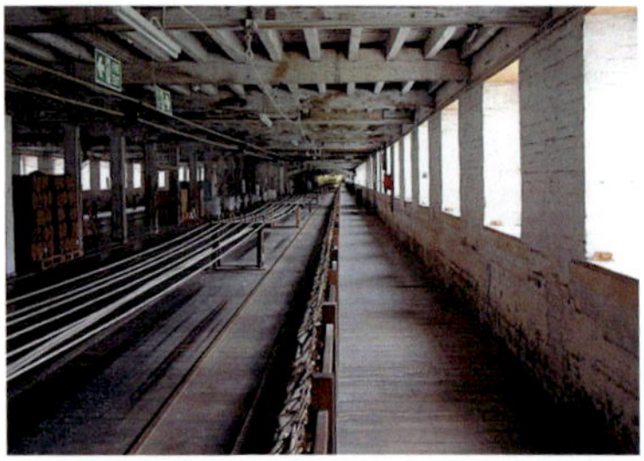

▲ The unique Chatham ropewalk is the oldest in existence (built 1786), making rope with machinery dating from 1811, in the largest building of its kind in the world.

educational charity which aims 'to advance, promote and encourage the education of the public in the method of traditional rope making'. See one of their public demonstrations in the longest building of its kind in the world at 338 metres (1,128 ft); the oldest ropewalk (built 1786) still in existence; rope being made using machinery dating from 1811; craftsmen employing techniques and materials that have evolved over 3,000 years.

- Visit boatyards, marinas and docks to see examples of knots and splices in action.
- Look out for ropes and knots in public places, for example: bell ropes in public houses; fishing nets and lobster pots on quaysides; ornamental knot boards in gift shops; Celtic knot patterns on tombstones; rope rigging in circuses and theatres; craft fairs and inland waterways.

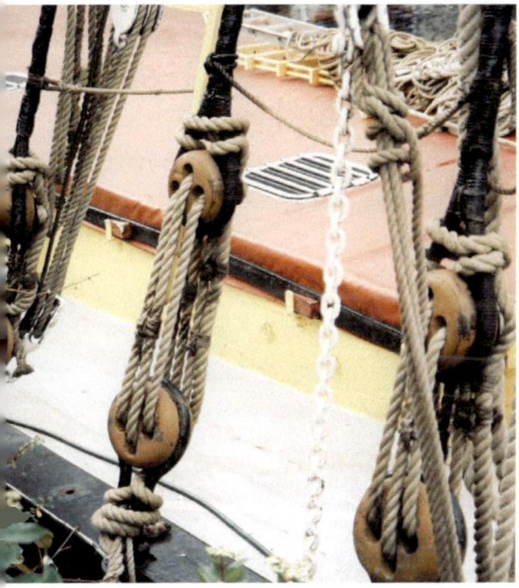

▲ Standing and running rigging aboard a sailing barge berthed in St Katherine's Dock, London, England.

Contact details

The International Guild of Knot Tyers (IGKT)

Knottology is a fundamental but fascinating art, craft and science, and one lifetime is barely enough to comprehend it all. But we devotees try, we truly do, and collectively we busy ourselves inventing or discovering new knots and knotting techniques. If you want to learn more about knots, join the Guild yourself.

The IGKT was established in 1982 and it is now a UK registered educational charity with a worldwide membership. Members

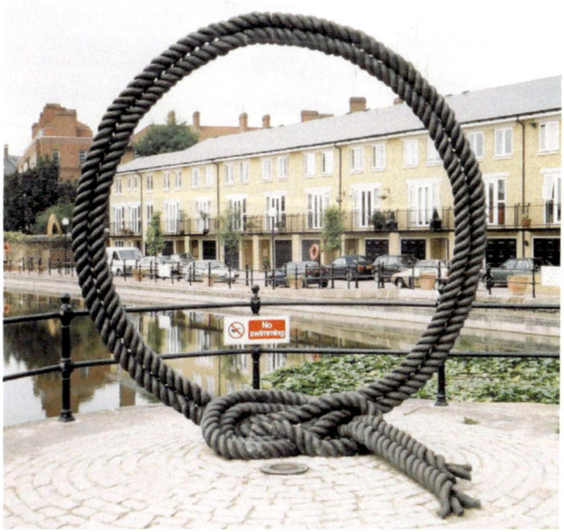

▶ This striking sculpture of a bowline-in-the-bight, standing 3 metres (9 ft) or more tall, is situated at one end of Hermitage Wharf, within the regenerated London Docks complex.

enjoy the quarterly magazine *Knotting Matters* which contains informed articles, expert tips, letters and editorial comment, as well as news and views on everything to do with knotting. In Great Britain, two large gatherings are held each year, but local groups (both in the UK and other territories) meet more often to enjoy lectures, demonstrations and workshops. Anyone interested in knots may join. To find out more contact: Nigel Harding, IGKT Honorary Secretary, 16 Egles Grove, Uckfield, East Sussex, TN22 2BY, England; tel +44 (0)1825 760425; email igkt@nigelharding.demon.co.uk;

IGKT websites

IGKT: www.igkt.craft.org
North American branch: www.igktnab.org
Pacific American branch: www/pab.org
Texas branch: www.texasknot.tripod.com

Other websites

Peter Suber[IGKT] (comprehensive treatment under three headings – knot tying, knot theory and knot art): www.earlham.edu/~peters /knotlink.htm

There are numerous other linked websites – a few of them animated – concerned with knotting and rope making; simply key in 'knots' or 'rope' and see where these searches take you.

Further reading

Ashley, Clifford W., *The Ashley Book of Knots* (New York 1944, London 1947) with a revised edition (1993), ISBN 0-571-09659-X

Edwards, Ron, *Knots for Horse-Lovers* (2001), ISBN 1-875872-63-9

Edwards, Ron, *Knots for Beachcombers and Mariners* (2003), ISBN 1-875872-69-8

Goodhind, Wendy, *The Girl Guide Association Knot Book* (1998), ISBN 0-85260-146-8

Grainger[IGKT], Stuart, *Creative Ropecraft* (4th edition, 2000), ISBN 0-7136-5377-9

Hopkins[IGKT], Richard, *Knots (2003)*, ISBN 1-84065-508-9

Judkins[IGKT], Steve and Davison, Tim, *Knot Know-How* (2003), ISBN 1-898660-98-0

Millodot[IGKT], Suzen, *Chinese Knots for Beaded Jewellery* (2003), ISBN 0-85532-968-8

Pawson[IGKT], Des, *Knot Craft* (2003), ISBN 0-7136-5441-4

Perry[IGKT], Gordon, *Knots* (2002), ISBN 1-84013-493-3

Shaw[IGKT], John, *The Directory of Knots* (2003), ISBN 0-7858-1629-1

Stetson, Emily, *Knots to Know* (2002), ISBN 1-885593-70-8

While some of the above are likely to be found on the shelves of specialist stores, many titles may have to be sought via secondhand and rare book suppliers or internet dealers before they can be ordered and obtained.

Index

Acknowledgements

Most of the cordage used in this book was generously donated by:

Marlow Ropes Limited (Marketing Manager Paul Honess), Hailsham, East Sussex, BN27 3JS, UK: tel: +44 (0)1323 847234.
Marlow is one of four business groups operated by The Rope Company Limited, designing and manufacturing specialized products for applications worldwide that include: aeronautical, civil engineering, climbing, commercial shipping, kites, military, the motor industry, naval and shipping markets, oil exploration, utility and work safety.

KJK Ropeworks (Kevin J. Keatley[IGKT]), Town Living Farmhouse, Puddington, Tiverton, Devon, EX16 8LW, UK: tel: +44 (0)1884 860 692.
KJK is a manufacturer of high quality ropes, cords and fittings, particularly suitable for craft work, and has build up an international customer base of expert knot tyers who appreciate and use its products.

Other UK cordage makers and suppliers

- English Braids, Spring Lane, Malvern, Worcestershire WR14 1AL, UK: www.englishbraids.com
- Jimmy Green Marine (ropes, rigging and safety equipment), The Meadows, Beer, East Devon, UK: www.jimmy green.co.uk
- Twistlink Ltd. (a large and varied stock of braids and cords, stock items and clearance lines), Stadon Road, Anstey, Leicester, LE7 7AY: www.fabmania.com

Picture credits

Thanks to the following for providing photographs for the book:

key: t = top, b = bottom, r = right, l = left

Geoffrey Budworth 187; Gail Fifett, Chatham Historical Dockyards Trust (www.chdt.org.uk) 186; Sam Chandler, Colletts Mountain Holidays (www.colletts.co.uk) 6, 9, 35(t), 114, 136; Vicky Culver (www.vickyweb.net) 177(l), 179; Martin Hendry/m&n publishing 1, 2(l), 3, 10, 18(t), 19, 35(b), 38, 62, 84, 166, 168, 169(l), 176; m&n publishing 13; Jennie A. Meares 182; David and Fiona McKenna 174; Briony Davis and Jason Knights, Nikwax Ltd (www.nikwax.com) 29, 181 (Photographer: Dave Willis); Karen Powell 7(t); Nina Sharman /m&n publishing 18(b), 177(b); Adam Spillane 2(r), 169(b), 178; Mary Taylor/Food Matters Tours (www.foodmatters.co.nz) 171

All studio photographs of knots and cordage: Colin Sherwin